Chicago Golf
The First 100 Years

Tom Govedarica

EAGLE
COMMUNICATIONS
GROUP INC.

Chicago

Eagle Communications Group, Inc.
1251 Wellington
Suite 110
Chicago, Ill. 60657

A Note to Readers: This book has been researched thoroughly, but information on local courses is subject to change. This is especially true for real estate prices at golf course residential communities. Specific questions on prices, membership eligibility, and other matters pertaining to private and public golf course sites should be directed to the course operator, proprietor or developer.

Edited by Mike Ryan
Cover and Book Design by Susan Hartill
Typeset by Arlene Sikora

Cover illustrated by Tom Lynch

Tom Lynch was selected as the featured artist for the 1990 U.S. Open at Medinah and the 1991 U.S. Open at Hazeltine. His distinguished credentials include being elected to the Society of American Impressionists and Who's Who in American Art. To order a limited edition print of the cover (14 in. x 21 in.), contact:

Tom Lynch Watercolors, Inc.
605 N. Chestnut
Arlington Heights, Ill. 60004
(708) 255-2011

ISBN 0-9630761-0-8
Printed in the United States of America

To my wife Sheryl and my sister Natalie—for their unwavering support, hours of personal sacrifice and attention to detail, this book is affectionately dedicated.

Contents

Acknowledgments

This book would not be possible without the assistance and cooperation of the local golfing community. I would like to express my gratitude to Dennis Davenport of the Chicago District Golf Association, Gary Holaway of the Western Golf Association, Paul Fullmer of the American Society of Golf Course Architects, John Barney of the Illinois Junior Golf Association and Mrs. B. Kenneth West of the Women's Western Golf Association.

I also wish to single out several other organizations who were helpful—the staff at the United States Golf Association Museum and Library (especially Karen Bednarski), the National Golf Foundation, the Professional Golf Association of Illinois, the Chicago Historical Society, the Wheaton Historical Society and the Chicago Park District (in particular, Bart H. Ryckbosch).

A special thanks goes to Adam Ritt at *Chicago District Golfer*. And for many kindnesses I am indebted to Carol McCue, Herb Mater, Bill Daniels, Bob Lucas, Dorothy May Campbell, Brad Holley, Dann Lobsinger and a host of club professionals, architects, course proprietors and individual club members.

Beyond the professionals who helped in this venture, I had invaluable encouragement from family and friends. I would like to acknowledge Bob and Elaine Bull, Sharon, Tim and Allison Bresnahan, Jeff Davy, John Reebel, Craig Smith, Dave Jern, Gary Voss, Robert Diftler and Suzanne Gorab.

Much of the credit for this project should go to the team who put it all together—my wife Sheryl, my sister Natalie, and Arlene Sikora, Tom Lynch and Susan Hartill. And also to my editor Mike Ryan, who was a believer from the very beginning.

Introduction

Mark Twain once said, "Golf is a good walk spoiled." Some local enthusiasts echo this sentiment, but they waste no time trying to schedule another "spoiled walk" for the following weekend.

It is because of this collective passion for the game, as well as the myriad of course options and a long-established tradition, that the Chicago area is probably the greatest golf market in the world. As golfers, we are part of this distinguished tradition.

Golf is, of course, just one of the many treasures that contribute to Chicago's greatness. Chicago has its magnificent architecture, it uniquely entertaining politics, its lovable professional sports teams (sometimes), its renown museums, its stately churches, and its cultural diversity. Walk into any bookstore and you'll discover a plethora of titles on these fine Chicago institutions. But until now, there wasn't a single book devoted exclusively to Chicago's great golfing legacy.

One of the greatest challenges I had in compiling *Chicago Golf: The First 100 Years* was collecting and sorting through the research. You would think that a game Chicagoans have enjoyed for one hundred years would be pretty well documented. It isn't. During my travels throughout Chicago and the suburbs, I visited more than 125 libraries, bookstores, second-hand bookstores, rare book conventions, estate sales, flea markets and even garage sales—all in the hope of finding nuggets of usable research data. On many days, I found only slivers.

I'm simply amazed by the minimal priority most authors who write neighborhood or village histories have afforded golf. Many of these residential areas have rich golfing traditions, but you wouldn't know it from the books that fill library shelves. It wasn't unusual to come across a book that had only a scant paragraph or two about the local golf club, which had served its community golfers from 60 or 70 years. The same book would then carry on for pages about its local bridge club, or town statue or even discuss in great minutia the importance of the town's first post office.

Believe me, I am not at all adverse to a good card game, respect art in all forms and appreciate the importance of a reliable postal system. But more than one half billion rounds of golf have been played by Chicagoans over the past century. This *has* to count for something.

Fortunately, there were early authors who did recognize golf's important local role. All are cited in this book's bibliography, including Joseph Ryan. As the author of the *Golfers' Green Book*, Ryan compiled a wealth of information on Chicago courses at the turn of the century. The illustrations of old course layouts in chapter five are from his book.

In assimilating my research, I ran across information that was, in fact, misinformation. As a reader, I was offended. As a writer, therefore, I put a premium on accuracy.

At this time, I'd like to clarify a few items you'll discover later. For example, in chapter seven, you'll note that when the Butterfield Country Club was established it was in Hinsdale. Although the club has never moved, it is today located in Oak Brook. Oak Brook is a relatively new village. When it formed, the Butterfield Country Club fell within its boundaries. There are other examples like this.

In my quest for accuracy, I found that golf club names presented something of a dilemma. Throughout most of the book, especially when there was no chance of misidentification, I was content to refer to a club by its popular name. But for the index, I wanted to use official, proper, correct, exact, full names. This was an exercise that absorbed many hours. Let me cite just one example.

I received a letter from a club—for purposes of anonymity, let's say it was called Bluebird—with its scorecard enclosed. The scorecard read: "Bluebird *Country Club.*" However, the letterhead had a "Bluebird *Golf and Country Club*" logo. Fortunately, a business card fell out of the envelope. Thinking it would resolve the issue, I picked it up and read—"Bluebird *Golf Club.*" (So I called them—the letterhead was right).

Although I first played golf in my teens, it wasn't until the last 10 years that I have become somewhat of a golf fanatic. And as my proficiency has improved, so has my appreciation and understanding of the Chicago golf scene and its illustrious past. I discovered the difference between a daily fee and a municipal course, who George May was, that the Chicago area is the site of the country's first 18-hole course and that Wilmette once had in the 1930s a nine-hole illuminated golf course. I even learned how to pronounce Cantigny.

So what this book attempts to do is to provide information and also perspective. On the first tee, you may not be thinking about Chicago's 100-year golfing heritage. Certainly, it won't be important on the last hole, as you attempt a 15-foot putt to break 90. But in between, as you enjoy your four-hour walk, you might find yourself thinking about the course you're playing (or others you've played) and wonder about the thousands of others who enjoyed the sport 25, 50 or 100 years ago. They, like you and me, are a small but integral part of the great Chicago-area golfing tradition.

Chicago Golf
The First 100 Years

Teeing It Up

The lazy afternoon pastime that grew into an obsession began on the rolling Scottish hills and dunes. By the time Chicago awoke to the game's charms in 1893, there were already about 760 golf clubs scattered around the world.

In Scotland, the game's birthplace, both kings and commoners succumbed to the sport's siren song. Indeed, King James II was once forced to ban the game; his subjects had become so smitten they were taking time away from a more critical endeavor—compulsory archery training. This was, after all, the 15th century, and Scotland needed archers, not golfers, to defend the realm from invasion.

The ban long lifted, Scotland of 1893 saw almost 200 golf clubs. England, Ireland, and France had similar venues. Canada, India, New Zealand, Australia, South Africa and other parts of the British Empire had been similarly enamored with the sport.

In the United States, the game was just catching on. No golf clubs had existed before 1888; by 1893, there were only 16. Most of these had Eastern Seaboard addresses, although there was one golf club out "West"—the Chicago Golf Club. (Ironically, the Chicago Golf Club took root, not in Chicago, but in the tiny hamlet of Belmont—today, a part of Downers Grove).

Golf was unknown to most Chicago residents in the late 19th century. Clearly, the sport had a lot of catching up to do.

During the ensuing years, it did just that. Now, almost 100 years later, there are more than 300 golf clubs throughout the local region. When it comes to golf, there are many who believe the Chicago area has no equal in the country.

No doubt, a claim of this magnitude is cause for debate. There is, after all, inherent pride in carrying the label of the country's "golfing mecca." It's not surprising, then, to see various cities and areas within California, Florida, New York and the Carolinas making their own pitch as the country's No. 1 golf market. Chicagoans take all this in stride, though, preferring to let the caliber and number of courses speak for themselves.

A few years ago, several PGA Tour players went so far as to suggest Chicago's courses could conceivably host a full year's tournament slate. While the number of Chicago-area courses is, in the words of PGA veteran Ben Crenshaw, "a mile long," the quality is equally impressive. As Bob Hope says of Chicago, "It may have more great courses than any in the country." As the sport's most famous octogenarian, he would certainly be a good judge. Not only has Hope played many of Chicago's layouts during the past five decades, he also has recorded two of his five lifetime aces here—at Bob O'Link and Butler National.

To see how far the Chicago area has come, note the remarks of Western Golf Association official Phelps B. Hoyt in 1899:

> *"While (I was) listlessly driving (balls) in Lincoln Park, a crowd of chaps who endeavor to monopolize the park for baseball gathered around me and began joshing about the 'sissiness' of the game. . .I invited one of the biggest and noisiest to try a drive and I teed up a ball for him. He made a swipe at the ball, missed it entirely. . .and nearly fell. He then made three or four vain attempts, but missed it every time. After his last effort, in which he succeeded in driving the ball about four yards, he threw down the driver in disgust and retired, using an expert golfer's vocabulary."*

What immediate effect this exercise had on those Lincoln Park skeptics is unknown, as is whether the "chaps" in question continued to joke about the "sissiness" of the game. It is clear, however, that many other Chicagoans knew little of golf, this point aptly made in an article carried in the May 14, 1899, edition of the *Chicago Inter Ocean:*

> *"Many people not familiar with the game of golf regard the terms golfer and dude as synonymous. They consider that the*

necessary attributes to constitute a thorough golfer are a red jacket, check knickerbockers and stockings, a tam o'shanter hat, and a bag full of clubs.''

But the newspaper report went on to remind readers "golf has made dozens of converts to the game in Chicago and judging from the present outlook, the golf fever is liable to become contagious." Golf did catch on quickly. By 1900, Chicago had 30 of the nearly 1,000 courses in the United States. It was clear the game was anything but the ephemeral fad some earlier critics had labeled it. Indeed, it was here to stay.

With courses popping up everywhere and the game's future looming bright, golf course architect Tom Bendelow issued a bold prediction in 1913. He stated, "The time is not far distant when there will not be a town of 10,000 which will not be able to boast of its (own) golf course." As it turned out, Bendelow's prediction didn't miss the mark by much.

By today's count, approximately 85 of the 122 municipalities within Cook, Du Page, Will, Kane, Lake and McHenry counties that have populations of 10,000 or more, according to the 1990 census, have at least one golf course. Not surprisingly, the city of Chicago leads the list with 13 course sites. Cicero has the dubious distinction of being the largest local municipality to miss the golf course trend. The area's 20 most populated cities and towns are listed, along with their course totals:

	Municipality	Population	Courses
1.	Chicago	2,783,726	13
2.	Aurora	99,581	3
3.	Naperville	85,351	6
4.	Elgin	77,010	4
5.	Joliet	76,836	3
6.	Arlington Heights	75,460	2
7.	Evanston	73,233	1
8.	Waukegan	69,392	4
9.	Schaumburg	68,586	2
10.	Cicero	67,436	0
11.	Skokie	59,432	2
12.	Oak Lawn	56,182	0

13.	Oak Park	53,648	0
14.	Des Plaines	53,223	1
15.	Mount Prospect	53,170	2
16.	Wheaton	51,464	3
17.	Downers Grove	46,858	1
18.	Hoffman Estates	46,561	3
19.	Berwyn	45,426	0
20.	Elmhurst	42,029	1

In addition to Chicago, Naperville, Elgin and Waukegan, nine other local municipalities have four or more separate course sites:

Municipality	Population	Courses
Glenview	37,093	5
Northbrook	32,308	5
Highland Park	30,575	5
St. Charles	22,501	5
Mundelein	21,215	5
Woodstock	14,353	4
Barrington	9,504	6
Oak Brook	9,178	4
Crete	6,773	4

While Bendelow expected larger sized towns to eventually tee it up, even he would have marveled at golf course proliferation in small towns. In particular, one Cook County municipality having just 454 residents AND a golf course immediately would have impressed Bendelow. The tiny village is named Golf. (Within its limits lies the private Glen View Club.) A list of the 10 smallest Chicago-area municipalities that can claim at least one golf course follows:

Municipality	Population
Golf	454
Richmond	1,016
North Barrington	1,787
Wadsworth	1,826
Sugar Grove	2,005
Huntley	2,453
Lake Villa	2,857
West Dundee	3,728
Burnham	3,916
Rosemont	3,995

Population and golf course totals aren't the only important numbers in evaluating a community's golfing interests. Another criteria is the number of golfers within the community. How do Chicago-area communities compare with the national average, which shows that approximately 18% of all U.S. households include at least one golfer? Listed below are several municipalities and the approximate percentage of golfing households:

Barrington	40%	Lemont	23%
Berwyn	18%	Maywood	11%
Cicero	13%	Naperville	35%
Elgin	22%	Olympia Fields	42%
Flossmoor	37%	Orland Park	38%
Glen Ellyn	32%	Robbins	4%
Kenilworth	40%	Winnetka	36%
Lake Forest	41%		

Is Olympia Fields the "golf center" of Chicagoland? About 42 of every 100 village households include a golfer. On the other hand, Olympia Fields has only one golfing facility. What about Chicago itself? Although only 18% of the city's households include a golfer, Chicago, with its much larger population, does have more courses than any other community in the area. Could Chicago be considered the "golf center" of the area? Finally, there is Lemont and its three golf facilities. Yet these three—Cog Hill Golf Club, Gleneagles Country Club and Mid Iron Club—provide 117 holes. No other local community except Chicago (with its 180 holes) has more. As Chicago's population is 378 times that of Lemont, could Lemont be called the "golfing center" of the area?

According to federal authorities, another Chicago-area community lays claim to this title. In fact, Orland Park is the officially recognized "World's Golf Center." Furthermore, the village has held this designation since 1964, when it acquired a copyright for the title. Currently, the title appears on all police uniforms and police cars. Each water tower is even painted in the form of a golf ball on a tee, advertising the village's moniker. Orland Park has only two golfing facilities—Silver Lake Country Club and the Crystal Tree Golf and Country Club—so why the tag line?

*Orland Park's
water towers
proclaim its official
designation
as the "World's
Golf Center."*

Originally, village leaders, among them Robert Johnson, based their logic on the number of golf holes within a 12.5 mile radius from Orland Park. In the '60s, more than 500 holes were within this 471 square mile area. Today, the number of holes is more than 1,000.

Other municipalities, including many in the local area, might also cite their reasons for believing they, and not Orland Park, are golf's worldwide center. Intramarket claims of No. 1 aside, most would probably agree that Chicago, in total, is the golfing center of the world.

More than 250 golf clubs, some featuring two, three or—in Cog Hill's example—four 18-hole courses, are found within the region's six major counties. For the purposes of this book, however, the definition of the Chicago district also will include portions of Grundy and Kendall counties plus Lake County, Ind. Furthermore, Lake Geneva, Wis., is also noted—it is a traditional playground for Chicago golfers who regularly return to its courses. Not included within the 5,000-square-mile mass are Rockford, Belvidere, De Kalb, Sycamore and municipalities east of Gary, Ind. By this broader geographic definition of the Chicago area, the golf club total surpasses 300.

At first glance, more than 300 total golf courses would seem to satisfy local demand. It certainly would if play were spread evenly throughout the week. Unfortunately, public course golfers are mostly preoccupied Monday through Friday, resulting in their flooding club phone lines to seek the limited weekend tee times available.

Frustrated in their efforts to secure a morning or early afternoon weekend slot, most local golfers wouldn't be surprised to hear that the National Golf Foundation considers

Chicago's metropolitan area "in need." With nearly one million players, the Chicago area should have at least 50%—or about 100—more public courses to meet demand effectively.

As golf's appeal continues to expand, attracting teens and pre-teens, retirees and seniors and—the fastest growing segment—women, the Chicago area will need additional golf clubs. Statistically, the demand is already present. From a practical perspective, however, it's doubtful even this golf-hungry region could support 100 new public courses—at least on a Monday through Friday basis. Today's economic realities prohibit such unabashed expansion.

Although golf started here in the 1890s, activities in the year 1833 laid a broad-based foundation for the game's debut. Chicago's incorporation as a town (pop. 200) was historically important and well documented, but—for golf—another event in 1833 was critical, providing land that, years later, would hold golfing treasures.

In 1833, Pottawatomie, Ottawa and Mohawk tribes negotiated a treaty with the federal government. In exchange for their ceded rights to 500 million acres of northern Illinois and southern Wisconsin wilderness, the Indian Nation received a promise of peace, $100,000 in cash and $100,000 in goods and annuities. The native Americans sold the land for next to nothing. In effect, the property transaction established a low-priced starting point, from which ensuing land values would slowly rise and then rocket during the 1960s and 1970s.

To put the original sale price in terms recognizable to a golfer, the government purchased each 200-acre parcel (the size of a typical Chicago-area country club) for approximately eight cents. Some 60 years later members of Chicago's first golf club purchased their 200-acre site for $28,000. Although the wholesale price index has increased approximately 10-fold from 1893 to 1991, land prices during the same period have gone up much more. Today, a 200-acre parcel of collar-county property is worth from four million to eight million dollars. The $28,000 price paid by Chicago's first club would barely buy enough land for a miniature golf course.

The price range of acreage during golf's 100-year evolution here is perhaps the most telling example of the game's escalating costs. By no means, though, can golf be labeled as exclusively a rich man's sport, regardless of what critics may suggest. While it is true men having the financial means participated almost exclusively in golf's earliest years here, the game is clearly within reasonable recreational spending limits. In relative terms, a four-hour round of golf is less expensive than watching a three-hour Bear game in Soldier Field or enjoying a two-hour dramatic production in the Chicago Opera House.

Still, the sport that critics once described as having a "silk stocking" following has an image of affluence. For example, current country club initiation fees often exceed $25,000. Some are now more than $50,000. In golf's first decade here, the highest initiation fees were $100 to $125.

Public golfers have also seen golf-related costs rise. Upscale championship-style daily-fee facilities charge $40 to $60 per round. Kemper Lakes, the area's priciest daily-fee course, is $90 (with cart). Even the more moderately priced daily-fee and municipal courses charge $20 to $40 per round.

Fortunately, most public courses feature reduced fees in the form of resident, twilight, senior or junior discounts. Then there's McArthur municipal in East Chicago— Chicago's least expensive 18 holes—where players only pay $3. Another bargain lies at the Barrington Park Golf Course. For just $2 a player can take in the five-hole, 675-yard course; for a dollar more, he or she can go around a second time. This is as close to free golf as there is in the Chicago area.

Actually, there was a time—in 1899 to 1920—when golfers played Chicago's municipal courses for free. When the city began charging nominal fees in 1921, players paid 10 cents per round or purchased a season pass for $2. As recently as 30 years ago, the nine-hole price at Chicago's city-owned courses was just 75 cents—$1.50 for 18 holes.

Golfers are also digging deeper into their pockets to pay for equipment. Improvements have pushed up equipment costs, in some cases into the $1,000 to $2,000 range.

While technology-driven clubs will improve a player's game, they will not mystically transform a high-handicap golfer into a scratch player. Nevertheless, it isn't unusual to observe less-skilled players exhibiting $1,000 clubs while registering 100-plus scores.

Shoes, gloves and other incidentals of the game do require upfront cash commitments. There is, however, a silver lining on the cost front. The price of golf balls has stayed remarkably constant throughout the past 60 years. That, in itself, is especially good news for local players who purchase about seven million balls annually. Of these, 25% wear out or are damaged; the other 75% are lost in thick cover, murky streams, trees or out-of-bounds areas. Many "lost" balls are retrieved by salvage crews or enterprising youngsters and are resold. Golfers usually lose these recycled balls, too.

Courtesy of Chicago District Golf Association

Arnold Palmer, member—Advisory Staff for Wilson Sporting Goods Co.

At least the beneficiaries of high-priced golf equipment and lost golf balls also are located in Chicago. Several of the game's major manufacturers headquarter here, including the largest—Wilson Sporting Goods.

Originally a meat-packing concern, the Thomas E. Wilson Company formed in 1914. In 1923, the company purchased the Western Sporting Goods Company. Two years later, their Advisory Staff concept debuted, incorporating the era's well-known golfers in Wilson's advertising programs. Those golfers—among them Gene Sarazen, Sam Snead, Ben Hogan, Patty Berg and Babe Zaharias—also offered suggestions in club design, a practice that continues today.

There were, of course, other local golf equipment manufacturers, but the majority have closed or been incorporated into other companies. Walgreen's is one company still in operation today that has lost its golf roots. In the '20s, the Walgreen's drugstore chain marketed its own house-brand golf ball, named the Po-Do. The company's founder, Charles Walgreen Sr., loved golf and belonged to several established clubs including Calumet and Beverly. At one point, he enlisted the services of professional Johnny Bulla to promote Po-Do balls, which led to Bulla's "Mr. Po-Do" nickname.

The Po-Do and Longway golf balls are long gone, as are the X- Ploder, Miss America and Shurput clubs and putters. All were manufactured by Chicago-based concerns. Today's local golf equipment manufacturers—Wilson, Ram, Tommy Armour, Pro Select and others—produce far superior products. Still, the names that spawn from space-age technology and modernspeak—for example, Ultra and Tour Lithium Balata golf balls or 845 S Silver Scot irons and Prism woods—do seem mundane compared to products of 50 years past.

Golf's 100-year march through Chicago's history has left many remnants in its path. Much of the game's early equipment has been tossed aside or even lost, much to the chagrin of current-day collectors who visit county fairs and garage sales in the hope of finding antiquated but valuable equipment and other golf collectibles.

As far back as the early years of the 20th century, equipment improvements aided golfers in lowering scores. This, in turn, influenced the definition of one particular golfing term, which had previously stood as the optimum score or standard of excellence on any given golf hole. The scoring objective today is to shoot par; however, years ago, the word "par" was nowhere to be found on the game's scorecard. Instead, players measured a hole's respective challenge by its "bogey" number. A 340-yard hole could be, for example, listed as a bogey 5. If by some fortunate event, a player registered a four, the hole total would be viewed as being one better than bogey. Predictably, the term "birdie" was also absent from early golfing jargon; besides, scoring "two under bogey" was about as common then as shooting a hole-in-one today.

USGA Museum & Library

Former Washington Park club pro, Fred Herd wears his U.S. Open medal. In 1898 he won the U.S. Open's first 72 hole event, going around the nine hole Myopia Hunt Club's course eight times.

Scores were higher 80 to 100 years ago, even among golf's early champions. Fred Herd, for example, then the club professional at the long-gone Washington Park Club, won the 1898 U.S. Open, his four-round score of 327 proved to be the best among 81 entrants. Two years later, the great English golfer, Harry Vardon, captured the 1900 U.S. Open at the Chicago Golf Club. Although his total equaled 313, it did include an opening round and precedent-setting 70. In the same tournament, however, John Harrison's four-round score of 393 still stands as the highest score recorded in U.S. Open competition. Harrison's infamous score is no doubt a record for the ages.

Since then, golf scores have drifted lower. When Hale Irwin and Mike Donald finished their four rounds at the 1990 U.S. Open at Medinah, they had identical totals of 280. While both had the advantage of employing modern clubs, they still had to play over a layout that was more difficult than venues of early Opens.

Medinah's No. 3 course is Chicago's most difficult. It receives the most attention, but there are other courses at area clubs that are nationally prominent, such as North Shore, Olympia Fields, Chicago Golf, Skokie, Midlothian and Onwentsia. Each has hosted at least one U.S. Open. Other clubs such as Glen View, Flossmoor, Hinsdale, Beverly, Idlewild, Glen Oak, Westmoreland, Calumet, Sunset Ridge and Butler National have hosted Western Opens. The market's newer residential golf course communities will only strengthen the local mix. Stonebridge has already played host to a Senior PGA Tour event—the 1991 Ameritech Senior Open. Certainly, the courses of Bull Valley, Royal Fox, Wynstone, White Eagle and Boulder Ridge are equally as impressive. And while the public is restricted at these private clubs, they can enjoy the courses at Kemper Lakes, Dubsdread, Forest Preserve National, Pine Meadow, Cantigny, Seven Bridges, Tamarack and Odyssey.

Actually, Chicago's golfing community never had it so good. Granted the weather limits the season to six or seven months, the costs to play a round have increased and weekend tee times are at a premium. Still, there exist immeasurable benefits to players here, which have clearly established Chicago as a user-friendly golfing market. Chicago even has the country's first club to add a sport's psychologist to its staff. Bud Gunn fills this roll at Glen-woodie. As the author of *How to Play Golf with Your Wife and Survive,* Gunn certainly has the qualifications to assist any golfer in taking a positive mental approach to the game.

For local enthusiasts looking for more than food for thought to improve their game, players at the Hilldale club in Hoffman Estates have a unique culinary option awaiting them after their round. There's a small clubhouse coffee shop available, but some may choose to dine at the on-grounds Nippon-Kan—it's the only Japanese restaurant at an area course. It's also the only area club owned by a Japanese company.

Chicago's reputation as a golfing mecca is not based on its Japanese restaurant or its sport's psychologist. Still, they and the charity events, golfing associations, club pros, per-sonalities, architects, periodicals, courses, tradition, oddities and the Chicago-area players themselves are the unique in-gredients that have blended nicely during the last 100 years to create Chicago's acclaimed golfing environment.

2

What's In A Name?

The Onwentsia Club takes its name from the Indian word that means "meeting place for sporting braves and their squaws." Stonehenge shares its name with an ancient monument more than 3,000 years old. Still others can trace their club names to an epic poem (Odyssey), a World War I battle site (Cantigny), a fictional character in medieval England (Ivanhoe) and a type of clothing (Tam).

Wm. Daniels/The Photo Partners

Cantigny's name still throws players for a loop. The correct pronunciation is Can-TEE-ney.

Before any club begins, it needs a name. Chicago names are as distinctive, unusual and fun as the clubs and courses themselves.

Sometimes they are even cause for debate. Just ask the five members who served on Naperville's Board of Commissioners in 1989. Before Naperville's new six million dollar championship-styled municipal course would officially open, it needed a name. Board officials carefully considered a list of suitable options: the alliterate Crego Crossing, amusing Bydew-Way, convergent Farmers Corners, pictures-que Pheasant Ridge and the open-vista Naperville Plains. In the end, the board chose none of these. Instead, *Naperbrook* gained board approval by a single vote. The two dissenters felt the name lacked "pizazz" and sounded "subdivision-like."

Some Naperville residents cried foul. To these unhappy taxpayers, the name Naperbrook sounded Bolingbrook-like. Considering that Naperville's neighbor to the south hadn't shared in the cost of the new golf course, a few Naperville folks seriously questioned their village board's selection of Naper"brook." The board deflated this mistaken theory by quickly pointing out the "brook" part of Naperbrook originated from Naperville's other municipal course—Springbrook.

If selecting a new name isn't hard enough, the process of renaming an established golf course can be downright inflammatory. This is precisely what occurred in 1991 at one of the area's famous layouts.

Golfers have played more than four million rounds at the Waveland Golf Course during its seven-decade run. But as of June 1991, the Waveland name became officially obsolete. Park District officials renamed the Lincoln Park course—the Sydney R. Marovitz Golf Course.

Here again, the selection of the new name created controversy. Proponents labeled the change as progressive. Marovitz was, they correctly declared, a distinguished labor lawyer and a champion of civil rights. Besides, they added, the Waveland name wasn't particularly meaningful—after all, it was just a city street. Opponents of the change did not question Marovitz's integrity. They were chagrined, however, that the one-time Chicago Park District official's name replaced Waveland with no public debate or prior notification. (Because it's more widely recognized, the Waveland name will continue to be used in this book).

*An aerial view of the
Waveland Golf Course
in 1948.*

*In 1991 Waveland officially became the
Sydney R. Marovitz Golf Course.*

Forest Preserve National, operated by Cook County's
Forest Preserve District, also appears ready to take a new
name. Opened in 1982, the tough 18-hole course is one of
the country's finest. There are indications the name of
former Cook County Board President George Dunne will
soon be added to the club's current designation. In all probability, though, the "George W. Dunne National" name
won't be seriously challenged. For starters, the current

name—Forest Preserve National—is less than 10 years old. More importantly, Dunne is recognized as one who spearheaded efforts to bring a quality county-operated course to the southern suburbs. The name change, to honor Dunne's leadership, seems justifiable. (At press time, the 18-hole course is still officially named Forest Preserve National.)

Actually, many Cook County Forest Preserve courses and Chicago municipal courses have taken their names from individuals. Few players would take exception to the old and recognizable course names. In the case of the Marquette, Jackson and Columbus golf courses, the names are natural extensions of the city parks in which the courses lie. Chicago's newest course is located on the far north side, in Warren Park. The park's nine-hole course is, however, named after Robert A. Black, a Park District employee of more than 50 years.

Of the 10 Cook County Forest Preserve courses, three are named after individuals. Two names are immediately recognizable: Chick Evans and Joe Louis. (They were both great champions—in fact, the official name of the Joe Louis course is Joe Louis the Champ Golf Course.) The third, Billy Caldwell, is probably a mystery to many Chicagoans. Although there is also a street named after him, Caldwell wasn't 1) Chick Evans' personal caddy; 2) Joe Louis' sparing partner; 3) an employee of the Cook County Forest Preserve District; or 4) a one-time Chicago politician. Caldwell was, instead, an important pioneer in Chicago history. The son of an Irish military officer and a Pottawatomie Indian maiden, Caldwell had the benefit of receiving a formal education. Upon completion, he went back to his mother's tribe and served as chief of the Pottawatomie Indians. As Caldwell was taller than all those he led, the tribe's members referred to him as Sauganash, an Indian word meaning "tall Englishman." Caldwell's most important contribution to Chicago's early history was in saving the lives of several white settlers against renegade attacks.

Before his and other friendly tribes sold their land to the government in 1833, Caldwell's tribe lived on what is now Chicago's northern border. This neighborhood today—Sauganash—includes the nine-hole Billy Caldwell golf course.

Several other golf clubs within the broader Chicago area can trace their names to individuals. One of the oldest facilities is at Elgin's Wing Park. Wing was an Elgin-based attorney. When he died early in the 20th century, his will specified his 100-acre estate should become a public park. Through the efforts of Elgin Mayor Arwin Price, a portion of the land was set aside in 1907 for a nine-hole municipal course. Price was partly motivated because many of his political enemies were members of the relatively new Elgin Country Club. In supporting development of the region's first municipal club outside of Chicago's city limits, Price endeared himself to Elgin's voters while still jabbing at many of his political rivals.

Peter N. Jans' motives weren't nearly as calculating. In organizing the course in 1916 (which was originally called the Evanston Community Golf Club), Jans had a noble objective. He wanted a course that north suburban caddies and Evanston residents could have access to, and afford. Today, the Peter N. Jans Golf Course is named for this civic leader.

The area's largest golf site is the 72-hole Cog Hill Golf Club. Its name comes from its founders, Marty and Bert Coghill. In the late '20s, the site had but two 18-hole layouts. Its current owner, Joe Jemsek, commissioned construction of courses No. 3 and No. 4 in the early '60s. Incidentally, when Jemsek acquired the site from the Coghills in the early '50s, there was tacit agreement between the parties that the Coghill name would remain.

Other Illinois-based facilities that take their names from their founders are:

Anets Golf Course (Frank Anetsberger)
Butler National (Paul Butler)
Craig Woods Golf Club
    (Richard and Mary Ann Craig)
Ravisloe Country Club (the Ravisloot family)
Zigfield Troy Par 3 (Zigfield Troy)

In Indiana, the Gleason Park Golf Course is named after U.S. Steel executive, John Gleason, and the Palmira Golf and Country Club takes its name from the grandmother of the club's founder, Dr. A.P. Vonazentura.

There is still another "person-named" club—the Richton Park-based Urban Hills facility, named for its founder John Urban. Without knowing the background, though, an uninitiated golfer might consider the name Urban Hills a contradiction in terms. In fact, several local clubs have anomalous designations.

It's always confusing for some area residents to discover the Evanston Golf Club is in Skokie and that the Skokie Country Club is in Glencoe. Dare they ask were the Glencoe Golf Club is? (It's in Glencoe.)

The historic Chicago Golf Club's clubhouse as it appears today.

In reality, only a handful of club names are geographic misfits; in each case, there does exist a logical explanation. In the Evanston example, the club had three different homes before it finally settled in Skokie. The Glencoe-based Skokie club has never moved, though; it took its name from the Skokie stream that once wound through the property. Then there's the region's first club, Chicago Golf. Originally located in Belmont (Downers Grove), the club moved to Wheaton in 1895. It took its name from the downtown-based Chicago Club.

Besides Evanston, Skokie and Chicago, the following clubs are also names of local municipalities. All, however, lie in communities different from their club name.

Bull Valley Golf Club (Woodstock)
Calumet Country Club (Homewood)
Calumet Golf Club (Gary, Ind.)
Glendale Golf Club (Bloomingdale)
Hinsdale Golf Club (Clarendon Hills)
Kankakee Elks Club Golf Course (St. Anne)
Oak Park Country Club (Elmwood Park)
River Forest Country Club (Elmhurst)
Riverside Golf Club (North Riverside)
Riverside Park Golf Course (Libertyville)

The background behind the Glen View Club, located not in Glenview but in Golf, Ill., deserves greater elaboration.

In 1898, the chairman of the Chicago, Milwaukee & St. Paul Railroad loved to play golf; one of his favorite clubs was Glen View. The train's engineers would take their boss, in his private car, to a dropoff site close to the course. After completing his round, he would be picked up at the same site along the train line. Engineers called the meeting place the golf station. A few years later, the railroad built a public depot on the site. By then, the area post office was also known as Golf. When the tiny village incorporated in 1928, the logical name for the community became Golf.

The Village of Golf has 454 residents and the private Glen View Club.

Although the village—Golf—did not take its name from the local country club per se, other newly formed communities did. Five examples are Midlothian, Olympia

Chicago Historical Society ICHi-22770
Photo by Earl Vilven

Built in the 1920s, the West Chicago-based St. Andrews clubhouse.

Fields, Medinah, Hickory Hills and Woodridge (although the original Woodridge golf course no longer exists).

For the most part, however, the opposite is true. There are at least 60 local clubs that share the same name as the municipality in which they are based.

Some clubs aren't shy about taking their names from areas beyond the greater Chicago region. While these include a club named after a state (Golf Club of Illinois) or a Minnesota lake (Itasca Country Club), most out-of-market name origins are international. In fact, a few take their names from famous Scottish and English golf clubs. From this list, local clubs such as St. Andrews (without an apostrophe, just like its namesake, and unlike the St. Andrew's Golf Club in New York), Turnberry and Prestwick serve as examples. In 1992, a new entry—Royal Melbourne—makes its Chicago debut. The Long Grove residential golf course community borrows its name from Greg Norman's favorite layout in Melbourne, Australia.

Many other clubs have names with a local flavor— names taken from the natural characteristics of the Chicago landscape. It is almost impossible to play golf locally and not run across a course with Pond, Stream, Creek, Spring, Highland, Valley, Riverside, Ridge, Meadow, Hill, Knoll, Field, Path, Run, Trail, Oak, Pine, Tree, Wood, Orchard,

Hickory, Apple, Walnut, Plum, Poplar, Green or Lawn in its name.

Typically, several of these natural characteristics double as golf course hazards. The sport's other major hazard—sand—while not technically a "natural" characteristic of any course is rarely used in club names. There is only one: the Sand Creek Country Club in Chesterton, Ind. In earlier days, Niles housed the now defunct Bunker Hill Golf Club.

While sand is not particularly popular, club names that have lake orientations are. These include: Shoreacres, Lake Shore, Ruth Lake, Kemper Lakes, Lake Bluff, Lake Barrington Shores, Lake Hills, Lake Park, Lakes of the Four Seasons, Twin Lakes, Lake Zurich, Country Lakes, Silver Lake, Americana Lake Geneva, the recently changed Waveland and the no longer existent Edgewater and Michigan Shores clubs.

Indian tribes, artifacts or words from Indian culture provide yet another bountiful source of club names. Billy Caldwell has already been noted. His tribe, however, is still remembered in St. Charles at their Pottawatomie Golf Course. At Bloomingdale's 36-hole Indian Lakes Resort, two other tribes are recognized: one 18 is named Iroquois, the other Sioux. Bensenville had at one time a club called Mohawk. Pistakee, as in Pistakee Country Club, is an Indian word for buffalo. Thunderbird, White Eagle, Minne Monesse, Indian Boundary, Indian Valley, Indian Hill and Arrowhead are further references to Indian heritage.

While at least 30 local clubs existed before the end of 1900, the Chicago area has only four that are "old" in name—Old Elm, Old Oak, Old Orchard and Old Wayne. All but Old Wayne have been around for more than 70 years. Old Wayne, however, started in the 1960s. Sometimes the '60s seem like ancient history, too.

The oldest of the four is Old Elm. The course opened in 1913 on a site that had been a virgin oak forest. So why did club organizers choose the name Old Elm? Near the clubhouse stood one magnificent elm tree, at least 193 years old back in 1913. It remained deeply rooted until 1958, when the then 238-year-old wonder died due to disease.

Lockport's Old Oak Country Club had its start in the '20s, though the club's original name was Kinsmans. Throughout the next four decades, the facility had several owners and various club names. When new owners purchased the then-named Eldorado Golf Club in the '60s, they changed the name to Old Oak. In part, the new name was picked because of cost efficiencies. One of Old Oak's new owners also owned the Old Orchard Country Club. Since he already had an ample supply of napkins, coasters and placemats with an "OO" insignia, the Old Oak name fit the bill.

A brief sampling of other course names and their origins not previously covered are:

- Arboretum Golf Club (Buffalo Grove)
  —once served as nursery grounds.
- Balmoral Woods Country Club (Crete)
  —named for Balmoral Racetrack.
- Beverly Country Club (Chicago)
  —part of the Beverly neighborhood.
- Bob O'Link Golf Club (Highland Park)
  —named for a farm on the site.
- Glen Oak Country Club (Glen Ellyn)
  —most early members lived in Glen Ellyn or Oak Park.
- Inverness Golf Club
  —named for the county in Scotland from which the ancestors of the club's founder had come.
- Kemper Lakes (Hawthorn Woods)
  —takes its name from the Kemper Insurance Group.
- Knollwood Club (Lake Forest)
  —named for the Knollwood Farm.
- Midlothian Country Club
  —takes its name from the middle county of a three-county area in Scotland called Lothian.
- Nordic Hills Resort (Itasca)
  —founders were Scandinavians.
- Seven Bridges Golf Club (Woodridge)
  —there are seven bridges on the course.
- Shiloh Golf Course (Zion)
  —biblical village in Palestine.
- Tamarack Golf Club (Naperville)
  —named after a 19th century post office.

- Wynstone (North Barrington)
  —"Wyn" is an abbreviation for the Windy City,
  while "stone" comes from the site's prior
  owner—W. Clement Stone.

Midlothian's clubhouse in the 1950s looks much the same as it did at the turn-of-the-century.

Knowing the names and origins of local clubs won't improve your golf game. The information cannot be exchanged for a better Saturday tee time. Still, the names of area clubs are important. Sometimes, they are hints of a club's genesis. Other names can provide clues to present day topography. A few pay homage to their organizers or early pioneers. Many signal geographic locales or are reminiscent of far away places. Some are odd, others are plain, but all are different and greatly enhance the texture of Chicago golf.

The Early Days: 1875-1893

Some may argue golf first arrived in the Chicago area in 1875. A makeshift three-hole "course" had been laid out on the deserted grounds of Camp Douglas, a Civil War internment facility for Confederate soldiers. Empty ration cans left behind served as the holes.

Charles Blair Macdonald provided the impetus behind this first Chicago layout. It represented an austere beginning for Macdonald's eventual contributions to the sport. By the time he died in 1939, C.B. Macdonald would be recognized not only as the father of Chicago golf but also the father of American golf course architecture.

The Camp Douglas experiment was nothing more than a two-or-three-time exercise—played in the twilight by Macdonald and Edward R. Burgess, a visiting chum. Any thought of course expansion was quickly ruled out due to the destructive antics of local ruffians. As soon as Macdonald and Burgess would leave the site, the neighborhood's bullies wasted no time in thrashing the holes and putting surfaces. This infrequent golfing activity did, however, signify for some historians the beginning of local golf.

During the 1880s, the pace picked up. For the most part, documentation of these early games is sketchy, though informal get-togethers were recorded in Geneva and Hinsdale.

As to the question of the first golf game within Chicago's city limits during the 1880s, local historians cite two incidents—in 1887 and 1888. Coincidentally, the details of each event include the presence of one Robert W. Chandler. In 1887, Chandler and three other Englishmen traversed Jackson Park engaged in a driving contest, aiming at stakes driven in the ground. Park police soon suspended the friendly competition.

In 1888, Chandler was at it again—this time alone on three improvised holes in Washington Park. An emigrant from Hoylake, England, two years previously, the former cotton broker was a serious student of the game—who often spent entire summers at the famous Royal Liverpool Golf Club. With no such organized golfing facility in Chicago, Chandler trekked out to Washington Park and set up three stakes as targets. His actions attracted first the quizzical attention of curious onlookers, then a policeman. Questioned by the uniformed Irishman on the meaning of Chandler's antics, the Englishman explained he was playing golf. Not at all familiar with the term, the policeman found the response unacceptable, which prompted him to order an immediate halt to further activity. Evicted but not defeated, the aroused Chandler fired off a parting comment, "This, the game of golf, will be known as the world's greatest pastime before Ireland becomes a nation."

It wasn't until the early 1890s that golf's development began in earnest. The Chicago area's first officially recognized, standard-sized golf course was created as part of the newly formed Chicago Golf Club. Three distinct factors led to the club's formation. One was the creation of a seven-hole mini-layout in Lake Forest. A second catalyst involved the opening of the Chicago World's Fair in 1893. The third, and perhaps most prominent influence, was Charles Blair Macdonald.

Born in Canada in 1856, Macdonald was the son of a well-to-do Scottish father and Canadian mother. Growing up in Chicago, young Charlie was sent overseas in 1872 to study at the United Colleges of St. Salvador and St. Leonard's in St. Andrews, Scotland. There, Macdonald's grandfather introduced the 16-year old to the sport by taking him to the famed golfing shrine—The Royal and Ancient Golf Club of St. Andrews.

Macdonald quickly became enamored with the game. With his grandfather pulling the right strings, Charlie was granted locker facilities within the club-making shop of "Old" Tom Morris. When he wasn't playing the famous course—sometimes as late as 10 p.m. in June and July—

Courtesy of Chicago District Golf Association

Tom Morris Golf Shop at The Royal and Ancient Golf Club of St. Andrews in more modern times.

Macdonald would spend spare hours at this unique shop. It was there he would listen to the luminaries in the sport, including "Old" and "Young" Tom Morris, a father and son duo who had won eight of the first 12 British Open titles.

The two years abroad were a personally fulfilling period—one that shaped his future attitudes on not only the game itself but also golf as a revered treasure. In 1874, he returned to Chicago and immediately began an 18-year crusade, preaching the sport's virtues to anyone who would listen. It was a calling that, for the most part, went unheeded. After all, many in his social and business circles knew absolutely nothing of the sport beyond what Macdonald told them. In his book, *Scotland's Gift: Golf*, Macdonald would later refer to this period as the "dark years." Frustrated in his inability to enlighten those around him, he would at least occasionally enjoy the game on business trips to Great Britain.

In April of 1892, Macdonald's dream of organizing a Chicago golf haven was nearing reality. The first step in this process was the formation of a tiny seven-hole course in Lake Forest. It ran along the Lake Michigan shore, occupying the grounds of two summer estates and adjoining park. The estates were owned by John H. Dwight and C.B. Farwell.

Farwell's son-in-law, Hobart C. Chatfield-Taylor, was a close friend of Macdonald. Though the two men shared many of life's interests, golf wasn't one of them. Considering that he had never played the game—indeed, only knew of its existence by what Macdonald had told him— Chatfield-Taylor at first was annoyed by Macdonald's preoccupation with the sport. Whether it was Macdonald's repeated chronicles of old St. Andrews or his persuasive power, Chatfield-Taylor's views on golf changed. He began to help Macdonald find land for a golf course. Lake Forest thus became the site of Chicago's first regular golf games during the summer of 1892. From Macdonald's perspective, the land was not exactly the embodiment of a classic golf course. For starters, the acreage was limited—only 20 acres. Second, there were too many trees and flower beds. To Macdonald, the finished product wouldn't serve the needs of a purist like himself, but would suffice as an initial golfing venue.

Driving stakes in the ground to designate where the seven future holes would lie, Macdonald laid out the course within two hours. Before doing so, however, Macdonald

Courtesy of Chicago District Golf Association

Hobart Chatfield-Taylor   *Charles Blair Macdonald*

took his friend to a point overlooking the shore. It would be at this locale the golf craze in the West began. As Chatfield-Taylor watched, Macdonald placed a ball on a sandy mound. Club in hand, Macdonald positioned himself toward the water—paused slightly—and then swung. His club whizzed through the air and hit the ball with a smack. They watched the ball's flight as it arced first skyward and then into the lake. Macdonald teed another ball—this time passing the driver to Chatfield-Taylor. Imitating his friend's actions, Chatfield-Taylor swung mightily at the ball. Several years later, Chatfield-Taylor documented the outcome of his initial golfing effort: ". . . after a series of contortions which would have done honor to the rubber man in Barnum's side show, (I) tore up a foot of turf without disturbing the equanimity of the little white object I had striven so viciously to hit. Macdonald laughed and I said damn. That was in April of 1892—and I have been saying it ever since."

Macdonald completed his Lake Forest assignment and returned to Chicago. Before leaving, he left behind several golf clubs and a generous supply of balls for his Lake Forest friend. A week later, Urban H. Broughton joined Chatfield-Taylor on the new links. Broughton was an English native—experienced with the game, and eager to play the only Chicago-area golf site. Playing conditions could have been better. Permanent hole cups were not in place. Furthermore, a heavy downpour continued throughout the afternoon. They toured the course anyway, allowing "holed" shots to be those hitting the stakes. By day's end, their enthusiasm remained high, although the same could not be said about their golf ball inventory, as most of Macdonald's leftovers from the prior week were lost.

That summer, Lake Forest served as the exclusive domain of golf in the Chicago area. However, only visiting Englishmen and a few locals took time to enjoy its enchantment. As Chatfield-Taylor noted, most who passed the in-progress activities "stared in amazement or as was more often the case laughed derisively at (the) antics."

Macdonald played the Lake Forest course too, though his visits were infrequent. He simply found it unchallenging.

That summer and fall, Macdonald continued to search

for a more traditional course site—one where he would organize the Chicago area's first golf club.

Golf historians agree that the 1893 Chicago World's Fair bolstered his efforts. Among the visitors who came here in 1892 and 1893 were English citizens, including the distinguished Sir Henry Trueman Wood, who was the British Commissioner General to the Columbian Exposition. The British delegation made it quickly known of their desire to play golf here; in fact, Wood had even brought his golf clubs. Prior to this official call for a legitimate golfing venue, Macdonald had never totally convinced his friends and associates of the need for a golf club, but, suddenly, many fellow members of the downtown-based Chicago Club became eager to fulfill Sir Wood's request.

Chicago Golf Club Incorporates in Belmont

With 30 contributions of $10 each, Macdonald used the $300 to lease 60 acres of rolling countryside 24 miles southwest of Chicago in Belmont (now Downers Grove). On July 19, 1893, the Chicago Golf Club was incorporated. Incorporators of Chicago's first golfing organization included Macdonald, Chatfield-Taylor and Urban H. Broughton.

The approximate 2,800-yard nine-hole layout attracted not only Sir Wood and other British dignitaries, but, more importantly, fulfilled Macdonald's dream to organize a golf club in this area.

While this club was the region's first, golf historians still debate two issues relating to the Belmont site. The first question is which year—1892 or 1893—marked the inaugural year of golfing activity at Belmont. The second question has even greater importance: whether Macdonald expanded the nine-hole course into one having 18 holes. There are some who claim Belmont did have 18 holes; if this is true, the course would have been the first in the country to feature 18 holes.

In my opinion, 1893 was the year that signaled initial play at Belmont. Joseph Ryan, the golf editor of the *Chicago Inter Ocean* newspaper, wrote in 1900:

"In 1893...Charles Blair Macdonald...laid out a crude course at Belmont...in connection with which the Chicago Golf Club was soon after established."

Additionally, Chatfield-Taylor, himself, wrote in a magazine article published in 1900:

"The Chicago Golf Club sprang into being...in 1893...too late (in that year) to bear visible fruits."

It is also my opinion that the Belmont site never had more than nine holes. Again, citing the *Chicago Inter Ocean* and its golf editor, Joseph Ryan, who wrote in 1896:

"By 1895 the (Chicago Golf) club thus founded had grown to such proportions that all the officers and wealthier members separated from their original organization (at Belmont) and purchased the Wheaton (site) and laid out the only full eighteen-hole course in the country."

Four years later in 1900, Ryan added these remarks:

"An option of land had been secured by the Belmont Club for the purpose of adding nine holes but the club never exercised the option."

Incidentally, the Belmont club, to which Ryan referred, was a new golf organization that had taken over the site vacated by the Chicago Golf Club when that club moved to Wheaton.

Here again, the words of Chatfield-Taylor are noteworthy. In the book, *Golf—A Turn-of-the-Century Treasury,* published in 1986, insightful golf-related articles from magazines of the 1895-1909 era are reprinted. Chatfield-Taylor's contribution entitled, "The Development of Golf in the West," refers to Chicago-area golf in the 1890s. He states:

"In 1895 there were but three golf courses near Chicago, with but one eighteen hole course."

The three courses he refers to are the 18-hole course at the Chicago Golf Club in Wheaton and the two nine-hole courses at Belmont and Lake Forest, the last named, an outgrowth of the mini-layout first played in 1892.

Ironically, there wouldn't be any debate on either of the

two issues in question if C.B. Macdonald hadn't created the controversy himself. In his 1928 published memoirs, *Scotland's Gift: Golf*, Macdonald claims that Belmont opened for play in 1892. He further states that a second nine holes were added in 1893. The course's present operator, the Downers Grove Park District, echoes Macdonald's claims. In fact, the village is scheduling a 100th anniversary ceremony in 1992 for what they believe is the site of the country's first 18-hole golf course.

Clearly, there is a difference of opinion regarding Belmont's original year of operation and whether it represented the country's first 18-hole golf course. All sides do, however, agree on one important point: Chicago Golf Club's Belmont site was the Chicago area's first nine-hole course. Its early success helped build a solid foundation for the sport's growth during the 1890s and into the 20th century.

The Nation's First 18-Hole Golf Course–At Wheaton

With funding of about $28,000, C.B. Macdonald really put Chicago Golf Club on the map in 1894—and into golfing history. Buying 200 acres of land one mile south of Wheaton in 1894, the Chicago Golf Club made its site ready for play by May 1, 1895. With all due respect to Macdonald's claim that he designed the country's first 18-hole course at *Belmont*, many historians consider the first 18-hole course in the United States to be at *Wheaton*. The original distance was 5,877 yards. By 1900, the club lengthened the course to 6,032 yards, although in doing so shortened its two longest holes.

Distances of the individual holes for both the original layout and (modified) layout are as follows:

#1	337	(460)	#10	129	(140)
#2	327	(330)	#11	242	(270)
#3	319	(340)	#12	308	(330)
#4	390	(415)	#13	513	(500)
#5	328	(320)	#14	334	(300)
#6	560	(520)	#15	350	(350)
#7	300	(285)	#16	317	(310)
#8	268	(260)	#17	347	(320)
#9	138	(160)	#18	370	(422)
	2,967	(3,090)		2,910	(2,942)

How important was the Chicago Golf Club in the development of local golf? That question may be too limiting in scope. A more appropriate question would be, "Is it true the Chicago Golf Club shaped the development of golf's growth nationwide?" The answer is a resounding yes!

Take a closer look at the club's résumé of major tournaments:

- Three U.S. Opens (1897, 1900, 1911)
- First U.S. Open anywhere outside Eastern locales (1897)
- First and only U.S Open won by the legendary Harry Vardon (1900)
- First U.S. Open won by a native-born American, John J. McDermott in 1911
- Four U.S. Amateurs (1897, 1905, 1909, 1912)
- One U.S. Women's Amateur and the first contested outside the East (1903)
- One Walker Cup competition (1928)

Macdonald patterned his design of the Chicago Golf Club's course after Scotland's St. Andrews layout. Grass-covered mounds, rolling terrain and pot bunkers—all traditional characteristics of a links-type course—were present. The Wheaton-based club also was similar in yardage to St. Andrews, a fact not ignored by those who suggested Charlie Macdonald always wanted to show Americans what a first-rate British course looked like. As a course architect, Macdonald was the quintessential traditionalist. He rejected the notion that hilly terrain enhanced a course's appeal and referred those who did to take up mountain climbing. He also considered trees a detriment, especially those close to the playing area.

Bunkers were a different matter, however; for Macdonald, they represented the only true golf course obstacles. In his opinion, any good golf hole should feature bold bunkers around the green and one or two more in the fairway. He explained their necessary presence this way, "The object of a bunker or trap is not only to punish a physical mistake, to punish lack of control, but also punish pride and egotism. If I had my way, I'd never let the sand (traps) be raked. Instead, I'd run a herd of elephants through them every morning." (Macdonald's pachyderms would have to rise early, though, at the present Chicago Golf Club course—it contains 120 sand traps!)

Though he took great care in designing the integral elements of each hole, Macdonald paid particular attention to the greens. He believed the soul of any golf course should lie within its putting surface. No doubt this conviction led to two Chicago Golf Club "firsts" in 1897. The Wheaton links became the first in the country to use bent

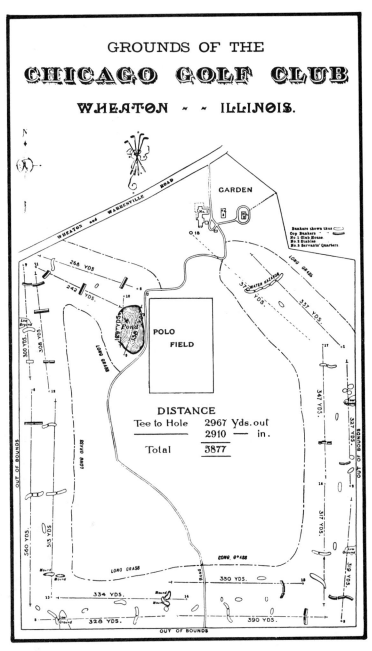

GROUNDS OF THE

CHICAGO GOLF CLUB

WHEATON ~ ~ ILLINOIS.

GARDEN

POLO FIELD

DISTANCE

Tee to Hole	2967 Yds. out
	2910 — in.
Total	5877

grass on its greens, the result of imported Holland seed. The second innovation saw the construction of a central watering plant that served as an irrigation source for the greens. Four miles of piping and two massive tanks fed by a steam-engine made it possible to pump 100,000 gallons per day to the club's 18 greens. Characteristic of the Wheaton course and other later designs, putts ran "true," an absolute requirement of any Macdonald creation.

Another first at CGC is also credited as a worldwide first—the out-of-bounds rule. Until the Chicago Golf Club established the out-of-bounds rule, the game's adopted practice had always been to play it where it lies. The new rule came about directly from Macdonald's design of the course.

Besides his skills as a course architect and general promoter of the sport, Macdonald was also an excellent golfer. He was, however, prone to slice off the tee. It therefore was no coincidence that CGC's first seven holes were arranged clockwise. Furthermore, several holes favored a left-to-right ball trajectory. In other words, slicing shots tended to be rewarded.

Conversely, players hitting balls right to left, or hooking, often faced second-shot lies from an adjoining farmer's field. Predictably, the "hookers" of the club weren't pleased with the course's apparent design discrimination.

At first, Macdonald fought any rule change. Remember, he had learned the game under the great masters at St. Andrews. There, the original 13 rules of golf were still being used. Under pressure, Macdonald came to endorse a rule-change compromise: All tee shots landing in the farmer's field would be considered out of bounds. Players would then be allowed to hit again from the tee area. For scoring purposes the re-hit would be considered their second shot.

Ironically, it would be Macdonald's strict interpretation of golf's rules that would lead in December 1894 to the formation of golf's first national governing body, the Amateur Golf Association of the United States. Five golf clubs formed this body, with the Chicago Golf Club being the only charter member not located in the East. Within a year, the organization changed its name to the United States Golf Association or USGA.

There was no USGA in September 1894 when Macdonald and 19 others competed in the first amateur championship in this country. He was favored to win the event at the Newport Golf Club in Rhode Island; with a medal-play format (best score) Macdonald's score of 189 over 36 holes fell one stroke short of winning. A month later at another amateur championship at the St. Andrew's Golf Club in New York, match play was the format (most holes won). Tournament organizers invited twenty-eight players, including Macdonald. Advancing to the final round, Macdonald and one other entrant were tied through 18 holes. The victor of this match would, of course, be the declared champion. After the first hole of sudden death, the outcome was the same: Macdonald had lost again.

Considered the best amateur golfer of the time, Macdonald was infuriated with two second-place finishes. He vehemently protested the results of both competitions, claiming each should be declared invalid. He said medal play should not have been the format in the Newport event, claiming match play should have determined the outcome just like the respected British Amateur championship. Macdonald's objection at the New York St. Andrew's-hosted championship didn't involve concerns of format but eligibility. A true national championship should include all qualified players, he suggested, not just those awarded entry by invitation.

First U.S. Amateur

One year later, in October 1895, the U.S. Amateur championship, now under the auspices of the USGA, took place at the Newport club. The format was match play. Thirty-two qualified entrants participated. At the tourney's conclusion, Macdonald had finally proved his playing prowess, winning the event easily. This time, no protests were filed.

The second USGA-sanctioned Amateur championship took place at the Shinnecock Hills Golf Club in New York the following year, and 58 players qualified. Macdonald did not win but his future son-in-law, H.J. Whigham, did.

In late 1896, Macdonald lobbied to bring the event to the Chicago Golf Club. He attempted to convince fellow USGA members that major golfing events could be contested outside the East. He forcefully suggested his Chicago Golf Club was the "only first class 18-hole golf course in America." (By then, other 18-hole courses did exist.) He won. In 1897, the USGA scheduled both the U.S. Amateur and the U.S. Open at the Chicago Golf Club. Both championships were played during the same week.

Early shot of original Chicago Golf Clubhouse.

Even in its early years, the CGC's course received innovative care and consideration. Grazing sheep were brought in to pare down the fairway grass. Several years later, the club used the first mowing machine on a golf course. Pulling the machine were two horses, their feet covered by boots to protect the fairway. The club even fined members $1 for not replacing fairway divots. It was a rule strictly enforced.

The layout today is still meticulously cared for and just as highly regarded. While CGC maintains a low public profile, golf's insiders know it well. Two of its par 4s—the second and twelfth holes—rank No. 13 and No. 14 respectively on *Golf Magazine's* 100 "greatest" American holes. As a group, the course's twelve par 4 holes are the most challenging fours of any American golfing facility.

Courtesy of Chicago District Golf Association

Harry Vardon won the 1900 U.S. Open at the Chicago Golf Club.

Any mention of CGC's current stature or illustrious past fails to underscore its impact on American golf. More than just the embodiment of Chicago-area golf, C.B. Macdonald and his club were the major forces propelling the game into rapid acceptance. From such a simple beginning—its original charter stated, ''pleasure and playing a game called golf''—the Chicago Golf Club continues to stand as the unquestioned shrine of local clubs. It was here that Bobby Jones and Harry Vardon came and triumphed. It was here that the McCormicks and Fields and Pullmans gathered—joined by other influential families of Chicago's elite. It was also here that C.B. Macdonald realized his earliest dream—to build a golfing jewel, whose luster shines as brightly today as it did nearly 100 years ago.

The Formative Years: 1893-1900

When the Chicago Golf Club incorporated in 1893, few could have guessed that eight years later 30 local golfing organizations would be operating. Golf's spreading popularity and rapid growth amazed even the sport's most avid proponents. As the 20th century dawned, the Chicago region had more courses than any other region in the country except New York.

Local expansion occurred through a combination of favorable circumstances, along with the contributions of several key individuals. One particular event—the World's Columbian Exposition of 1893—provided an incalculable boost. C.B. Macdonald later wrote, "Extraordinary as it may seem, the birth of golf in the states, and the conception of the World's Fair in Chicago were simultaneous."

The Fair, with its "White City" designation, was more than just 350 buildings occupying former swamp land in Jackson Park. Held to celebrate the 400th anniversary of America's discovery, the Columbian Exposition attracted exhibitors from five continents and millions of attendees—28 million to be precise! Though acclaimed as the "miracle of the day," the Fair's true worth transcended the ornate architectural structures; it represented a symbol of regeneration. Chicagoans swelled in pride, their spirits lifted, their collective energies soared.

Almost overnight, Chicago's image became glorified not only on the Eastern Seaboard but internationally as well. Consequently, a migration of Easterners and overseas immigrants began to flood the local area—throughout the 1890s and the early 20th century. Among these diverse groups were Scottish, Irish and British natives. Speaking with thick accents and often penniless, they did have one gift which they gladly shared. They were familiar with golf and eager to promote the sport's virtues. Some became club professionals or club makers. In fact, the accepted belief in 1900 was that no respectable area club would have anyone else but a Scottish pro.

Still, the Fair and those whom it attracted would have been less successful in seeding golf's future had not land been so abundant. The many parcels that dotted Chicago's environs were inexpensive and, even more importantly, accessible to Chicago's advanced railroad system. Rail lines were clearly the lifeblood of any club's successful development.

Beyond land and easy access, certain individuals took the lead in building the game's local foundation. Either through their respected influence in the community or their monetary support, they advanced the game of golf. The efforts of C.B. Macdonald and Hobart Chatfield-Taylor have been noted but there were, of course, other pioneers. Arthur B. Bowen of the Riverside Golf Club was perhaps the one person most responsible for the Western Golf Association's debut in 1899. Individuals such as Angus Hibbard (Glen View), Charles F. Thompson (Flossmoor), W.A. Alexander (Exmoor) and A.C. Allen (Skokie) were critical in their respective club's development. Certainly, Joseph Donnersberger's support of Chicago's first public facility—Jackson Park—was noteworthy, as were the design efforts of early course architects such as H.J. Tweedie and Jim Foulis.

Not surprisingly, the names of golf's early pioneers are foreign to many who enjoy the sport today. Nevertheless, their legacy is real as were the 30 clubs they and others challenged Chicagoans with by the end of 1900:

- Belmont Golf Club
- Bryn Mawr Golf Club
- Chicago Golf Club
- Du Page County Golf Club
- Edgewater Golf Club
- Elgin Country Club
- Ellerslie Cross Country Club
- Elmhurst Country Club
- Evanston Golf Club
- Evanston King's Daughter Golf Club
- Exmoor Country Club
- Geneva Golf Club
- Glen View Golf Club
- Hinsdale Golf Club
- Homewood (Flossmoor) Country Club

- Jackson Park Public Links
- Kenilworth Golf Club
- La Grange Country Club
- Lake Zurich Golf Club
- Maywood Golf Club
- Midlothian Country Club
- Newspaper Golf Club

- Onwentsia Club
- Ouilmette Country Club
- River Forest Golf Club
- Riverside Golf Club
- Skokie Country Club
- Washington Park Club
- Westward Ho Golf Club
- Wheaton Golf Club

Establishing the chronological order of these early clubs is a difficult task. Complicating the process is the question of what benchmark constitutes a club's official beginning.

From a legal perspective, an incorporation date can be used—however, not all early clubs filed for incorporation. Another option would be to use the "established" date—a reference to a club's beginning prior to official incorporation. A third view would consider any "informal" golfing activity played even before a club's "establishment" date.

While there may rightfully be an attitude of "who cares?" the issue of seniority is an important one among local clubs. Consider the definitions used by some area facilities in addressing their longevity. One suggests it is the oldest local club at its *original* site. Another 18-hole club admits four other organizations are older but adds those four were built originally as *nine*-hole layouts. Others refer to founding dates and exclude incorporation dates or vice versa.

This preoccupation is understandable, considering many early clubs no longer exist. Of the 30 around at the turn of the century, 15 ultimately folded. A few details about the pioneering clubs that are no longer with us follow:

Belmont Golf Club

After the Chicago Golf Club vacated its original Downers Grove site, another golf club quickly formed. Organized by among others, H.J. Tweedie, the Illinois Golf Club lasted three years. A third organization to occupy the property incorporated in 1899 as the Belmont Golf Club.

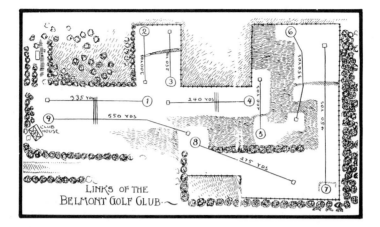

Members played over a nine-hole 2,900-yard layout. In 1968, the Downers Grove Park District purchased the site and with it acquired the oldest nine-hole course in the Midwest.

Bryn Mawr Golf Club

This golf club was an auxiliary of the Bryn Mawr Social Club. Golf started in 1897 on a site just south of Jackson Park near 72nd Street and Seipp Avenue. Designed by H.J. Tweedie, this nine-hole course measured 2,287 yards over 50 acres. It was such a tight layout, two holes crisscrossed two other fairways. The club was not affiliated with the Bryn Mawr Country Club, which was later established in Lincolnwood.

Du Page County Golf Club

When this club incorporated in July of 1900, it represented Wheaton's third golfing site. Only the city of Chicago could claim more facilities. The Du Page club leased 40 acres of grazing land. Livestock roamed the fairways, stopping occasionally to satisfy their appetites by chewing on fairway grass. They would have enjoyed the greens, too, had not wire netting surrounded every one of the course's nine greens. The 2,133-yard layout bordered the Chicago Golf Club; James Foulis, the Chicago club pro and greenskeeper, designed the course.

In reality, Du Page's layout barely qualified as a golf course. Even a $5 initiation fee attracted just 21 members by 1901. The club closed shortly thereafter, its members joining the Wheaton Golf Club.

Edgewater Golf Club

Organized in 1897 and incorporated the following year, Edgewater was a long-time and prominent fixture of local golf. Occupying two sites during its 70-year existence, the club was first situated at the corners of Devon and Broadway in Chicago. The nine-hole course measured 2,804 yards, though the length was increased to 3,008 yards by 1900. One hole ran 593 yards and was considered the longest hole in the entire district. Several other Edgewater holes featured extremely narrow fairways bordered by rows of mature oak and birch trees. The members referred to these slender fairways as "bowling alleys." An early grounds improvement cost the club $757—a fence was purchased to encircle the 55-acre grounds. Within two years, however, the expenditure had been totally recouped through a new revenue source—the outside of the fence was sold as an advertising medium. The layout itself represented another Tweedie design.

In 1912, Edgewater moved to its second locale at Pratt and Ridge Avenues, where it stood until its final days in the late '60s. Edgewater was a charter member of the Western Golf Association. Several local tournaments were contested on its links, including one of major prominence—the 1943 Chicago Victory National. The club is also notable for its most famous member, Chick Evans.

Ellerslie Cross Country Club

Organized and incorporated in 1899 at 91st Street and Western Avenue, the Ellerslie Cross Country Club could offer its members both golf and equestrian activities. The course itself was a respectable nine holes, measuring 3,025 yards, though two fairways did cross railroad tracks. Club initiation fees were a pricey $100. Women golfers had access to the course every day, a liberal characteristic of the era. Interestingly, the course and clubhouse architect was Zachary T. Davis, who later served as the architect for Wrigley Field and Comiskey

Park. By 1908, the Ellerslie club disbanded. During the '20s a portion of the property would yield another golf course—the Evergreen Golf Club.

Elmhurst Country Club

Incorporated in late 1900, the Elmhurst Country Club first had a nine-hole course in Elmhurst, measuring 2,960 yards on 75 acres. Eventually moving to Addison, the Elmhurst Country Club survived into the 1980s before being sold for $6.4 million to the Du Page County Forest Preserve District, which renamed it Oak Meadows.

Evanston King's Daughters Golf Club

Golfing was started at the Evanston King's Daughters Golf Club in 1899 to provide additional revenue for the organization's Fresh Air Home in Evanston. The housing facility was designed for young women in need. The golf club itself was the only one in the Chicago area operated by women. While access to the course was non-discriminatory, initiation fees were $5 less for single women than for single men. The nine-hole course, which measured 2,775 yards on 40 acres of rent-free property, was laid out by Colonel Henry Kidder.

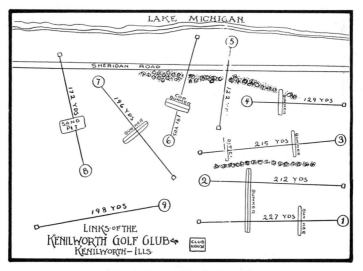

Kenilworth Golf Club

Founded in 1894 primarily as a social club, Kenilworth added golf links in 1899. Twenty-five acres of land were used for the nine-hole facility, which measured 1,662 yards. All holes ranged from 122 to 227 yards in length. Fairways crossed Sheridan Road three times in the H.J. Tweedie-designed layout. The club's golfers searched for a more conducive locale and found it in 1908 near the present-day train station in Kenilworth. Reorganizing into the North Shore Golf Club, members successfully secured a lease on 40 acres. By 1917, they had purchased the property for $100,000. Just six years later, the nine-hole course was sold to developers for $262,000.

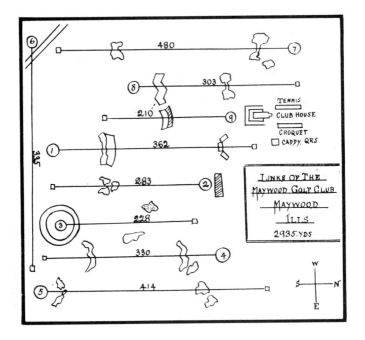

Maywood Golf Club

Organized in 1900, Maywood's club uniquely employed no membership cap, welcoming any applicant willing to pay the $1.50 initiation fee. It was easily the least expensive country club investment within the Chicago district. Maywood featured a surprisingly long layout—almost 3,000 yards. Designed by a relative unknown, Philip Brockles, the course had cross-bunkers on nearly every hole. Unfortunately, the lease expired in 1910, the land sold to a real estate developer and the club disbanded.

In 1923, a reorganized Maywood club opened in Hillside—its layout exemplifying modern golf course architecture. Designed by the architecturally prolific Tom Bendelow, the new Maywood site featured one island green, other raised and well-trapped greens, double-terraced tees and plenty of fairway bunkers. Membership at this club was limited to 275—each paying a $100 initiation fee. Early in the '30s, the 6,406-yard facility became a public-fee course. Maywood survived into the '60s before being sold. The land currently holds a shopping center on Mannheim Road.

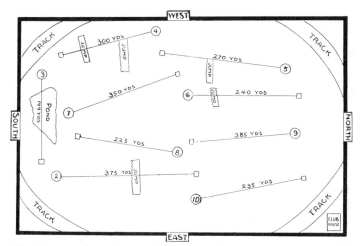

The layout of the Newspaper Golf Club.

Newspaper Golf Club

Incorporated late in 1899 by employees of several Chicago newspapers, the club occupied two separate leased sites during its four-year existence. In its inaugural year, the members played in Oak Park. A year later, the club moved to a new home at 7400 West Roosevelt, its nine-hole course located within the Harlem Park track's oval. Designed by 1896 U.S. Open champion James Foulis, the 2,524-yard course had one small pond and no sand bunkers. Other hazards did exist, specifically in the unconventional form of five steeplechase jumps. Furthermore, the entire course was pock-marked with divots created by horses entered in equestrian competitions.

All nine holes were individually named. While this practice wasn't in itself unusual in golf's early days, the
names of the holes were. All were taken from Chicago
newspapers of the period: *The Record, Tribune, Inter
Ocean, Times-Herald, Chronicle, Daily News, Journal,
American and Evening Post.* Ultimately, the Newspaper
Golf Club was unable to honor its five-year lease and
folded in 1904. By 1910, however, the site—minus the
defunct race track—re-emerged as the Harlem Golf Club.
This was Chicago's first daily-fee course.

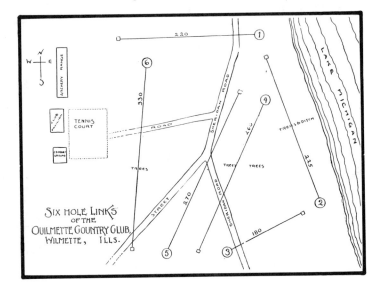

Ouilmette Country Club

Organized in 1898, this Wilmette-based club's primary appeal was social, though recreational activities weren't totally excluded. A mini six-hole layout was in place equal-
ing nearly 1,500 yards. Four holes crossed Sheridan Road.
One other fairway closely bordered Lake Michigan. H.J.
Tweedie is "credited" with the design.

Increasing traffic proved annoying to players, with the
serious enthusiasts going on to join other area golfing
clubs. Ouilmette's property was subdivided and the club
eventually merged with another—the Evanston Century
Club—in the '20s. Attempts by the remaining members
to start a golf club were successful in the early '40s. The
Michigan Shores Golf Club took root in Wilmette, at the

corners of Lake and Michigan Avenues. The club no longer exists; the site is today Gillson Park.

River Forest Golf Club

Organized in 1898, the River Forest Golf Club officially incorporated in 1901. Four years later, the club closed, with many of its members who were Oak Park and River Forest residents joining Westward Ho. Although River Forest's club featured a challenging 2,934 layout, it was its clubhouse that drew acclaim. Its architect was Frank Lloyd Wright.

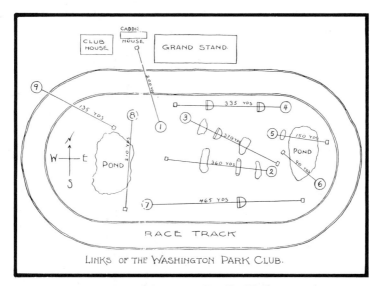

LINKS OF THE WASHINGTON PARK CLUB.

Washington Park Club

Though the club organized in 1883, it was not until 1896 that golf was added. Located near Chicago's Jackson Park, the facility's primary draw was its racetrack. Most of the nine-hole course was inside the 85-acre oval perimeter—only the first tee and the ninth green were outside the track's surface. No golf games on the 2,315-yard course were allowed during the racing season. The co-designers were Richard Leslie and, to a lesser extent, C.B. Macdonald.

Because of the park's gaming nature, the golf club attracted influential citizens of the era. The $100 initiation fee represented no concern for many of the 600 members, including J. Ogden Armour, Reuben H. Donnelley, A.B. Dick, Montgomery Ward, William Borden, Marshall Field and Robert Todd Lincoln. The club professionals were the Herd brothers—Fred and James. Fred had won the U.S. Open championship in 1898. In 1905, the complete facility closed due to the strong anti-gambling movement within Chicago.

Westward Ho Golf Club

Incorporated in 1898 as the Oak Park Golf Club, the organization changed its name by year end to Westward Ho Golf Club. This club was a charter member of the original 10-club Western Golf Association. In its 60 year existence, Westward Ho occupied three separate venues. The first was a leased site in Oak Park, on Madison and Home Avenues. Its second locale, ready for play in 1899, bordered Chicago—in an area today called Galewood. Also leased, the Galewood location provided enough space for a full 18-hole course. The 6,103-yard facility was laid out by Tweedie and club professional David McIntosh. During the early years, the club experienced two major clubhouse fires that almost led to financial collapse. In 1905, however, the River Forest Golf Club merged with Westward Ho, thus adding an important source of income. One of the earliest members was A. Haddow Smith, the original land owner of Chicago Golf Club's Belmont site.

In 1922, the club purchased 200 acres for $72,000 at Wolf and North Avenues in Melrose Park. The seller was the Albert Amling Company, which had intended to use the land to raise roses and other flowers. Amling himself became a member in 1923, when the new site opened. Designed by club professionals Frank Adams and Stuart Gardner, Westward Ho evolved into one of the region's most beautiful and challenging courses. The club's zenith occurred in 1947, when it hosted the Chicago Victory Tournament, which was won by Ben Hogan. A little more than 10 years later, Westward Ho closed.

Wheaton Golf Club

Organized in June of 1900, the impetus behind Wheaton's formation could be traced to the 1897 U.S. Open and Amateur championships played at the town's

other golf club—Chicago Golf. Local residents simply
wanted a golfing facility of their own. In 1900, James and
David Foulis laid out a nine-hole course on leased land
that was formerly a fairground. It measured first 1,706
yards, then in 1902, 2,860 yards.

While the Wheaton Golf Club was private, the facility
was more like a community course. Initiation fees were
$10. The limited acreage prompted club members in 1910
to seek a larger venue. Another Wheaton site was found
and under reorganized management the club changed
its name to the Green Valley Country Club. The 1929
stock-market crash and ensuing Depression forced
Green Valley's conversion in 1931 to daily fee. Though
the club limped along throughout the 1930s, its ownership eventually sold the property to real estate
developers.

In addition to the previously detailed Chicago Golf
Club, the other 14 clubs started in the 1890s that still exist
today are: Elgin, Evanston, Exmoor, Geneva, Glen View,
Hinsdale, Homewood (now Flossmoor), Jackson Park, La
Grange, Lake Zurich, Midlothian, Onwentsia, Riverside
and Skokie. A brief look at the early days of these clubs
follows:

Photo by Dr. Roy P. Wilcox
Chicago Historical Society ICHi-22769

First Clubhouse at Elgin Country Club, 1901.

Elgin Country Club

Though officially incorporated on April 1, 1901, the Elgin
Country Club has roots that go back to 1898. During 1898
and 1899, a crudely designed mini-layout was played on
gravel hills just behind the state asylum building. There
were no greens to speak of and tin containers were used

as cups. In 1901, the club built a nine-hole course on property west of Elgin on Highway 20. The 109 acres were owned by Mrs. Owen Weld and leased to the club for $2 per acre.

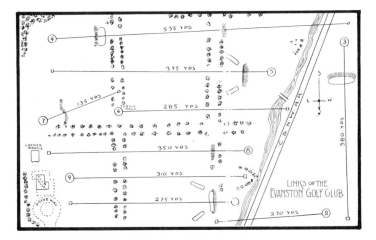

Evanston Golf Club

Organized in 1898, the club has had four homes, its first in north Evanston. In 1899, it moved to west Evanston on an 80-acre site that included nine holes plus a five-hole auxiliary course. Distance of the nine-hole course was 2,935 yards. One imposing hazard was the Chicago & North Western Railroad tracks. In particular, the second and fourth holes required lofted shots to clear the slightly elevated railway. Club members who comprised the greens committee laid the course out. A third locale was found soon after at Ridge near the Wilmette border. Finally, in 1917, the Evanston Golf Club, then under reorganized management, moved to its current site in Skokie. The club has had several notable names among its membership including William A. Dyche—whose name is now immortalized by Northwestern University's Dyche Stadium.

Exmoor Country Club

Incorporated on Oct. 14, 1896, Exmoor is one of the very few early clubs that has remained at its original location. The club was the first of the current five Highland Park facilities. Originally, the organization incorporated as the Highland Park Golf Club, but changed the name to Ex-

Exmoor Country Club

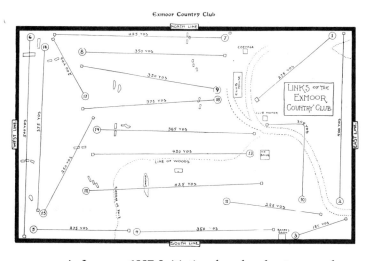

moor in January 1897. Initiation fees for charter members were $25. William A. Alexander, recognized as the "father" of the Exmoor club, was by occupation an insurance man. The club has been often called the "Securities Club," since many of its members are associated with various financial organizations. From 1897 through 1901, the course was limited to nine holes. In 1902, the 18-hole course came into play at 6,005 yards. Exmoor's No. 10 hole is a dogleg right, almost configured at a right angle, one of the few in Chicago's early years that "bent." In 1907, the club purchased the formerly leased 100-acre site, and later an additional plot of 40 acres, bringing the total property cost to $90,000. Members included the Cudahy family, A.B. Dick, W.C. Pullman and H.C. Chatfield-Taylor. Exmoor's course was designed by R.H. McElwee, Harry Towner and W.A. Alexander. H.J. Tweedie provided his expertise when Exmoor expanded to 18 holes.

Geneva Golf Club

Organized in 1897, the Geneva Golf Club saw only limited activity in its earliest years. A six-hole course was used in 1899—though the following year no golf was in evidence. In 1901, the sparse membership leased a 40 acre site just west of town, where a rough nine-hole course was laid out. For the next 13 years, informal play became the regular pattern. Not until 1914, the year the club incorporated, did it purchase the property for

$14,000. A new nine-hole course was crafted under the supervision of Jim Foulis.

Well-dressed crowd gathers at Glen View Club in 1902.

Glen View Golf Club

Incorporated on March 29, 1897, the Glen View Golf and Polo Club has remained on its original site in the tiny village of Golf as an 18-hole layout. By 1900, polo was dropped from the club's activities, as was the designation within the club's name. Another nine holes were built, primarily for women, on the former polo field. Early founders were from Evanston, several being faculty of Northwestern University. Interestingly, founders gave no consideration to locating within Evanston. The city's dry status and temperance attitudes were not endearing to Glen View's forefathers.

The club paid $18,000 to the Dewes family for the 200 acre wooded site. In later years, the club sold property located south of Golf Road. Today, this land is owned by the Cook County Forest Preserve District, which operates the Chick Evans municipal course.

Designed by club professional Richard Leslie, Glen View's 18-hole course measured 6,051 yards. The 17th hole was called "Log Cabin," because of its log cabin that had once been the home of a pioneer family. Early club members included many associated with the railroad industry. Perhaps coincidentally, a one-car trolley operated from Evanston to the club. Other members were Daniel Burnham, Michael and John Cudahy, Charles Deering and even a couple of ex-presidents—William Howard Taft and Warren G. Harding.

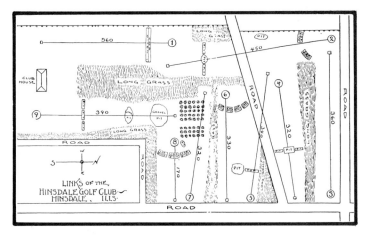

Hinsdale Golf Club

While play in the area was reported as early as 1883, the Hinsdale Golf Club was not incorporated until Oct. 15, 1898. The club has had at least two venues. First located on the west end of Hinsdale, the 3,040-yard course had nine holes on an 80-acre site leased from Henry Middaugh. On the club's 170-yard eighth hole, a bunker 60 yards wide fronted the green. The largest bunker in the area, it was aptly named "Hell." Hinsdale's inaugural day of golf occurred on May 13, 1899.

In 1901, the Hinsdale course added nine more holes. The second Hinsdale course was designed by H.J. Tweedie. In 1909, Henry Middaugh, wanting to subdivide and sell the property, refused to renew the club's lease. A new 134 acre site found literally next door was purchased for less than $19,000. The new course opened on Oct. 9, 1909. In 1920, the Hinsdale clubhouse burned down, a loss of more than $75,000. The following year, their still-uncompleted new clubhouse also was destroyed. In 1924, the current clubhouse was built, this time constructed of brick at a cost of $123,000.

Homewood Country Club
(Now Flossmoor Country Club)

Founded a year before officially incorporating in 1899, Homewood's course was built from day one as an 18-hole layout on its current site. The course measured 6,110 yards and featured one hole playing at 570 yards. Dr. H.W. Gentles, club pro J.S. Pearson and the ever-present

H.J. Tweedie shared in the design responsibilities. The Homewood club also included an auxiliary nine-hole course. Homewood was one of several early clubs constructed near Illinois Central Railroad tracks. Before choosing their eventual property site east of the railroad lines, club organizers were given assurance by railroad officials that a new passenger depot would be quickly built. The railroad not only honored their commitment but added housing lots known as the Illinois Central Sub-Division at Flossmoor, just west of the tracks. Not surprisingly, several early members of the club were executives of the Illinois Central Railroad.

Jackson Park Public Links

History was made on May 11, 1899, as the first golf course west of the Alleghenies opened to the public. The site of the nine-hole facility was on a landfill laden with bricks, pillars and other debris from the demolished structures of the old Chicago World's Fair. With the opening of Jackson Park's course, perceptions of golf for only the affluent began to slowly change. The *Chicago Inter Ocean* at the time wrote:

> *"The course at Jackson Park is a long stride forward in the popularizing of the royal game. When first imported to America, golf received no mark of popular approval; its peculiarities were ridiculed more mercilessly than even tennis, when that was a novelty. Golf was called a fad of the upper ten, and all the paraphernalia of clubs and caddies and its initiated jargon of 'tees' and 'halved holes' and 'stymies' were food for laughter. But the sturdy, breezy game has made its way, and today the progressive policy of the South park board has put it within reach of the plain people."*

Newspaper accounts of the new public course were so complete, specific details of each hole's characteristics were reported.

At the formal opening ceremony, three dignitaries had the honor of teeing off first at the new course. Play began on the second hole as the first hole was deemed too difficult and potentially embarrassing. This was due primarily to a 30-to-50-yard water hazard located immediately in front of the first tee. At the second hole, the trio—consisting of the president of the South Park Board, Joseph Donnersberger; South Park Board Superintendent Frank Foster; and Judge Murray Tuley— were ready to commence play. While Tuley belonged to the Riverside Golf Club, Donnersberger had before that day never even seen a golf ball. First up, he sliced into the rough. Foster followed with another slice. Tuley was up next. The group's third slice was recorded, this time so extreme a spectator was nearly struck. The judge hit again, this time landing in the fairway a scant 50 yards out. It was felt at the time that history would remember Donnersberger and Foster as respectively the grandfather and father of public golf in Chicago, but the reality is that their memory has long been forgotten.

Others who were also instrumental in the development of the Jackson Park facility were members of the Quadrangle Club from the University of Chicago. Comprised chiefly of professors and students, these advocates of the game performed yeoman services in promoting golf for the masses. Members of the Delta Tau Delta, Alpha Delta Phi and Phi Delta Theta fraternities were regular participants on the links.

With so many novices flooding the public course, the adjoining golf shop sold clubs in rudimentary fashion. Customers buying a four-club package were advised the "brassie" was for drives, the "iron" for long fairway shots, the "mashie" for approaches and finally the "putter" for greens play.

Originally a nine-hole layout, Jackson Park's facility expanded in 1900 to 18 holes. The following year, a separate nine-hole course was constructed. Though the combined 27-hole facility featured clay teeing areas, sandy fairways and greens—often with more pebbles than strands of grass—the site always attracted huge followings. But then Jackson Park's municipal courses were the only public golfing facilities in the area until 1907. Additionally, the price was right—golf was free until 1920.

La Grange Country Club

Founded in 1899, the La Grange Country Club originally had a nine-hole facility at La Grange Road and 47th

Street in La Grange. Occupying 80 acres, the course had a playing distance of 2,960 yards, with all greens guarded by bunkers or pits. The course was laid out by H.J. Tweedie. In 1913, the club moved to its current site on Brainard Road in La Grange.

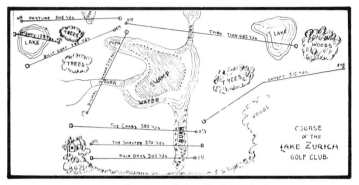

Lake Zurich Golf Club

When the Lake Zurich Golf Club organized in 1895, its Hyde Park founders sought to establish a relaxed and peaceful environment. Used mostly as a summer retreat for University of Chicago professors, the club created a nine-hole layout measuring 2,865 yards and designed by Robert Foulis. Unlike other clubs, the Lake Zurich organization never placed too high a priority on the competitive aspects of the game. Local rules were not strict or cumbersome—best illustrated by the club's first rule: "Don't take the game too seriously." Other rules exhibited a further unconventional approach toward the sanctity of the sport's guidelines. For example,

> *"Any ball lying in any gopher, rabbit or crab hole may be lifted and redropped within a club's length.*
>
> *"A dandelion or weed may be plucked (on the green) without penalty."*

It's safe to say no other Chicago club has placed as high a priority on humor as Lake Zurich. Consider, their ruling for lost golf balls:

> *"The missing ball will eventually be found and pocketed by some other player, in which case it becomes a stolen ball. There is no penalty for a stolen ball."*

While other clubs engaged in formal affairs to celebrate respective club milestones, Lake Zurich's members never succumbed to pomp and circumstance. What other club would schedule the "Learned and Informative Discourse on Newspaper Typographical Errors" on an annual dinner program? In another year, the dinner menu included "entree of prime ribs of tadpole and butterfly livers."

Perhaps this sense of humor is what attracted members such as Chester Gould, the creator of the Dick Tracy comic strip, or Leo Burnett, the founder of the worldwide advertising agency bearing his name. Other members ran in literary and educational circles. Of the latter, so many had PhD's that it was common to hear members refer to their colleagues as "Doctor." Books authored by Lake Zurich's members were so numerous the clubhouse included bookshelves filled exclusively with works written by its members.

Still, Lake Zurich has never had a membership roster of more than 50. Furthermore, all share in club duties. Maintenance is performed not by paid laborers but by club members. There is no bartender or staff; thus, each member pours his own drink from his own identified bottle. At their family-style dinners, the member with the least seniority carves and serves the food.

Early in the club's history, an attempt was made by the Chicago & North Western Railroad to condemn part of the facility's property for railroad expansion. Taken as a serious threat to its future, Lake Zurich plotted an ingenious defense that was eventually successful. Four cadavers from Rush Medical College were donated to the club and subsequently buried on the grounds complete with tombstones. Incorporating part of its property as a cemetery, the club had found the legal loophole to avoid any further challenge from the railroad.

Today, the course is still nine holes and its distance of 2,651 yards represents even less playing yardage than almost 100 years ago. Course activity is extremely limited; some members consider the course to be busy if there is more than one foursome playing at any one time.

The Midlothian Clubhouse in 1899.

Midlothian Country Club

Organized in 1898 and incorporated in January of 1899, Midlothian's layout was considered to be among the best in the region. The H.J. Tweedie-designed facility included 27 holes on its 200-acre site. No trees were present on the 18-hole course, which measured an unusually long playing distance of 6,387 yards. One hole, running 550 yards, was surprisingly called "Easy Street." A nine-hole layout measuring 2,778 yards was considered a qualifying course, in that members had to score under 73 to be allowed on the main layout. In the early days, shooting 72 or better was no small feat. To avoid the embarrassment of continually not qualifying, many members proposed the nine-hole course be donated to the female members. A short time later, the women returned it. Perhaps most unusual about the layout were the names assigned to each hole. In order, they were called: England, France, Russia, Turkey, Japan, Italy, Germanie, Switzerland and America. During Midlothian's long history, the club has remained on its original site. Though within the city limits of Blue Island, the adjoining train depot took its name from the club. And years later, when the village that included the club's property was being incorporated, village founders chose the name Midlothian.

Members of the club have included R.H. Donnelley, Marshall Field, John G. Shedd, A.G. Spaulding and

Montgomery Ward. Midlothian's primary founder was
George R. Thorne.

The Onwentsia Club

The Onwentsia Clubhouse in 1899.

Along with Chicago Golf Club, no other organization
was as influential in shaping the early days of local golf
as was Onwentsia in Lake Forest. Though the two clubs
were geographically separated, they were close-knit
organizations, often staging tournaments or hosting
social gatherings at each other's club. The bond naturally followed the relationship between its two founders,
C.B. Macdonald and Hobart Chatfield-Taylor, who were
credited with creating the seven-hole Lake Forest course
in 1892. While Macdonald moved on and formed the
Chicago Golf Club at Belmont, Chatfield-Taylor remained
in Lake Forest. One of the region's first club handicap
tournaments was held there on July 4, 1894. Among the
participants was one Reginald de Koven, a left hander.
But since there were no left-handed clubs available, he

chose to compete using only a putter. While the others sliced their balls into Lake Michigan or hacked and needlessly uprooted yards of turf, de Koven's "putts" weren't long but they were true—and good enough to win the championship.

The club decided to expand in 1894, leasing land on the western edge of Lake Forest; the nine-hole facility was named the Lake Forest Golf Club. It was a crude layout. There weren't any bunkers at all, though the first hole did contain a water hazard immediately in front of the tee that caused an inordinate amount of jitters among members. But of paramount concern to members were train tracks bordering several holes. Players complained of too much noise. So the following year about 180 acres of adjoining property were leased and on Oct. 25, 1895, the Onwentsia Club was formally incorporated.

First, nine holes were built. By 1898, an 18-hole course measuring 5,984 yards was opened. Robert Foulis and H.J. Whigham were the credited architects.

Onwentsia always has been a club that has attracted notable families. Early members included the Armours, Swifts, Cudahys, McCormicks and Farwells. C.B. Macdonald and H.J. Whigham were also members.

By 1899, Onwentsia, then a member of the USGA, was selected to host the 5th annual U.S. Amateur. Besides the Chicago Golf Club, no other local club at the time had ever entertained a national tournament.

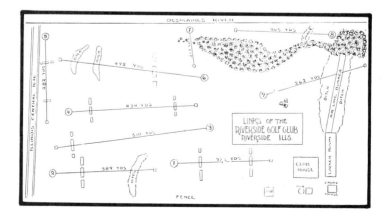

Riverside Golf Club

Organized play at Riverside began in 1893 on a three-hole layout in a park near the home of an early founder. By 1894, another site for nine holes was secured and the club incorporated three years later. The course measured 3,217 yards and was designed by W.A. Havemeyer, J.S. Driver and Thomas Hannah. In 1919, additional property was purchased and fused into an expanded 18-hole facility.

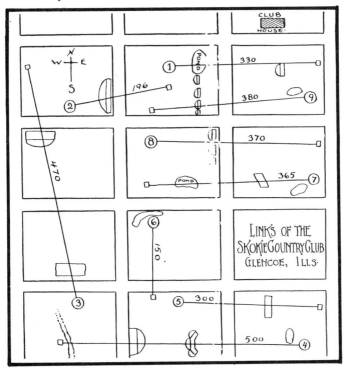

Skokie Country Club

Organized in 1897 and incorporated the following year, the Skokie Country Club remains today at its original site. Initially designed by George Leslie, the nine-hole course measured 2,700 yards. With 117 charter members by 1898, the club drafted plans for a clubhouse, which cost $1,930. Skokie's course measured 3,061 yards in 1900 and in 1904 the club added nine more holes. A decade later famed architect Donald Ross redesigned the 18-hole layout. Hosting its only, thus far, U.S. Open, in 1922, the club's course has continued to rank among the Chicago district's premier layouts.

So influential were the glamour clubs of Chicago's early history that national tournaments stopped there regularly. Of the first seven Chicago-hosted U.S. Opens, all were played at the Chicago Golf Club, the Glen View Golf Club, the Skokie Country Club, the Midlothian Country Club and the Onwentsia Club. These along with the Exmoor and Homewood Country Clubs were also the hosts of the first 12 U.S. Amateur and U.S. Women's Amateur championships played in the Chicago region.

So, while some of the 30 different local clubs that emerged from 1893 through 1900 proved to be more successful than others—all contributed in introducing the game to Chicago's citizenry. Collectively, these early clubs formed the solid foundation from which local golfing interest would grow.

The Evolutionary Period: 1901-1920

If the 1890s represented local golf's formative years, the ensuing two decades could be termed its evolutionary period. By 1920, 70 different organizations featured a golf course. Of this group, 50 were 20th century creations; the other 20 were survivors from the 1890s. With its course facilities increasing annually, the Chicago area strengthened its position as the country's golfing hub of the West.

USGA Museum & Library

Playing golf on the first day of the new century—January 1, 1901.

Still, local expansion didn't come without growing pains. While a handful of clubs steered clear of troublesome hurdles, the majority stumbled occasionally. Not surprisingly, money-related concerns were common. This was especially evident with the many clubs that occupied leased property. Impending expiration dates forced members to make important decisions on the future of their organization. Could club membership afford the increased costs of a new lease? Would another site offer a more cost effective alternative? Should attempts be made to purchase outright the club's current acreage? Faced with these options, club members often moved as a group to another location or even decided to disband the club. In a few cases, they even stayed put, either as a lessee or as the new owner of the property.

There were other monetary concerns, too. These often involved the size of the club's course and the lavishness of the clubhouse. Budgetary limitations had to be adhered to, but members disagreed on what construction projects should be given priority.

While financial concerns were common, they weren't the exclusive topics of members' debate. In at least two examples, voting minorities left their original clubs to form new ones. The issues that forced these early 20th century disputes would hardly draw a yawn today.

One issue involved the question of liquor. The Scots, in particular, would find this matter amusing if not totally ironic. After all, they invented the game, but are even more well known for their other famous export—whiskey. For centuries, the Scots have incorporated golfing and drinking into their society—apparently with little controversy. Closer to home, libations were clearly present at America's first golf club. Members of the New York-based St. Andrew's Golf Club celebrated their club's founding (as recorded in meeting minutes) to wit: "success to the club was drunk."

Locally, founders of the Glen View club—most of whom were Evanstonians—searched for a future club site "not closer than four miles to Northwestern University with the conviviality of liquor in mind." They never considered their own community for the club's eventual home, not as long as the Northwestern four-mile prohibition district remained in place.

North of Evanston, in another dry community, Hobart Chatfield-Taylor's experience from the late 1890s would validate one of golf's adages—the 19th hole's discovery tripled the sport's popularity within a week. It seems he became convinced that the Lake Forest citizenry needed an incentive to try the new game, so in his words—"with malice afterthought, I invited younger residents for a game of golf. They came...golf clubs and balls were distributed...started to their doom in pairs. When they (finished) hot and tired, I lured them to the dining room where decanters of Scotch whiskey were placed enticingly before their innocent eyes. Alas, they fell, to a man. Whether it was owing to the game or the whiskey I would not venture a guess—but on the following Saturday the number had doubled, and from that day to this, except on Sunday, golf has flourished at Lake Forest."

Not all local clubs endorsed the notion that liquor's availability ensured success. Several local organizations—for example, the Homewood Country Club—allowed no presence whatsoever. Members at these clubs were hardly inconvenienced by the absence.

An opposite viewpoint prevailed at the Ridge Country Club, which was organized in 1902. Located in a south side Chicago neighborhood considered "dry," the club found its membership divided. The issue of allowing liquor into the clubhouse had Ridge members taking sides, the pro-wet group a minority, but a vocal minority nevertheless. Unable to tilt the balance in their favor, the dissidents resigned their Ridge memberships and joined a nearby club, Auburn Park, which was unencumbered by any alcoholic restrictions.

Auburn Park had formed in 1901. Designed by T.R. Brocklesby, the 2,337 yard nine-hole course covered 80 leased acres in Chicago's West Auburn Park. A single sand bunker existed—the other hazards were wide ditches. The course proved unfulfilling, however, and at the lease's conclusion, club members moved to another site in 1908—renaming the club Beverly. The Ridge club also moved—relocating to its current location in 1916. Ridge and Beverly disputes have long since been forgotten. Today, the liquor issue is a moot point for Chicago's only two south side private clubs.

Besides the relative merits of clubhouse beverages of choice, the era's other major controversy involved Sunday play. More clubs than not prohibited golf on Sundays, their reasons a kind of public relations gesture to spouses and local ministers alike. It's debatable which group club organizers aimed most to please. Still, there's agreement the clergy and the members' wives fought hard to stop golfing activities from spreading to Sunday. On the other hand, many men who could only find time to play Saturday rounds became frustrated by long waits and that their course lay quiet on Sundays. Throughout the period, clubs began to open for play on Sunday.

The La Grange Country Club, which had formed in 1899, had members who believed the Sunday moratorium should continue. There were dissenters, though, and each year a vote would be taken—the result was always the same. Fed up by this lack of progress, several La Grange members announced their intention to start another club—one permitting Sunday golf. In 1910, they formed the Edgewood Golf Club in La Grange. Ironically, remaining members of the La Grange club took another vote the following year. This time, the motion allowing Sunday play passed—by a single vote.

While some ministers questioned the morality of playing golf on Sundays, many of Chicago's citizens found even greater concern in widespread gambling activities. Their objective was to put an end to its most visible symbol: the racetrack. This strong crusade forced Washington Park's track to close. The park's golf club also closed, an innocent victim in the process.

Just beforehand, though, Lawrence Heyworth was trying unsuccessfully to form a new club on Chicago's lakefront. Early in 1905, he sent out letters proposing his plans to approximately 1000 prominent citizens. When the returns came in, he counted only 21 acceptances. Not yet willing to abandon hope, Heyworth sent out a second mailing. As fate would have it, the letters arrived to prospective applicants just as Washington Park's proprietors announced their racetrack and golf course would close. In less than 30 days, Heyworth received several hundred responses, each containing commitments for the $100 initiation fee. The South Shore Country Club thus began.

South Shore's nine-hole course operates today as a public facility, managed by the Chicago Park District. No other Chicago-based private club, past or present, enjoys as illustrious a history as South Shore. The club hosted formal affairs for President Taft, King Peter of Yugoslavia,

Edward-Prince of Wales and Buffalo Bill Cody. It was here Chicago's elite would gather for dinner dances or to be entertained by the artisans of the era—among others Will Rogers. South Shore's early years deserve special mention.

Since the site was essentially all sand, top soil had to be hauled in—a painfully slow process. More than 4,000 cubic yards of rich black dirt was transported by train and

Chicago Historical Society DN 52,788

Chicago Historical Society ICHi-22772

The South Shore Clubhouse in 1908.

Aerial view of the South Shore Country Club.

wagon from Momence, Ill. Two years after course construction had begun, the ninth hole hadn't been developed. Fairways of four of the remaining eight holes were incomplete, though greens were in place. They had been purchased for one cent per square yard from the old Washington Park facility. Another memento from the former club were the member's lockers, purchased for 50 cents each. Indeed, these lockers were among the least expensive items within the club's $285,000 clubhouse. Charles Fox designed the Spanish-style structure but is perhaps more famous for his design of the Drake and Blackstone Hotels.

Courtesy of Chicago District Golf Association

Aerial view of the Calumet Country Club in the 1940s.
Within ten years, an expressway cut through it, prompting a
redesign of the layout.

During South Shore's 69-year history as a private club, its course stayed at nine holes, amazing, considering the club's membership topped 2,000 at its peak during the 1950s. But as sociological changes swept the neighborhood, the core membership—primarily south side Irish—migrated to the suburbs, joining more convenient clubs. By 1973, membership had slipped to 731. In 1974, the Chicago Park District purchased the 58-acre site for $9,775,000. Included in the property transfer were the club's original wooden lockers—the 50 cent relics Heyworth had procured in 1905.

While South Shore is no longer private, at least the course is still played. Other south side clubs have been long shuttered. These include 1890s-built Bryn Mawr and Ellerslie, plus the early 20th century golf clubs—the West Pullman, Windsor, Normal Park and Armour (built for employees of Armour and Company).

Ridge and Beverly have survived as has Jackson Park. Another early south side club also thrives today, although at its second location. The Calumet Golf Club was organized in 1901. Fifteen years later, the land owners advised the club of their intent to end the lease in order to develop the property. Finding no suitable city parcel available, Calumet's members purchased 160 acres in Homewood. Originally, members played three nine-hole courses, but in 1921 Donald Ross restyled the site into a challenging 18-hole course. Also important, their new club and signature course lay near Illinois Central Railroad access, a key consideration for their membership, most of whom still lived in Chicago.

While the Midlothian and Homewood Country Clubs had forged the way during the 1890s, the Ravisloe Country Club was the first golf club in the 20th century to have a south suburban address near railroad lines. Opening in 1901, it was located in Homewood. In 1908, the Idlewild club also built its new club near the rails—settling in nearby Flossmoor. Further down the lines, clubs in Kewanee, Chicago Heights, Dwight and Kankakee formed respectively in 1911, 1912, 1913 and 1915.

Northern Expansion

Similar development was also sprouting along the north suburban lines of the Chicago & North Western Railroad. At least 10 more clubs took root from 1902 to 1918.

Waukegan-based Glen Flora is the oldest of north suburban clubs established in this century. Before 1900, the area's most visible attraction had been the Glen Flora mineral springs. Originally, bubbly community leaders believed the natural resource would attract a large tourist trade. The idea fizzled and instead a country club was formed in 1902; nine years later, the Glen Flora course opened.

Further to the south, in what was then considered the Fort Sheridan community, the Old Elm Club opened its 18-hole course June 20, 1914. It was one of the first clubs (some say the first) in the country to exclude women from its clubhouse and grounds. Unlike today's mood, where calls to open all private club gates even wider are heard, Old Elm's policy in 1914 created little controversy. Certainly, the wives of Old Elm's members didn't object, since they and their husbands were already on the membership scrolls at other so-called family-oriented country clubs.

With a playing distance of 6,305 yards, the early layout was considered one of the area's finest. A little history is also associated with Old Elm's two course designers, H.S. Colt and Donald Ross. Colt was the first accomplished golf architect not to have been a professional golfer. As for Ross, he was to become the best known and most prolific golf architect during the sport's first 50 years in America.

USGA Museum & Library

*Donald Ross was
America's best known
and most prolific
designer during
golf's first 50 years.*

There is today another all-male golf club in Chicago's northern suburbs but, unlike Old Elm, the Bob O'Link Golf Club was originally formed as a facility open to the whole family. In 1921—four years after opening—club members voted 110 to 69 to limit the club to men exclusively.

Two theories have been suggested for this sudden change in philosophy. The first involves a lack of funds to keep the club open. The rumor was another north suburban family club would provide needed cash on the proviso that Bob O'Link exclude women. Supposedly, the unnamed club's course had been overrun with wives and daughters, leaving many of the club's male members in the lurch.

Theory No. 2 suggests Bob O'Link's members wanted a club comprised of men who had the financial wherewithal to join two clubs. One would be Bob O'Link; another would be the more traditional family-oriented country club.

The club remains all male, a fact that is readily apparent. At what other facility would the clubhouse's front door open into the male locker room? The on-course restroom is identified with a "we men" sign. All club employees are male. Only once since 1921 have women been allowed on club property. During the 1928 Western Amateur, women were included among the gallery.

Bob O'Link wasn't the only Highland Park-based club to open during this time. In December 1918, the Northmoor Country Club formed. Less than a year later, the club purchased 164 acres of land for $225,000. Donald Ross designed the 18-hole course. Northmoor became the second predominately Jewish country club on the North Shore. Ten years earlier, other organizers had started the Lake Shore Country Club at a 300-acre site near Lake Michigan.

A few miles up the lake's shore, another club incorporated in 1916, though its course opened a couple of years later. Shoreacres attracted an exclusive and very affluent membership—its roster reading like a Chicago version of Who's Who. Among the families at Shoreacres were the Armours, McCormicks, Ryersons, Swifts, Donnelleys and Chatfield-Taylors. The club's first president was Stanley Field, nephew of Marshall Field. Unquestionably, Stanley Field was a powerful force behind the club's formation and continued to provide strong leadership during his presidency—from 1916 to 1926.

Reportedly, members spent $500,000 to acquire the property and build the course and clubhouse. Shoreacres also intended to make use of the recreational opportunities provided by Lake Michigan, creating a kind of "boating country club." The plan was to develop an informal linkage with its neighbor to the north—the Great Lakes Naval Training Center—for the purpose of providing its members with recreational boating activities. For whatever reason, the water-oriented sports idea was never fully implemented.

While many North Shore clubs weren't exactly blessed with lake shore vistas, they did have important access to nearby train depots. Members of Indian Hill (the club's original name was the Winnetka Country Club) could easily walk from Winnetka's train station to the club in minutes. In 1912, club members purchased 234 acres for $25,000. About 100 acres were set aside and later sold for housing—all homes occupying at least one acre. Members used the remaining property to build a clubhouse and a golf course. Donald Ross designed the 18-hole layout that officially commenced play on July 10, 1914.

South of Winnetka, in Wilmette, the Westmoreland Country Club opened during this time. Club professional Joe Roseman designed this course and others in the northern suburbs. He also went on to become a golf course owner, but is probably remembered most as an early pioneer of underground course-watering systems.

On Chicago's north and northwest borders, there were three private clubs. One was Edgewater, which had formed in the 1890s, and is no longer in existence. The other two, the Irving Park Golf Club and Edgebrook Golf Club, remain in operation—although Edgebrook is now a public facility and the Irving Park club is now known as Ridgemoor.

In 1901, residents of the Irving Park community organized the Irving Park Golf Club. Occupying 40 acres, the flat 2,600-yard course featured four holes over 400 yards. Originally, the membership was capped at 40, with each paying a $10 initiation fee. When the leased property fell into the hands of a real estate developer, the club had to move. By 1905, club members found a 70-acre plot on Chicago's northwest side. During the following years, the Irving Park club saw its membership roster expand to 150. Members purchased more property and the course took shape as an 18-hole layout. The club's management also changed as did the club's name. In 1913, the organization officially became the Ridgemoor Country Club.

Chicago's other private club was Edgebrook. In 1919, however, Edgebrook's 10-year run as a private club ended when the newly formed Cook County Forest Preserve Commission acquired its first golf course for use by the public.

Western Expansion

West of Chicago, the Aurora and the Oak Park Country Clubs were each chartered in 1914. Tom Bendelow designed the Aurora layout; Donald Ross crafted Oak Park's course. Incidently, members of Oak Park's organization have shown good financial sense throughout the club's long history. In 1914, members purchased the 190-acre site for $190,000. Forty-one years later, Elmwood Park paid the club $200,000, purchasing a 20-acre site on the club's northwestern boundary, where the town built the Elmwood Park High School.

If only members of the 1909-established Pickwick Golf Club had shown a similar appreciation of sound financial practice. Doomed from inception, the Glen Ellyn-based organization choked on its own insatiable appetite. Expectations proved to be unrealistic. Within 24 months, the club went into bankruptcy.

Although short on cash, Pickwick's organizers did have a generous supply of imagination. For example, members planned on building not just any clubhouse but one that would be U-shaped in design, 550 feet long and occupying eight acres. Plans for the building's interior included 24 small dining rooms and another one capable of seating 500. Organizers envisioned 200 separate sleeping rooms, a 1,000-seat auditorium, an indoor pool, four bowling alleys and the largest locker room facility in the area. The club's 18-hole course would ultimately be the highlight of the grandiose facility—at least, that was the plan.

When Pickwick's club declared bankruptcy in 1911, a new group of practical-thinking members took over and incorporated as the Glen Oak Country Club. Upon property transfer, the new owners took control of a 130-acre parcel, which included a poorly maintained nine-hole course. Two structures stood. One was a rundown farmhouse which Glen Oak's members used as a temporary clubhouse. The other structure served as a locker room—it was originally a barn. The property's former owners couldn't even build a hot water heating system for shower facilities, let alone a clubhouse and a course that was intended to turn heads.

USGA Museum & Library

The Olympia Fields Clubhouse is one of the largest in the world.

It fell to another to develop into this country's most massive country club ever. Olympia Fields will always stand tallest in American golfing history as the biggest of them all.

The name alone suggests the grandeur to follow. Founders chose the word "Olympia" because of the association with the ancient games of Greece. "Fields" became a natural suffix since the south suburban site occupied a huge area, almost 1.5 miles by 1.0-mile wide. Total property costs were nearly $215,000.

The club formed in 1915 and immediately attracted interested applicants. First, 500 charter members joined. By 1930, the club had more than 1,400 names on its membership roster. Club members authorized construction of four 18-hole courses. The first, Course No. 1, opened in June 1916; the last, Course No. 4, in May 1923.

While four 18-hole courses did monopolize much of the 750-acre complex, Olympia Fields wasn't just a large country club but a small community. Fifty summer cottages dotted the grounds, along with a hospital, school, ice-making plant and fire station. None of these structures compared, however, to the club's centerpiece building—the huge clubhouse. Built in 1925, at a cost exceeding $1 million, the mammoth edifice stretched the length of a football field. The main dining room alone was large enough to seat 1,400. Locker facilities for 1,200 were available, as were 70 private sleeping rooms. Naturally, there was also a lounge where beverages of choice were served—it was referred to as the club's "73rd" hole.

Olympia's grounds were a naturalist's delight. The property was home to more than 60 species of birds, including many that were relatively uncommon, such as rusty blackbirds, ruby-crowned kinglets, solitary sandpipers, yellow-billed cuckoos, hermit thrushes and red-headed woodpeckers. These and other more common varieties settled in any one of 10,000 trees—comprised themselves of 70 different species. Including the 25 varieties of shrubs and 200 varieties of blooming plants, the entire landscape was as picturesque a setting as any country club in the country.

There was, in fact, a call to establish the grounds as a state game preserve. Already enriched with high populations of deer, wild turkey, pheasants, geese, ducks—even foot-long turtles—the club had hoped the state would stock fish in the club's streams and build a large lake on Olympia's property. Though eventually authorized as an official game preserve, Olympia Fields never fully developed the game preserve program.

Because of its membership volume, the club served the diverse interests of "Olympians" through committees—20 of them. There was, of course, one for birds and forestry along with an art, insurance, road and magazine committee—which published the monthly _Olympian_.

The club's recognized founder is Charles Beach, though its first president was Amos Alonzo Stagg. There is some question whether these two men along with other early organizers intended Olympia Fields to grow quite so large. This reference relates mostly to the gigantic clubhouse. Clearly, its construction cost led to a downsized Olympia Fields complex in later years.

In 1924, club membership assumed a $500,000 mortgage to build the country's largest clubhouse. Interest charges alone totaled $100 per day. The debt coupled with the financial straits of the '30s led club directors to a drastic but unavoidable solution. Courses Nos. 2 and 3 were sold to real estate developers. In 1944, exactly 20 years after the clubhouse's ground-breaking ceremony, the club retired all debt.

As large as Olympia Fields was, it did share one common trait with most of the local clubs—even the smallest—they were all private. Up until 1907, the region had but one public course, at Jackson Park. In 1907, Elgin doubled the number of Chicago-area public courses with its introduction of Wing Park. Elgin thus became the smallest city in the country to feature a public course. Although Wing Park and Jackson Park weren't especially challenging, they attracted a regular cadre of participants that limited still others who wanted to give the game a try.

After 1907, more public courses opened, including the area's first privately owned, public-fee layout in 1910 at the Harlem Golf Club. The critics laughed at the premise that public golfers would support such a concept. Note the following excerpt taken from the _Chicago Daily News_ in 1932 as it recalls comments directed to Harlem's organizers in 1910:

> _"Who will pay to play golf at so much per round? Golf will never go over in this town to such an extent as to furnish a place for the ordinary individual to play. It's a rich man's game."_

While Harlem charged a nominal fee, a trio of new Chicago-operated municipal courses promoted free play. The first opened in 1908 and immediately began to serve its west side constituency. Local residents had asked West Chicago Park commissioners as far back as 1900 to provide a local golfing outlet but not enough open space had been available within Garfield Park. In 1905, commissioners resolved the space problem by authorizing the dismantling of an old concrete bicycle track. Tom Bendelow was brought in to design a golf course. On Aug. 17, 1908, Garfield Park's nine-hole public course opened—surprisingly with little advance publicity. The commissioners explained later that they didn't wish to detract from attendance levels at the Cubs-Giants baseball game. The death knell for Garfield's course came in 1935. Pressure to extend Jackson Boulevard through the park, eliminating a more circuitous path around the southern perimeter, gained enough local support to signal Garfield's end.

Chicago's next municipal course debuted at Marquette Park in 1915. Built as an 18-hole course, it offered southwest side residents an alternative to either Jackson or Garfield Park layouts. While Marquette Park's facility exists today, it is limited to nine holes, the other nine being eliminated in 1936.

Of the three new municipal courses built from 1908 to 1916, the course at Diversey (in south Lincoln Park) attracted the most attention. Though the Diversey site had a six-hole course from 1911 to 1913, the primitive layout may best be remembered for its tin can cups. This era in Diversey's history is commonly referred to as the "Tin Can" period. Nevertheless, the course represented the sole outlet for north side residents. By all accounts, the Lincoln Park commissioners weren't anxious to fund construction of a new nine-hole course at Diversey. Instead, they had bigger plans. Specifically, the commissioners proposed the building of a regulation-sized 18-hole golf course on a site between Montrose and Waveland Avenues. This property was, however, still under water and at least 10 years away from being thoroughly reclaimed. Facing a mounting call to satisfy area enthusiasts, they reluctantly approved plans to build the Diversey nine-hole layout. On Sept. 9, 1916, the official dedication ceremonies were held—the guest of honor, Illinois Governor Edward Dunne.

By 1920, Chicago and Elgin had been joined by other local municipalities eager to establish golfing facilities. Aurora, Evanston and Winnetka were among the earliest communities to offer public links.

Establishment of the Cook County Forest Preserve in 1915 also aided the public golfer's plight. Edgebrook, as has been noted, was annexed, while the Palos Hills 18-hole course was carved out of preserve-owned land in 1919. But still more than 80% of the Chicago's district courses by 1920 were private.

Demand for more golfing venues was fueled by interest in national tournaments. Newspapers and magazines filled their pages with detailed accounts of championship events. Local media coverage increased dramatically when Chicago clubs hosted.

Tournaments came to the Chicago area on an almost annual basis from 1901 to 1920. The U.S. Open, U.S. Amateur and U.S. Women's Amateur were each locally contested four times during these years. The Western Open was played on Chicago-area courses nine times and the Western Amateur, eight. With the PGA Championship held in 1920, this becomes the most active 20-year period of Chicago tournament history.

USGA Museum & Library

Walter Hagen on the left and Jock Hutchison. Each won a PGA Championship on a Chicago course.

USGA Museum & Library

Evans won the U.S. Open and U.S. Amateur in 1916.

But Chicagoans had a greater reason to follow these events—their own favorite son. While the area produced several fine players, no one was superior to Charles "Chick" Evans. His impact upon the game was so pronounced, any attempt to define his contributions seems incomplete.

Born in Indianapolis, Evans was four in 1894 when his family moved to Chicago's northside. Four years later, he noticed a sign in Rogers Park that read "Edgewater Golf Grounds." Curious, he asked his father about its meaning and was told that golf was a Scottish game that many Americans were attempting to learn. Within six months, Evans began to caddy at Edgewater's club.

During the next eight years, the club had no better caddy. Earning caddy badge No. 1, Evans' reputation around the club became legendary to club members. By then, he had become a pretty good player himself and often provided tips to members, if they so requested. Additionally, his prowess in finding "lost" golf balls gained him acclaim and extra tips. Evans' strategy in finding lost balls was really quite simple. He would first lie down in the area he believed shielded the missing ball. He then began to roll his body over the tall grass until something created pressure on his back, legs or arms. The missing ball was, of course, the cause of this pressure.

In 1906, Evans quit caddying and began to enter locally held amateur events. In the second event he ever entered— the Chicago City Championship—Evans finished second. Amazingly, his success had been achieved through the exclusive use of two clubs, a mid-iron and a putter.

A year later, the then 17-year old won his first golf championship—the Interscholastic tournament at Onwentsia. Before 1907 ended, Evans had won the Edgewater Open, the Chicago City Championship and the Western Junior. It represented the beginning of a brilliant golfing career, spanning five decades.

USGA Museum & Library

Evans on the left and 1913 U.S. Open winner, amateur Francis Ouimet.

Gifted with a fluid swing, Evans had no peer from tee to green. His putting proficiency was another matter, however. This shortcoming prevented him from dominating the golf scene through the teens and '20s. Poor putting stopped him from winning several major tourneys from 1910 to 1915, including the 1914 U.S. Open at Midlothian, where he lost to Walter Hagen by a stroke. The same year, Evans also finished second in the prestigious U.S. Amateur championship.

Two years later, Evans turned the tables—stepping into golfing immortality. Ironically, Chicago's favorite son zoomed into national prominence by winning outside of Chicago. His first big triumph came at the 1916 U.S. Open, held in Minneapolis. Recording a four-round total of 286 (70-69-74-73), Evans' record score stood until the 1936 Open.

Evans' triumph at the 1916 Open was accomplished with only seven golf clubs in his bag. He later admitted the clubs cost him $20.75. By comparison, Evans paid his U.S. Open caddy $20. The clubs more than proved their minimal investment later in 1916 as Evans won the U.S. Amateur championship in Pennsylvania. The double wins were a golfing first. Not only had no other golfer achieved this feat before, but only one would ever duplicate it. (The great Bobby Jones did it in 1930).

Evans' amateur career included other great victories. He captured eight Western Amateurs, four City Championships including the one he won at 17, one Western Open and even won the French Amateur. While truly a golf immortal and easily considered Chicago's best golfer ever, Evans' financial and inspirational contribution in tuition-assistance programs for former caddies is his most important legacy. With the help of the Western Golf Association, the ongoing Evans Scholars Foundation is testimony today to Evans' philanthropy. (The foundation's specific objectives are more closely examined in a later chapter.) Twelve years after his death in 1979, more than 5,000 Evans Scholars have graduated from college—each of them owing a debt of gratitude to Chick Evans. His triumphs fueled golf's expansion during the early part of the 20th century. The fact that he started as a caddy and remained unpretentious throughout his career contributed to his appeal and that of the game of golf.

The Golden Era: 1921-1930

The scope of golf's enormous popularity in the 1920s does stretch the imagination. Consider, for example, that Chicago's Jackson Park 27-hole course averaged more than 220,000 rounds per year. In 1925 alone, the facility drew an almost unbelievable 259,843 rounds. During the '20s, the other city courses weren't quite as busy, but they still averaged almost 100,000 rounds per year. Local golfers were so eager to hone their skills, waits of three to four hours were commonplace.

Seeing the need for more area courses early in the decade, developers embarked on an unprecedented construction boom. When it finally stopped in 1930, the local region had more than 120 new golf courses—an average of more than one new course per month over the 10-year period. The Chicago area has not experienced, either before or since, such a prolific rate of growth of new courses. And, for the most part, these were well-planned, well-constructed facilities. Indeed, nearly one of every three currently operating courses is a product of golf's golden era.

To understand the reason for the game's heightened interest during the 1920s, we need to look at what else was happening outside the world of golf. This was a time of fun, almost euphoria, and certainly contrary to the mood felt during the war years 1917 to 1919.

The Roaring '20s found Chicagoans joining the rest of the country in celebrating their newly found prosperity. An age of consumerism dawned. With the shorter work hours being introduced, recreation increased. Nightclubs flourished. Hollywood introduced talking pictures. Dances like the Charleston and black bottom were the craze.

Chicago golfers wait their turn at Jackson Park's first tee.

The sport scene had its converts, too. Baseball attendance soared—in part because of the exploits of Babe Ruth.
More than 150,000 Chicagoans watched Gene Tunney and
Jack Dempsey square off for the heavyweight championship in Soldier Field. Meanwhile, the era's golfing greats—
among them Evans, Jones and Farrell—captivated local
followers.

While not everyone in Chicago played golf, the game's
skyrocketing popularity attracted new enthusiasts from a
diverse populace. Cardinal Mundelein heard golf's calling
and built a private course for seminarians. Local manufacturing plants organized intracompany golf clubs. Women
players took full advantage of Ladies Day discounts. Doctors played on Wednesdays. Judges often cleared afternoon
dockets to squeeze in a round, which also allowed lawyers
to get in more practice time.

Presumably for reasons other than having a good alibi,
Chicago mobsters also took up golf. Joe and Pete
Gussenberg enjoyed the game up until their untimely death
in 1929 on St. Valentine's Day. Ralph Capone, on the other
hand, lived long enough to score a hole-in-one on Sept.
15, 1930, at Indian Head's 140-yard 7th hole. Ralph's infamous brother, Al, wasn't nearly as skilled. Still, Al visited
enough local courses in his time, always preferring ones
with wide open layouts. He avoided courses where tree-
lined fairways might tempt intruders to hide in their cover.

Chicago's law-abiding citizens had fewer restrictions in
choosing where to play. In fact, as the number of new

courses increased, so too did a golfer's difficulty in choosing a course to play. Enter here the wonderful world of advertising, whose use by golf clubs became widespread during the 1920s. Unfortunately, many club proprietors touted the same claims—often using identical buzzwords:

Pickwick   "Unexcelled Accommodations"
Oak Hills   "Unexcelled Accommodations"
Vernon Ridge "Unexcelled Facilities"
Northbrook   "Unexcelled Accommodations"

For some golfers, the quest for a golf site that was truly "unexcelled" would not have been resolved by these claims. Who knows? They may have opted instead to play Techny Fields, which billed itself as "unsurpassed."

If the dilemma in finding a unique course wasn't difficult enough, consider the myriad of options for golfers also wanting a facility with good food. While Techny Fields featured "exceptional food," Vernon Ridge had "home cooked meals at moderate prices." Were the meals better at Northbrook? That club offered the "finest meals at exceptionally low prices." On the other hand, White Pines advertised "famous home-cooked meals" in a "cozy, friendly clubhouse," no less. But then again, Golfmoor had a "high class restaurant." With so many choices, some golfers may have avoided making the tough decision and gone to Hillcrest. There "ample picnic grounds" were available.

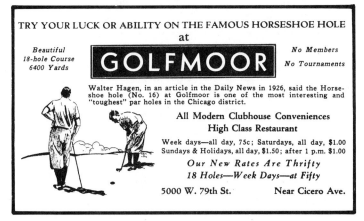

Ads from local courses included testimonials—this one from Walter Hagen.

When the ads weren't espousing specific course or clubhouse virtues, they sought to increase the market by targeting appeals to beginners, advising them to forget "the science of the game and play for the outing." These appeals registered only partial success, since much of the targeted audience seemed satisfied with bowling and billiards. Taking the gloves off, the followup advertisements warned these indoor-sport enthusiasts that their activities took place in "poorly ventilated" and "illuminated artificially" environments. Offering an alternative, these messages stressed the healthfulness of golf—using ad copy such as: "invigorating air, in the sunshine and within the beautiful countryside."

Commenting on golf's popularity during the '20s and the unparalleled increase of participation, the locally published *Chicago Golf and Country Club Review* reported in its March 1930 issue:

> *"Eventually, if not already, Chicago will be the center of golf in the United States. In and around this city are or will be located more golf courses than are to be found around any city in this country or any country.*
>
> *"At the present time there may be more golf courses in the New York District than there are in the Chicago District. But Chicago is very rapidly gaining; in a way which foretells very clearly the coming supremacy of our city. One of these clear indications is the rapid growth of public and semi-public courses in the Chicago District. At the present time, there are almost 50 public fee courses in or near Chicago, and in addition the many public parks and forest preserve courses.*
>
> *"These unequalled facilities for the playing of golf at a cost of from 15 cents to prices higher but still within the price range of almost every person's pocket, are resulting in the creation of a very large public ripe for membership in private courses. No other city employs such an ideal condition for the increase in its golfing public and consequent increases in its clubs.*
>
> *"It is important that the official bodies which have to do with the guiding of golf in this district be prepared to cope with a growth which interest in the sport makes inevitable."*

The editorial mentions semi-public courses. Specifically, these were private clubs that welcomed public play at off-peak hours during the week. Including these semi-public options, along with the area's privately owned daily-fee courses plus available municipal courses, the public golfer could pick and choose from among 100 different courses by 1930.

In 1920, only 15 public courses existed. All were municipally operated except for Harlem Golf Club in Forest Park—Chicago's first daily-fee course. From 1921 to 1926, 16 more daily-fee courses appeared:

Big Oaks (Chicago)	Fairlawn (La Grange)
Budlong Woods (Chicago)	Galewood (Oak Park)
Evergreen (Chicago)	Hickory Hills (Oak Lawn)
Golfmoor (Chicago)	Hillside
Greenview (Chicago)	Dixmoor (Homewood)
Mid City (Chicago)	Oak Hills (Orland)
Cedar Lake (Indiana)	Oak Shore Beach
Chain O'Lakes (Antioch)	(Waukegan)
	Villa Olivia (Elgin)

Of the six new daily-fee courses in Chicago listed above, five lay near the city limits. Besides being less expensive, land there was more readily available. On the other hand, operators of Chicago's sixth daily-fee site—the Mid City Golf Club—discovered moderately priced property at the corners of Western and Addison Avenues.

Before Mid City opened in 1924, the property served as a city dumping ground. Littering its landscape were rusted automobiles, bedsprings and mattresses, iceboxes, and a multitude of old shoes and tin cans. When Bill Langford announced his intention to create a golf course on the site, the critics laughed. But, in time, a popular 6,080-yard course evolved. Within a few years, however, the city targeted some of the course property (the parcel south of Addison on Western) for the new site of Lane Technical High School and, by 1931, construction began. With less acreage to work with, Langford redesigned Mid City into another 18-hole course, albeit one measuring only 4,735 yards. There wasn't enough space for any par 5s so the course featured nine par 4s and nine par 3s.

While Mid City remained a popular and busy site, its grounds were always well-maintained. Still, the older patrons, remembering the original refuse dump, would always be alert when divots were taken. They half expected to unearth something unusual, though of course, they never did.

By contrast, the Evergreen Golf Club arose from farmland that once functioned as the site of the old Ellerslie Cross Country Club. Evergreen's founders Walter and Arthur Ahern knew the parcel intimately, having long viewed the land from their back porch. Intuitively, the Aherns felt a golf course could succeed and they were proved right. Today, Evergreen's layout is the sole survivor of the six daily-fee courses built in Chicago during the early '20s.

Of the district's other 10 daily-fee courses built from 1921 to 1926, five operate today: Cedar Lake, Fairlawn (now Fresh Meadow), Hickory Hills, Oak Hills and Villa Olivia.

What started in the '20s as a rush turned into a torrent of daily fees between 1926 and 1931. There were 27 new courses that, from their inception, were built as daily-fee operations:

Bonnie Dundee (Dundee)	Minne Monesse (Grant
Brae Loch (Grayslake)	Park)
Burnham Woods	Old Orchard (Arlington
(Burnham)	Heights)
Cedar Crest (Fox Lake)	Orchard Beach (McHenry)
Cog Hill (Lemont)	Pickwick (Glenview)
Crystal Lawns (Joliet)	Pipe O'Peace (Blue Island)
Dan-Dee (Dundee)	St. Andrews (No. 2)
Dixie-Hi (Harvey)	(West Chicago)
Glenbard (Glen Ellyn)	Shady Lawn (Beecher)
Hillcrest (Barrington)	Silver Lake (Orland)
Hunter (Richmond)	Walnut Hills (Palos Park)
Indian Head	Westgate Valley (Worth)
(Western Springs)	White Pines (Bensenville)
Indian Ridge (Gary, Ind.)	York (Hinsdale)
Lansing Airport (Lansing)	Zurich Heights (Lake
	Zurich)

But Chicago's golfing public had still more options. Unable to compete with more established private clubs or impacted severely by the changing economic climate in 1930, many private clubs built during the 1920s dropped their "membership-only" policy. A few converted entirely to daily-fee; some became semi-public clubs. These 36 private clubs opened their courses to the public in this period:

Antlers (Wheaton)
Bartlett Hills (Bartlett)
Bellaire (Wauconda)
Bonnie Brook (Waukegan)
Cary
Casa Del Mar (Dyer, Ind.)
Cedardell (Plano)
Chapel Hill (McHenry)
Cherry Hills (Flossmoor)
Columbian (Wheeling)
Countryside (Mundelein)
Cressmoor (Gary, Ind.)
Crystal Lake
Fox Lake
Glen Acres (Glenview)
Glendale (Bloomingdale)
Gleneagles (Lemont)
Glenwood
Indian Wood (Matteson)

Kinsmans (Lockport)
Laramie (Chicago)
Libertyville
Lincoln Hills (Gary, Ind.)
McHenry
Middlebrook (Northbrook)
Midwest (Hinsdale)
Mission Hills (Northbrook)
Momence
Naperville
Rob Roy (Arlington Heights)
Round Lake
Sportsman's (Northbrook)
Techny Fields (Northbrook)
University (Northbrook)
Vernon Ridge (Deerfield)
Woodridge (Hinsdale)

While there were many private clubs that converted to public play in one form or another, the majority of private clubs built in the '20s stayed private. And what a superb group they were! Clubs such as Kildeer (now Twin Orchard), Butterfield, Sunset Ridge, Tam O'Shanter, Knollwood and Illinois (now Green Acres) were all formed in the decade. But the most famous example from this era was Medinah.

Medinah, the site of the last three locally held U.S. Open championships, is Chicago's eminent club. Still, its well-deserved reputation didn't come easily. Certainly, it didn't come quickly.

Only three years after Medinah first opened, a major financial crisis erupted. Members met the challenge, but not without experiencing the sting of a $300,000 shortfall.

Entrance to Medinah.

In 1930, members felt another pain, this the result of Harry Cooper and Gene Sarazen scoring 63 and 65 respectively on Medinah's newest course—No. 3. The two scores put an immediate end to member claims that No. 3 was one of the toughest layouts nationally. Digging a little deeper into their wallets, members spent money to make the course harder. Within five years, experts considered No. 3 among the country's best.

Even later, when a new generation of Medinah members served as hosts of the 1975 U.S. Open, the club drew negative post-tournament reviews for its handling of the event. By the time members could interest the USGA to again schedule the Open at the club, nine years had passed. And the USGA would only offer the Open to Medinah with an important proviso. Specifically, the USGA suggested that a new 18th hole be built, and, furthermore, that the seating capacity around the finishing hole be expanded. Still remembering the 1975 affair, Medinah's members vowed to spare no expense to first, satisfy USGA requirements, and, second, host the best organized U.S. Open in history. Both objectives were ultimately met, in 1990.

Throughout the club's history, Medinah's members have paid the price. Unlike many other Chicago-area clubs built before it, Medinah's membership wasn't comprised of Chicago's richest or socially prominent families. In fact, the working-class club, during its early years, was just trying to build a respectable membership base. In April 1924, a local newspaper brief reported that the club sought new members, specifically, those who already belonged to the "noble of the Ancient Arabic Order of Nobles of the Mystic Shrine of North America"—Shriners, for short.

The club's membership requirements were just one of the unusual characteristics that suggested Medinah's operation was beyond the franchise of a traditional country club. For example, the club's organizers had purchased a 650-acre wooded property site near Roselle; the land was about three times the size of a typical Chicago-area golf club site. Building their own informal country escape, the grounds soon included not only the usual golfing, swimming and tennis facilities, but also a polo field, skeet range, equestrian trail, ski-jumping hill and other recreational venues.

Organizers also commissioned the construction of a clubhouse. Though it wasn't as large as the colossal building at Olympia Fields, Medinah's clubhouse featured an architectural uniqueness that stopped first-time visitors in awe-inspiring delight. The $750,000, three-story building included a 1,000-plus capacity locker room, huge ballroom and smaller rooms for lodging and indoor recreation activities. The structure's architectural thumbprint, however, was the mosque-like interior of its rotunda entrance. Incorporating a design that blended Italian, French and Byzantine elements, building architect Richard Schmidt—also a Shriner—crafted a work of 20th century art. Today, the building has a $20 million replacement value.

But the club was, after all, a golfing facility, too. When construction began in 1926 of its third course, the club put into practice its philosophy that women members were important to Medinah's success. The third course would be used exclusively by its women members. Most people know Medinah's No. 3 course, completed in 1928, proved to be too difficult for the ladies. Soon thereafter, Medinah's No. 2 layout was designated to be used exclusively by the distaff side, with Nos. 1 and 3 reserved for men only. If there is irony in the fact that Chicago's toughest current-day course was originally intended to be for women only, there is even greater irony that Tom Bendelow designed it.

Bendelow's reputation as a golf course architect had been anything but illustrious—at least before his work on Medinah's three courses. Though he had laid out several hundred courses nationally from 1900 to 1924, most were municipal projects that he completed in a day. As an architect, Bendelow certainly lacked the creative genius of a Donald Ross, an Alister Mackenzie or a Charles Blair Macdonald. Still, Bendelow's design and workmanship on Medinah No. 3 were as fine as could be found on any course in the country. Unquestionably, the end product represented Bendelow's lifetime best.

Medinah's No. 3 course still is the club's most visible symbol. Today, the layout ranks among the top 20 in the country; most judge No. 3 to be one of the 50 greatest in the world. While the course is its key drawing card, with applicants waiting up to seven years to gain full playing privileges, the club's primary resource is its membership. For almost 70 years, its early members and those who came after them worked to build an even greater organization. In the process, they faced adversity and overcame it. Today, while members recognize and are proud of their club's national and international acclaim, they continue in the Medinah tradition of seeking excellence. Perhaps this explains why it has been and continues to be revered by so many Chicagoans.

While Medinah's No. 3 course started to gain its well-deserved recognition in the 1930s, another Chicago-area course that had also been built in the 1920s gained immediate plaudits. This was the No. 4 course at Olympia Fields. Completed in 1922, it was the site of the PGA, Western Open and U.S. Open championships in 1925, 1927 and 1928, respectively. Asked in 1928 to name his favorite course nationally, pro golfer Johnny Farrell selected Olympia Fields' No. 4. Personal sentiment influenced him, no doubt. Just a few weeks earlier, Farrell had won the U.S. Open championship on it.

Farrell's top 10 list included a second Chicago course—Mill Road Farm. Though long gone, the course was not only the most exclusive facility in the region, but also the toughest.

Advertising executive Albert Lasker operated the 7,000-yard par 72 course on the grounds of his 500-acre Lake Forest estate. Reportedly built at a cost of more than $3 million, the grounds of the estate included a 55-room mansion, 12-car garage, greenhouses, riding stables and a movie theater. But it was the golf course that drew the era's best golfers, including Farrell and Bobby Jones. The course's rating difficulty was 76.32, the highest of all area courses (Medinah's No. 3 had the second highest rating of 76.08). Even the era's greatest golfers could never shoot par. As part of a private estate, Mill Road's golf course was spent in brilliant obscurity. Lasker sold the property in the 1940s. Today, single-family homes cover the site.

Chicago Historical Society Photo by Trowbridge, Box 423, #31.

A view of the private Lasker Estate and its tough 18 hole course.

Fortunately, another challenging Lake Forest course from the same era survived. The Knollwood Club rests on 220 acres that the club's organizers purchased for approximately $600 per acre. Using 180 acres, famed designer Charles Hugh Allison designed the tough Knollwood course in the mid '20s. Its shining moment came in 1956 when it hosted the U.S. Amateur.

Allison had also designed another north suburban course that entertained two U.S. Amateur competitions. The Glenview-based North Shore Country Club opened at its second site in 1923, a year after members vacated their original club site in Kenilworth. Actually, members of the Edgewater Golf Club had coveted the Glenview property, but, in the end chose to remain at their Chicago site. Consequently, North Shore's members purchased the property option from Edgewater. In 1928, the North Shore club entertained the Western Open. Five years later, it hosted the 1933 U.S. Open. Also noteworthy is that this marked the last time an amateur—Johnny Goodman—won the Open.

USGA Museum & Library

The North Shore Country Club's first tee as it appeared in 1933.

Courtesy of Chicago District Golf Association

Ralph Guldahl and his son "Buddy." Guldahl finished one shot behind Johnny Goodman at the 1933 U.S. Open at North Shore.

Here are the private clubs that were built in the 1920s and remained private throughout the decade. Some, such as North Shore and Westward Ho, had been established prior to 1921 but moved to new facilities in the 10-year period and so are listed here:

Acacia (La Grange)
Barrington Hills
(Barrington)
Biltmore (Barrington)
Briergate (Deerfield)
Brookwood (Addison)
Bunker Hill (Niles)
Butterfield (Hinsdale)
Edgewood Valley (La
Grange)
Euclid Hills (Orland)
Fox Valley (Batavia)
Illinois (Glencoe)
Itasca
Kildeer (Long Grove)
Knollwood (Lake
Forest)
Lake Hills (St. John,
Ind.)
Lincolnshire (Crete)
Maywood (Hillside)
Meadow Grove
(Palatine)
Medinah
Melody Farm (Lake
Forest)
Mill Road Farm (Lake
Forest)

Mohawk (Bensenville)
Navajo Fields (Worth)
Nordic (Itasca)
North Shore (Glenview)
Northwest Hills (Mt.
Prospect)
Olympic (Arlington
Heights)
Pistakee (McHenry)
River Forest (Bensenville)
Rock Island (Chicago)
Rolling Green
(Arlington Heights)
Ruth Lake (Hinsdale)
St. Andrews (No. 1)
(West Chicago)
St. Charles
St. Mary's (Mundelein)
Southmoor (Palos
Park)
Sunset Ridge (Winnetka)
Tam O'Shanter (Niles)
Twin Orchard
(Bensenville)
Westmoor (Roselle)
Westward Ho (Melrose
Park)
Wilmette

In contrast to the increase in the number of new private and daily-fee clubs, the future municipal course explosion had to wait. During the 1920s, however, three north suburban villages did introduce nine-hole courses to their citizens. Highland Park (Sunset Valley), Glencoe and Lake Forest (Deerpath) thus joined Evanston and Winnetka with this community perk.

The Cook County Forest Preserve Commission also added a north suburban layout by acquiring the Northwestern Golf Club. Once the site of an auxiliary nine-hole course at the Glen View Club and then later sold to Northwestern University, the course was purchased by the county in the early '20s. Edgebrook and Palos Hills were the only other Forest Preserve courses before 1921.

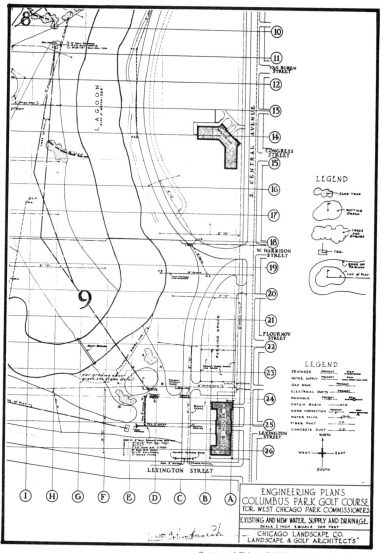

Architect Tom Bendelow's design plans for Chicago's
Columbus Park Golf Course.

Chicago's Park District added two more courses—Columbus in 1921 and the Jacob A. Riis Park in 1928. The Riis Park addition had come after heated debate between proponents (Riis Park Golf Club) and opponents (Riis Park Golf Club Elimination Association). Eventually siding with the pro-golf group, a local community newspaper was credited with tilting the balance toward course construction.

One other change at Chicago's Park District courses was the introduction of greens fees. Prior to 1921, the rounds were free. Still, the new fees were nominal. At Diversey's course, for example, a nine-hole round in 1921 cost 10 cents. A season's pass only cost $2. Throughout the '20s fees did rise, but by 1928 a round for 25 cents to 35 cents was common.

Publicly owned facilities in Chicago, along with those in Elgin, Joliet, Aurora, Gary and the northern suburbs, drew approximately one million rounds in 1928. It's a staggering total, since publicly owned sites represented less than 15 percent of all local courses. In total, public and private courses experienced over four million rounds in 1928. Chicago's two baseball teams by comparison drew fewer attendees, even though the Cubs led all of baseball with 1,485,000 in home attendance. In an era without televised sports, a case can be made that Chicago's summer pastime wasn't baseball but rather golf.

Indeed, 1928, and the decade in general were about as totally golf-oriented as any period in Chicago's history. Several major tournaments were hosted locally. The 1922 U.S. Open at Skokie produced the first major victory for the then 20-year-old Gene Sarazen. It marked another first of sorts—spectators were required to buy tickets. In 1925, Olympia Fields played host to the PGA Championship, a match-play format won by Walter Hagen. Two years later, Hagen won the Western Open, again at Olympia Fields. No year in Chicago's tournament history will compare to 1928. The U.S. Open, Western Open, Western Amateur, Women's Western Amateur and Western Junior Championships were all contested in the area. The year's final event, an international competition no less, saw Bobby Jones' American team soundly beat a group of English amateurs in the Walker Cup at CGC. It's the only time the Walker Cup competition came to the Chicago area.

The decade had other golfing firsts. Chicago's first International Golf Show was held in 1926 and attracted 200 exhibitors. Later that year, WGN radio aired reports of a locally held U.S. Open qualifying round. Listeners received 10 minutes of detailed coverage from the Calumet Country Club every hour. This marked the first time local radio afforded such in-depth coverage.

But then came 1929 and the $15 billion stock-market crash. Few individuals could predict at the time that there would be a Depression, and that it would be as severe as it was. It signaled the end of local golf's 37-year ascent.

Golf Takes A Step Backward: 1931-1950

Less than two years after the stock market crashed, 2,300 banks failed nationwide; in Chicago, only 51 of 228 remained open. Thousands of other businesses also closed their doors for good. Companies that survived did so by scaling down work forces, sending unemployment soaring. With 750,000 Chicagoans unemployed, the merriment of the '20s gave way to economic turmoil, in the process slashing the public's recreational pursuits. Golf was devastated. After nearly 40 years of continuous growth, the game's momentum had come to a stop.

Private clubs took the hardest hit with membership declines averaging 25 percent annually in the early and mid '30s. A few organizations held their own. Knollwood, for example, showed a "respectable" 14 percent drop, going from 324 members in 1929 to 278 in 1938. Other clubs experienced more severe losses. The Homewood-based Ravisloe Country Club saw its roster base cut in half, prompting discussions of a potential merger with the nearby Idlewild Country Club.

To combat the effects of declining membership, club officials tried several counter-maneuvers. One was to lower initiation rates dramatically. In 1927, for example, the typical Chicago-area club had an average $1,800 initiation fee. In 1932, the average fell to $500. Consider that Olympia Fields' initiation fee in 1933 stood at $300, or $900 less than the club's pre-Depression fee. During the same time, the Skokie Country Club's fee dropped from $1,600 to just $225. Ridgewood experienced one of the most dramatic declines—having its membership fee fall from a peak of $2,000 to $110. Clearly, membership bargains were available.

In addition to cutting initiation fees, several area clubs introduced new types of membership programs to attract prospects. One example saw clubs offering one-year memberships. In fact, the Bob O'Link club had one for out-of-town visitors and employees of Chicago's Century of Progress Exposition of 1933. The Highland Park club offered these fair "specials" for $50.

The early '30s also saw the area debut of another atypical type of membership—one that featured social privileges exclusively. The Columbian Golf Club in Wheeling was the first to offer a social membership, for $100. Shortly thereafter, the Midlothian Country Club also announced that it, too, was accepting social memberships.

While private clubs cut initiation fees or introduced various one-year membership opportunities, some clubs, ironically, embarked on costly renovation programs to attract new members. Remaining club members dug deep into their pockets to fund capital improvement projects, hoping to gain competitive advantages. The strategy paid off handsomely in several cases.

Perhaps the most common course improvement during the period was the construction of underground watering systems. Before 1926, only two area clubs featured such systems—the Chicago Golf Club and the Illinois Country Club in Glencoe. Starting in the late '20s and continuing throughout the '30s, this addition became the prerequisite for a first-class course. Specifically, a $52,000 system proved to be the key selling point in attracting new members to Midlothian. The North Shore Country Club spent $110,000 on theirs in 1931. Its presence attracted new members, but more importantly paved the way for the USGA to select it as the host site of the 1933 U.S. Open. The same year, 33 Chicago courses featured underground watering systems—more than any other region in the country.

Clubs made improvements off the course, too. Nongolfing recreational facilities, designed for the whole family, became a priority. St. Charles Country Club founder, Lester Morris, had observed the family oriented concept working successfully at California country clubs. Instituting the changes at his St. Charles club, he was able to increase its membership during the 1930s.

While some area clubs enjoyed modest success in neutralizing the Depression's effects, other organizations weren't so lucky. Some closed for good, while others shut down operations for periods up to 10 years. Still others went the daily-fee route.

. Daily-fee courses had one clear advantage. They were inexpensive to play and unencumbered by annual dues or initiation fees. Recognizing this strength, the Chicago Daily Fee Golf Club Association agreed to the establishment of a uniform pricing structure in 1933. The rates and the 27 member clubs were as follows:

$1.00 All day, weekdays
 .75 18 holes, weekdays
 .50 Twilight, weekdays

$1.00 Mornings, Saturday
 1.25 All day Saturday
 .75 Twilight Saturday

$1.50 All day Sunday
 1.25 Afternoons, Sunday
 1.25 Twilight Sunday

SOUTH SIDE CLUBS	NORTH SIDE CLUBS	WEST SIDE CLUBS
Chicago Meadows	Big Oaks	Arrowhead
Cog Hill	Elmgate	Harlem
Evergreen	Mid City	Hillcrest
Golfmoor	Northbrook	Indian Head
Hickory Hills	Pickwick	Glenbard
Kinsmans	Rob Roy	Midwest
Oak Hills	Techny Fields	White Pines
Pipe O'Peace	Vernon	Woodridge
Walnut Hills	West Wilmette	
Westgate Valley	Illuminated	

Most of the time, these clubs accepted phone reservations. For some daily-fee clubs, tee times could also be made off-site—including Walgreens!

Still, it wasn't enough. With the golden days of the 1920s gone, it became evident to course operators that steps be taken to rebuild daily attendance. To illustrate just how far levels had plummeted from 1928, in 1933, Chicago's municipal courses drew but 258,000 rounds. In golf's earlier heyday, Jackson Park's facility alone topped this attendance.

Weekday play at courses—public and private alike—fell precipitously during the early 1930s. It wasn't unusual for private courses, in particular, to stand nearly empty on some weekdays. Imagine eight foursomes representing the entire activity at Olympia Fields four-course complex or similar scant weekday gatherings at Medinah's 54-hole facility. It was clear that area courses needed some kind of boost to reestablish golfing interest.

Chicago Tribune Golf School

In 1933, there was one major innovation: a golf school sponsored by the *Chicago Tribune.* Free weekly lessons, over a five-week period, were offered at all member courses of the Chicago Daily Fee Association. Local club professionals donated their time to serve as instructors.

Two local pros are given credit for initiating the golfing school concept. Tom Walsh of Westgate Valley and Julius Lambert of the Northbrook Golf Club felt golf's future status was tied directly to introducing novices to the sport. Early support of the concept came from several sources, including the Chicago District Golf Association and its president, Harry Radix. Although the CDGA had primarily private clubs as its members, Radix felt the free lessons would serve "as the most novel stimulus, golf as a game, has had in years. (The) innovation will stimulate interest...among all classes."

With funding and promotional support from the *Chicago Tribune,* the classes commenced; all that attendees were required to bring was one club, preferably a 5-iron. The classes attracted not only novices, but intermediate golfers as well. Juniors, seniors and women learned the basic tenets of good golf. The correct grip and proper swing techniques enlightened attendees, but they also took note of suggestions pertaining to course etiquette, especially slow play.

All told, Chicago-area enthusiasts received 15,000 lessons during the first year. The number increased to more than 20,000 in 1934. By 1936, organizers switched school sites—holding classes exclusively at Chicago's municipal courses. The lessons continued every year throughout the '30s and '40s; in fact by 1950, more than 700,000 lessons had been offered to local residents. The informal golf school easily became the largest and most successful operation of its type anywhere in the world.

Still, other than the novel golf school concept, the '30s *and '40s* produced few highlights. Looking back, it's unlikely two consecutive decades could ever again be as problematic. With the Depression, three other recessions and World War II, the 20-year period was golf's first and only regressive era. Nationally, the number of facilities dropped from 5,700 in 1931 to 4,931 in 1950—a 14 percent decline. Private club numbers that had stood at 4,500 in 1931 crashed to the 3,000 level by 1950. While some became daily-fee sites, the majority simply ceased to exist.

The Chicago area—long a golf course sanctuary—suffered even more. In 1931, about 200 courses dotted the local landscape; twenty years later, only about 160 remained, a 20 percent attrition rate. For every new course built locally, three to four facilities closed. In reality, most of the course additions occurred early in the 1930s—the mid-to-late '30s and the '40s showed little construction activity.

Notable additions from the early '30s that currently operate include Big Run, Timber Trails and a reorganized Sportsman's. While technically the Northbrook-based course first took root in the '20s as Sky Harbor, its 1931 debut as Sportsman's featured a rather unique opening ceremony.

Chick Evans represented just one of several well known area amateur golfers to christen the "new" layout. By day's end, none bettered par. Evans himself posted a 76. The highlight of the proceedings, however, took place at the 8th hole—a 206-yard par three. Using a wood, Robert Griffin hooked his tee shot off an out-of-bounds post. The ball ricocheted toward the green and rolled into the cup.

Evans also took part in Big Run's introductory ceremonies in Lockport one year later. Three weeks after that, he played at another course opening, this one eagerly awaited by many Chicagoans. On June 15, 1932, the new nine-hole course in north Lincoln Park officially opened. Among those on hand to join the festivities was the state's governor, Louis T. Emmerson. Emmerson, in fact, had first ball honors at the new course.

With financial assistance provided from the state, Waveland (as it soon became known) took more than two years and nearly $2 million to build. Part of the cost went to reclaim the land from Lake Michigan. Originally, plans called for the creation of an 18-hole course—stretching north to Montrose. Although the expansion never materialized, the nine-hole course with its hundreds of American elms and Norwegian maples and colorful flower beds, all against the backdrop of Lake Michigan's blue waters, drew immediate plaudits.

Park District authorities took pride in sculpturing one of the most beautiful municipal courses nationally. But they also worried about how public players would treat the manicured grounds. Specifically, their worries centered on images of inept hackers and golf's neophytes trudging through flowered landscapes. They visualized seedling trees being bruised by the wild swings of novices.

Courtesy of Chicago Park District Special Collections

Chicago's Waveland Golf Course in its early years.

Obviously, some form of action had to be taken to preserve Waveland's landscape. But what? A suggestion to allow access to only proficient golfers seemed reasonable; in effect, the quasi-official 1932 policy prohibited beginners.

This rather weak discriminatory effort soon met with vociferous objections and threats of legal action against the city. You could say that this ruckus represented Chicago's first and only "golf-in." Protesters said a municipal facility could not bar access to any individual and certainly could not legislate access based on proficiency. Quietly, the commissioners rescinded their attempts to save Waveland from its own players.

By the mid '30s, Waveland was the most active of the city's municipal courses. The Park District even constructed horseshoe pits and Ping-Pong tables near the first tee for waiting golfers. In those days, Waveland's greens fees were a quarter; today, the cost is $6 weekdays and $7 on weekends. Although the Ping-Pong tables, horseshoe pits and most of the original 50 sand traps are long gone, Waveland still is Chicago's busiest and most beautiful public golf course.

City-operated Waveland wasn't the only municipal or county course to emerge out of the 1930s. Cook County's Forest Preserve Commission added the Indian Boundary course in 1931. Its construction contract featured a clause whereby building contractors worked at their own expense if construction went beyond 90 days. Amazingly, the course's completion occurred exactly 90 days after work began. The county also introduced a new nine-hole course—Billy Caldwell. In truth, this layout had been the third nine of Edgebrook's 27-hole site.

In 1931, Waukegan's Park District purchased the former daily-fee course, Bonnie Brook, for $160,000. Today, the 140-acre site remains a municipally operated course.

Much of the funding to build or acquire golf courses came from state and federal sources. In particular, the Franklin Roosevelt-created Works Progress Administration (WPA)—or jobs program—spurred development of several area public courses in the '30s.

One example was in St. Charles. Here a nine-hole course evolved under the watchful eye of designer, Robert Trent Jones. The Pottawatomie Golf Course represented the early works of perhaps the most accomplished golf course architect ever.

The WPA also funded in 1935 a municipal course in Gary, Ind. Nine new holes thus joined the already existent 18 at Gleason Park. The new nine, however, would serve only black golfers—the other 18 had been a "whites-only" venue for years.

Interestingly, only two years earlier a story in the *Orland Park Herald* announced the coming of a proposed new country club for "negroes only." The rather brief item told of a Negro organization leasing or buying property just east of Orland Park—with plans calling for an elaborate clubhouse and adjoining 18-hole course. Strangely, no further mention of the exclusive black country club ever again appeared in the local paper.

Meanwhile, some 40 miles to the north, another oddity took place in Wilmette. The bright idea of proprietor Joe Roseman, a nine-hole illuminated golf course was added just west of the Wilmette Golf Course. Called West Wilmette Illuminated, the layout featured nine par 3 holes—ranging in length from 90 to 165 yards. Its 1932 debut marked the start of night-time golf in Chicago. Unfortunately for Roseman, the course failed—closing within three years.

Before the decade ended, a handful of public courses formed—among them Inwood, Dempster, Crete and East Chicago. The private course additions totaled zero.

Jemsek Buys St. Andrews

Private courses were instead coping with financial realities. Actually one club's demise opened the door for purchase by Joe Jemsek. St. Andrews 36-hole layout had originally served two markets. One 18-hole course was membership only; the other, daily fee. In 1939, however, both became the property of Jemsek for reportedly $100,000. Chicago's "father of public golf" has gone on to purchase other courses, but St. Andrews represents his first.

A collective sigh of relief probably echoed loudly throughout Chicago-area golf clubs as the 1930s ended. Renewed optimism for the coming decade prevailed. Unfortunately, World War II put a sudden halt on any dreams of better times ahead.

The war's effect on the local golf course scene was different than the Depression's but just as damaging. For starters, many men left for overseas. Those who remained had to live with severe war-time rationing programs—the two affecting golf the greatest were gas and rubber conservation. Suddenly, the rubber golf ball became hard to find—at least at prewar prices. Gas rationing curtailed travel to outlying clubs. Consider Knollwood's Lake Forest-based club. It had come through the 1930s in relative ease—losing a net total of just 48 members. During the middle '40s, however, Knollwood's membership plummeted from 278 to 100. Another north suburban club, Sunset Ridge, saw its membership drop from 300 to 130 in a six-month span in 1941 alone.

In the western suburbs, the River Forest Country Club, near extinction, had but 78 members in 1944. Eventually, the club's finances stabilized, but only through cost-cutting steps, whereby members literally rolled up their sleeves and assumed most maintenance responsibilities.

For other private and public clubs, still reeling from the earlier Depression, the war and its effects represented the knockout punch. Some took a long count, lying motionless throughout the '40s.

The Woodridge Golf Club, for one, closed between 1943 and 1948. The site even had a new owner in 1945. The Elmhurst-Chicago Stone Company purchased the old course and began to dig deep for gravel. But the gravel supply was found too far below ground to be economically recovered. This resulted in Woodridge's "second coming" as it reopened for public play in 1948—about the same time it built one of the earliest lighted driving ranges in the area.

Another facility sprang to life after a seven-year hiatus. Originally called Columbian, then Bon Air in the '30s, the club was reborn as Chevy Chase in 1949. In its heyday in the '30s it was infamous as a gambling haven. In 1949, though, the new general manager declared Chevy Chase "is going to feature golf, swimming and very fine dinners. There will be absolutely no gambling." This was a far cry from earlier days when Sunday morning players would arrive at 5:30 a.m. just in time to pass other friends on their way to their cars after visiting the Wheeling-based night club and gambling the night away. It was, as earlier noted, built in 1924 by the Knights of Columbus, a Roman Catholic fraternal group. The club certainly has had a diverse history.

Though Chevy Chase and Woodridge recovered, they were the exceptions, as 30 other clubs passed quietly into extinction.

Despite two decades of setbacks, the period did have some memorable moments. In particular, the tournament circuit frequently chose Chicago as clubs continued their tradition of hosting prestigious national championships.

Courtesy of Chicago District Golf Association

Macdonald Smith won three Western Opens in his lifetime— the last in 1933 at Olympia Fields.

Courtesy of Chicago District Golf Association

Johnny Goodman was the last amateur to win a U.S. Open— in 1933 at North Shore.

In 1933, Chicago golfing enthusiasts witnessed three major tourneys. In the process, they saw a little bit of history being made. This was the year Johnny Goodman etched his name into U.S. Open annals by winning the event as an amateur, a feat that still stands. The same year Virginia Van Wie—considered the finest female player from the area —won her second consecutive U.S. Women's Amateur at the Oak Park Country Club. Olympia Fields hosted the final major event of the season, the Western Open. Winning the tourney was future golfing Hall of Famer Macdonald Smith.

One of the most unusual contests took place in 1935 at the Melrose Park-based Westward Ho club. There, a match-play exhibition was held between six recognizable local PGA professionals and six foreign stars. It's doubtful that any of the more than 1,000 spectators who gathered had ever seen these foreign-born players.

At day's end, the U.S. team had soundly defeated their guests by a score of 8 to 1. Interestingly, the visitors made no attempt to hide their objective of perfectly emulating the American players' swings. They predicted that their countrymen would one day embrace the sport enthusiastically and that golf's popularity would reach mammoth heights in their homeland. The international players—Tommy Miyamoto, Bob Asami, Jack Yusuda, Sesui Chin, Kanekichi Nakamura and Toichro Toda—came from Japan.

In 1939, Medinah hosted the Western Open. (Strangely, it would be the last Western played on an area course for 23 years.) Although it was Medinah's first national golfing championship, the facility's fame had grown throughout the decade by its successful staging of other championships. Among them were the Illinois State Amateur in 1933 and the inaugural Chicago Open in 1937.

Two other events also debuted in the decade: the Illinois Open and the Illinois Women's Amateur, in 1931 and 1934, respectively. Clearly, while the 1930s were tough, such contests kept the sport within the public's eye.

Courtesy of Chicago District Golf Association

Harold (Jug) McSpaden and Lt. Ben Hogan. McSpaden beat Hogan in an 18 hole playoff at the 1944 Chicago Victory Tournament.

In large degree, the war years saw a suspension of most major championships. Even with their eventual resumption, only one was played at a Chicago club by the end of the '40s, when Medinah hosted the 1949 U.S. Open.

Bob Hulbert, Ben Hogan, and Sam Snead. Hogan won 1947 Chicago Victory Tournament at Westward Ho.

One locally staged tournament did gain national prominence during the war period. In 1942, tournament organizers changed the name of the Chicago Open to the Hale America Open. Proceeds were directed to the Navy Relief Society and United Service Organizations. Although Ben Hogan collected the championship trophy at Ridgemoor in 1942, the true benefactors were the country's military personnel.

From 1943 through 1947, the annual charitable event continued. Renamed the Chicago Victory National Golf Championship, it helped to raise nearly $500,000, which was distributed to area veteran's hospitals and rehabilitation centers. It should be noted everyone connected with golf during those days contributed. This includes the CDGA, the Illinois PGA and public golfers who participated in the "Golfer's Dime-a-Round" program. Even an exhibition match between Bing Crosby and Bob Hope during 1945 raised nearly $19,000.

Courtesy of Chicago District Golf Association

Hogan blasting out of trap on Westward Ho's 18th hole as the crowd looks on.

One other note on Chick Evans before leaving the '40s. In 1944, Evans won the Chicago Amateur Championship— quite a feat for the 54-year-old veteran. Amazingly, he successfully defended his title the following year.

Other prominent championships during the '40s were held at Tam O'Shanter. It wouldn't be until the '50s that these golfing tournaments and their fabled promoter would capture worldwide attention. This ensuing decade would mark the earnest development of the George S. May era.

TEN LEADING SCORERS			
ROUND	NAME	PAR	AT HOLE
4	NELSON.	5 UNDER	18
4	IC SPADEN.	3 UNDER	18
4	.. HARPER	2 UNDER	18
4	HARBERT.	EVEN	18
4	L. MANGRUM	1 OVER	18
4	HARRISON	1 OVER	18
4	HOGAN.	2 OVER	18
4	BULLA	3 OVER	18
4	PALMER	5 OVER	18
4	LAFFOON.	5 OVER	18

Final leader board from 1946 Chicago Victory Tournament. Tied for 9th was Palmer, not Arnie but John.

Courtesy of Chicago District Golf Association

9

The George S. May Decade: 1951-1960

During any year in the 1950s, the top money-winner on the PGA Tour got there one of two ways. He could have captured seven or eight of the Tour's 25 to 35 sanctioned events—an unlikely accomplishment. More plausibly, he won one, most important tournament, the World Championship of Golf at the Tam O'Shanter Country Club in Niles. It was no coincidence that every leading money winner on the Tour from 1952 to 1957 won this championship—and golf's biggest paycheck of the year.

This tournament was golf's first big money event. As such, it attracted the sport's greatest names. Considered Chicago's headline event, this annual contest more than made up for the lack of other major Chicago tournaments throughout the '50s. Indeed, this decade was the only one in which Chicago did not host a single U.S. Open, PGA Championship or Western Open. In truth, none was missed by local enthusiasts, not as long as George Storr May continued to hold his numerous Tam O'Shanter tourneys.

In an era where the average tour purse equaled $18,000, May's events averaged $150,000. During 1954, for example, a champion of any of the Tour's 25 to 35 other contests would win about $3,000. At the World Championship, the victorious golfer received $50,000. Furthermore, the winner could pocket an additional $50,000 for taking part in 50 golfing exhibitions around the country. A $100,000 payday in 1954 was an inordinate sum of money. Was there any wonder why the most accomplished golfers of the decade automatically penciled in the Chicago stop on their itineraries?

Tam's annual championships were always eagerly awaited. George Storr May's innovations clearly left an imprint on the sport. There can be no argument May's contributions enhanced the game's future. Though he was often controversial, certainly unique and even called the P.T. Barnum of golf, his accomplishments put his name among the legends of the game.

Though the 1950s in Chicago were the George S. May decade, his first tournament dated back to 1941. The All-American Golf Tournament was actually two concurrent contests, played by a field of men's professionals and amateurs. But while the amateurs were playing against each other in a match-play format, the professionals engaged in the more traditional medal play. Since pros and amateurs played in the same foursomes, with essentially two different scoring systems, there was often confusion in the gallery as play on each hole was completed. Only those who were concentrating were able to keep track of what was really happening.

The professionals knew exactly what was at stake. With the winner receiving $2,000, the event even then was golf's biggest prize of the season. First place was worth exactly double that won earlier by the 1941 winners of the U.S. Open and PGA Championship. Byron Nelson won May's inaugural event and in 1942 repeated as champion.

Chicago Historical Society DN alpha

Babe Zaharias (second from left) and Beverly Hanson watch Patty Berg tee it up at Tam in 1953.

By 1943, a couple of wrinkles were added. First, a professional women's tournament was scheduled along with the men's professional and amateur contests. Secondly, May announced a second championship scheduled for one month later. This event became the World Championship of Golf. While it later was referred to as golf's richest tourney, the 1943 version offered no prize money. The winner took home a pennant.

Not until 1944 did the World Championship tourney's first-place prize exceed that of the All-American Golf Tournament. Byron Nelson won both events, collecting checks of $5,000 and $6,662.50.

By 1948, the World Championship's top prize was worth $10,000. Lloyd Mangrum pocketed this amount in addition to the $5,000 for winning the All-American event. Three years later, Ben Hogan collected a combined $7,000 for winning the U.S. Open and Masters tournaments. At Tam O'Shanter, his first-place showing in the World Championship netted $12,500.

Each succeeding year, May would boost the World's purse so that by 1952 first prize equaled $25,000. Julius Boros was the Tour's leading money winner that year; of his $34,000 in winnings, $25,000 came from the World Championship. In 1955, Boros won again; his whopping $50,000 winner's prize pushed his 1955 leading earnings to $65,122.

After a dispute with PGA Tour operators, May abruptly canceled the 1958 championships. Not the first time May had been involved in a dispute, this squabble centered on players' entry fees. May's objection wasn't that the PGA had the right to retain such fees, but rather other tournament promoters on the Tour were allowed to keep their field's respective entry fees. The dollars themselves were not the issue to the Chicago millionaire. What troubled May was the inconsistency—enough so that he ultimately focused national attention on the debate by canceling all his tournaments.

May later indicated in 1958 he would be willing to sponsor a "new and improved" tourney for the following year. This one would include a total purse of $250,000, with the winner collecting an unprecedented $100,000. There was, however, one proviso attached. May wanted PGA tournament director Ed Carter fired. The termination never occurred, and the 1959 version of the world's richest golfing event was dropped.

Perhaps May's most memorable dispute originated with his mandate to require all players to wear identification tags on their backs. Designed for easy gallery recognition, most golfers went along with May's unusual dictate. Some professionals didn't; Ben Hogan, for one, strongly objected. Ultimately, the nonconformists chose one of several alternatives—the simplest being either to wear the tags or not to enter. Others who entered and didn't conform had their prize money halved. One thing is certain, however. Today's practice of caddy identification tags used at all tournaments is a direct offshoot.

Courtesy of Chicago District Golf Association

George May presents $5,000 check to Ben Hogan for Hogan's win in 1947 at World Championship.

Other golfing firsts are attributed to May. For example, he is credited with attracting foreign professionals to the PGA Tour. Two Canadian stars played his 1945 tourney. By 1954, the international contingent included 25 pros from as many countries.

A couple of factors contributed to the 1954 tournament

having so many foreign contestants. One of May's events in 1954 was the first International Cup Match—between U.S. and foreign players. Although the competition was only held in 1954 and 1955, it represented still another tournament held on Tam's grounds during a two-week period. Keep in mind it was in addition to the All-American Tournament for men and women pros plus the events for men and women amateurs. Add to these the annual World's Championship of Golf for professional men and women players.

All told, there were 713 entries in May's All-American Golf Tournament in 1954. Four simultaneous events were held between Aug. 5 and 8, attracting 396 male professionals, 241 male amateurs, 26 female professionals and 50 female amateurs. There were so many contestants on the Tam grounds, starting times began at 5:30 a.m. Many of these players were also present at the World Championship—starting on Aug. 12.

Nationally Televised

There was another reason why the 1954 tournament drew so much interest—a direct result of the 1953 World Championship of Golf. Leave it to George May to recognize the promotional opportunities of an emerging medium—arranging to have his event broadcast live on national television. It was the first golf event televised across the country.

As fate would have it, the contest remained in doubt until the final hole. Lew Worsham needed a birdie to tie Chandler Harper's earlier posted score of 279. Off a wedge from 104 yards out, Worsham's ball hit the green and rolled toward the hole as the camera followed. From living rooms, taverns and inside Tam O'Shanter's clubhouse, viewers watched in disbelief as Worsham's ball disappeared into the cup. Scoring an unbelievable eagle, he had won the tournament along with $25,000. Worsham's effort, which was later referred to as the "shot heard round the world," is considered today one of the greatest in golfing history.

As a golf promoter May had no peer. His ticket prices were kept deliberately low. Parking costs were waived. If advance sales were judged unsatisfactory, May would hire a private plane to drop thousands of discounted or free tickets into inner-city neighborhoods. Once on Tam's

Chicago Historical Society ICHi-22771 Dr. Frank E. Rice

View of Tam O'Shanter's finishing hole.

grounds, the spectator was treated to additional entertainment by May in the form of masked trick-shot golfers or clowns for the children. He made sure guests had opportunities to win door prizes. Asked why he offered such prizes and discounted tickets, May responded logically, "I can't sell those people hot dogs and beer if they're downtown." Clearly, George May was the gallery's favorite impresario.

The crowds attended the numerous Tam tournaments in droves, constantly setting new attendance records. Unbelievably, more than 60,000 attended the last round of the 1956 World Championship. While most moved from hole to hole watching their favorite performers, others perched themselves in bleachers situated at prime viewing spots. The grandstands were but another of May's innovations to tournament golf.

May's accomplishments range from the use of short-wave radio operators at each hole communicating player's scores, to his initiation of minimum spending policies by Tam's club members. He also commissioned a film on the Tam O'Shanter's tournament history, which included the use of a helicopter for unique aerial perspectives of the beautiful 6,900-yard layout. May guaranteed Tam's grounds appeared lush, even if it meant spraying green vegetable dye on burnt-out fairway patches.

Courtesy of Chicago District Golf Association

Sam Snead in
his sartorial splendor.

His creative and visionary genius places his name along sports pioneers like Bill Veeck, Charlie Finley and George Halas. These were men who dared to be different. More importantly, they all believed progress required stepping beyond the boundaries of the status quo.

Though May died in 1962, he did earn in his final years the recognition of several golf associations. Perhaps the most important award came from the Golf Writers of America in 1955. May was then named the "outstanding contributor to golf" a year after President Dwight D. Eisenhower.

Eisenhower's association with the sport spotlighted the game like never before. His involvement—coupled with Arnold Palmer's charismatic nature—electrified the public's golf interests in the '50s. Television helped provide the bridge to the masses. With the nation following the triumphs of golfing's first mass media-created superstar, while at the same time identifying personally with Eisenhower's upper double-digit mediocrity, the sport was suddenly "in." After nearly two decades, growth was again evident. Expansion took the form of greater participation and new facilities.

In 1951, less than 2% of the U.S. population played; by 1960, this percentage doubled. Courses had numbered less than 5,000 in 1951. In 1960, more than 6,300 were in existence nationally. But while more Chicagoans were taking up the game, the construction rate of new local facilities during the 1950s was strangely far below the national construction average.

The George May tournaments always attracted large crowds.

This lack of new area course construction could be traced to the flight to suburbia. This in turn created a ripple effect, proving counterproductive to course growth. With developers acquiring large tracts of suburban acreage for new home construction, open land was less available. Additionally, escalating land values dissuaded many potential entrepreneurs from investing in such a limited-profit venture.

Residential and commercial real estate developers also found existing course operators agreeable to sell out. Long-established layouts such as Westward Ho and Big Oaks ceased operating, giving way to commercial and residential structures. Other suburban clubs also closed, though their sites were not developed. The widespread suburban building boom had placed a premium on retaining some open acreage; hence, the former Bunker Hill and Lansing Airport layouts became forest preserve property. Today, these two sites comprise respectively the Clayton Smith and North Creek Meadow Forest Preserves.

Suburban flight also necessitated one other change in the region's topography. It was during this decade a majority of the area's expressway systems would be built. Some clubs found their properties directly in line with progress' path. In Calumet Country Club's case, Interstate 294 chopped off one half of the club's 18-hole layout. Members agreed to rearrange the site's remaining property into a newly designed 18-hole facility. Noted architect Edward Lawrence Packard performed the task admirably. Mannheim Golf Club's public-fee site was also in the same interstate's projected path. Unlike Calumet, Mannheim closed for good.

Part of the reason Chicago-area growth did not compare favorably with other parts of the country was that the region's long-established golfing tradition already had created a sizable number of layouts. With the exception of weekend morning activity and the business or so-called trade golfing events, existing properties were not exactly swamped with players. Essentially, supply had outpaced demand, especially during the weekday slots.

Still, there were notable additions to the local scene. Among those new early 1950s entries is one facility that really was not new at all. Originally constructed in 1927, the then-private Olympic Country Club in Arlington Heights was one of several organizations to suffer during the Depression years. Converting to a public course and operating under a new name, the Arlington Golf and Country Club struggled for survival until 1941 before expiring.

From 1941 to 1950, the property resembled anything but a private club. Much of the 150-acre site was pasture land and the ornate clubhouse became home to 10,000 baby chicks and their 17 Japanese tenders. The chicken farm itself fell under the ownership control of the Curtis Candy Company. In 1950, Dan Taggert began to change all that. Convincing company executives he could make the former course profitable, Taggert entered into a leasing agreement. Two years later, the remodeled 6,245-yard facility opened for public play. Initially, the trapless layout featured the region's only par 6 hole. Later in the course's "second coming" the 620-yard hole became a par 5. Taggert—who eventually acquired full ownership—operated Arlington's site for two decades before turning over the land to developers.

Most of the other nine and 18-hole courses emerging in the early-to-mid '50s still operate today. Salt Creek and Fort Sheridan are but two examples. Hickory Hills doubled its facility in 1954 to 36 holes. More than 20 years later, developers purchased half the land, with the remainder returning to a regulation 18-hole course.

The O'Hare Field Golf Club, occupying the southern portion of O'Hare International Airport, knew its existence would be a short one as the airport grew. It was somewhat analogous to a parking lot occupying the future site of a downtown high-rise building. Ironically, the country's busiest airport during the 1950s lay on the south side of Chicago at Midway. Three decades prior, on its way to necessary expansion, Midway had gobbled up the Chicago Meadows golf course.

Business transactions involving golf course properties, and there were several during the 1950s, did not necessarily result in a course closing. To the contrary, new owners believed the sport's economic potential outweighed the initial dollars required to purchase existing layouts. One believer, who had owned St. Andrews since 1939, garnered enough capital to buy Cog Hill's 36-hole facility in 1951. Joe Jemsek then added another, Fairlawn, in 1953. Leasing the grounds, Jemsek made improvements to the course and renamed it Fresh Meadow.

Courtesy of Chicago District Golf Association

A young Joe Jemsek.

Southmoor's new owner, Ben Stevenson, had no prior experience with operating golf courses; in fact, he ran a south side bowling alley. Like Jemsek, however, he thought golf's better days lie ahead, and, in 1951, Stevenson purchased the 196-acre site for $180,000. By 1953, an additional nine holes were constructed. In 1960, Stevenson sold the

27-hole site to Bill O'Conner and George Sullivan. The public facility operates today, known as the Palos Country Club.

Municipalities also joined in the golf course pursuit. Even with escalating prices, the village of Glenview agreed to pay $550,000 for the former daily-fee Chesterfield facility. While the 1955 expenditure seemed extravagant, city fathers had done their homework. With open land in Glenview expensive and rare, land acquisition and construction costs of a brand new course could easily have topped $1.5 million. Thus, the Chesterfield site represented quite a value. Less than a decade later, other municipalities were paying three to four times as much as Glenview had paid.

The 1950s could never be categorized as a prolific building era. Even with the debut of three new nine-hole facilities—Apple Valley (now Apple Orchard), Crystal Woods and Par Three Golf—toward the decade's end, the period's net course growth was negligible. In retrospect, it would be the last local dry spell in the game's one-hundred year existence here.

Irrespective of the rate of course growth, the 1950s proved the dominion of one man, George Storr May.

With his familiar proclamation every August to "Hurry, hurry, hurry, ladies and gentlemen," golfing's first significant promoter and former Bible salesman would bellow, "This way to the biggest show in the great game of golf." In person or through the media, local fans heard his annual invitation—and followed. Big name golfers from around the world also responded to his call, as did the news media. Officials from golf's national governing boards attended; so did the Pinkertons, who would patrol Tam O'Shanter's grounds. And documenting it all was network television—and millions of viewers.

May propelled the sport's visibility into a higher strata. Coming at a time during the 1940s, when a boost was so desperately needed, and continuing right through the following decade, May singlehandedly provided the necessary spark. What, of course, resulted was an explosion of interest, not only in his tournaments but also in the man himself.

Although every passing day erodes the memory of Tam's glory years and its unique host, vestiges of each are still present today. In particular, one cannot think of the current PGA Tour's biggest money events without recalling those years Chicago staged golf's richest golfing championships.

10

The Public Gets A Chance: 1961-1980

With golf's popularity on the upswing, an explosion of new courses ripped through local landscapes during the '60s and '70s. This increase was long overdue. Not since the 1920s had there been anything resembling a building surge and that was primarily for private club expansion. On the other hand, the 1961-1980 period featured a different objective: aimed to satisfy the public's need for more layouts. By 1961, it was apparent public demand had surpassed supply. Recognizing the imbalance, municipalities and privately financed daily-fee operators began what can only be described as the most aggressive public course construction ever seen in local history. Twenty years later, municipal facilities had doubled from 1961 levels. Privately controlled daily-fee sites had similarly increased, helped in part by par 3 and executive course additions and the debut of hotel and resort-oriented golfing facilities.

But the construction highlight from the era was the emergence of championship-style public courses. With the widespread introduction to the Chicago area of quality golf facilities accessible to all, public golfers finally could play on grounds every bit as challenging and aesthetically pleasing as their private country club counterparts.

Predictably, an increase in the number of private clubs did take place, but it was surprisingly low. In fact, only about one of every seven new courses built had a "Members Only" designation. Many of these facilities were associated with real estate developments. Nevertheless, one of the region's greatest golf courses opened during this period in Oak Brook—Butler National.

In spite of the relatively high construction rate of new courses, the characteristic of golf's cyclical nature remained: established courses continued to be sold. Even with the escalating interest in golf, several operators were barely showing a profit. Maintenance and insurance expenditures grew, but the primary concern centered on real estate taxes. Three and fourfold percentage increases had taken their profitability toll. In addition, their effect was slowly pushing operators into a selling mode.

Real estate developers eventually acquired layouts at Acacia, Midwest and Arlington and converted these daily-fee sites into subdivisions. Other public courses also fell into extinction. The list includes Walnut Hills, Arlington Park, Maywood, Navajo Fields, Dixie Hi, Mohawk and Dempster. Today, office buildings, retail establishments and a cemetery occupy the various grounds.

For still other courses changing ownership, the golfing facility remained intact. Indeed, many of the new proprietors were municipalities, quite cognizant of the inherent advantages of community golf course ownership. One immediate benefit was the preservation of open land. During the suburban rush of the late '40s and '50s, the inventory of available land had steadily decreased. As a result, there was a heightened emphasis to maintain at least some undeveloped acres. A golf course satisfied the objective along with the ancillary benefit of offering recreation. Additionally, ownership eliminated any chance of the property being developed, while at the same time providing a new income source to the village. Lastly, the attraction of a golf course enhanced the community image and for neighboring homeowners maximized real estate property.

Funding for acquisition or new construction was reasonably inexpensive—especially in light of the many pluses existent. Money could be easily generated through local bond issues. In some examples, state and federal assistance was available. Operating a course had some sobering financial constraints but at least the burden of real estate taxes was not one of them.

One of the earliest municipal acquisitions of the '60s saw the once private Mount Prospect Country Club converted to municipal control. The purchase, with its sale price of $1 million, did raise more than a few eyebrows, but, as in nearly every example of municipal golf course properties, proved to be a sound investment. Today, the northwest suburban acreage is appraised at several times the initial cost. More importantly, the course itself is an appealing recreational facility for community residents and considered one of the Chicago area's most successful operations.

The same could be stated about Bensenville's $1.68 million acquisition of the 36-hole White Pines complex. Purchasing its first municipal courses in 1967, Bensenville assumed management control in 1970 from the Branigar organization.

During the 1970s, more municipalities took over former daily-fee facilities. In 1972, Aurora purchased the Fox Valley Country Club for $900,000. The same year, the village of Wilmette paid five times as much to acquire its municipal course from Northwestern University.

Considering the ownership trend, it wasn't surprising two adjoining communities engaged in a legal tug of war over the former Maplecrest Lakes. The course itself lay in an unincorporated area between Downers Grove and Woodridge. Each village applied for federal matching grants to help defray the nearly $2 million cost. Woodridge eventually won out, purchasing the facility in 1973, renaming it Village Greens of Woodridge. But Downers Grove shouldn't have been too disheartened. In 1968, the village purchased the Chicago Golf Club's original site. As noted earlier, this historic site remains the Chicago district's oldest existing golf course.

Two famous Chicago-area club conversions occurred in the 1970s. In fact, respective accounts of the Tam O'Shanter and Edgewater clubs show several parallels. Each had once shaped Chicago's rich golfing history. Each had been closely associated with one towering golfing legend. Yet sadly, both clubs were also on a downward spiral.

Niles-based Tam O'Shanter had been George May's personal platform. Open since the mid-1920s, the private club garnered local and national attention since 1941. For the next 17 years, May distributed two million dollars in prize money to the top finishers of his All American, World's Invitational and Women's All American Tournaments. Though May died in 1962, Tam continued on, holding its last major championship in 1965 as Billy Casper won the first of his four Western Opens.

Edgewater had the longevity edge on Tam. The Rogers Park club could trace its roots to 1898. While Edgewater hosted its share of championship events, the club's association with Chick Evans is most remembered—going back to the great amateur golfer's days as a caddy. Edgewater's sunset years included a diverse membership, among them a handful of unsavory types, reportedly mobsters. It wasn't at all unusual to note these characters bullying their way past respectable members, who waited patiently for their turn on the first tee. If that wasn't distasteful enough, they sprinkled their vocabulary with profanity in full earshot of all who mingled about.

These incidents in the club's final years became moot when Edgewater's equity members agreed to sell the 94-acre property to a developer for $8 million. Each member would receive about $21,000.

While the circumstances that led to Tam O'Shanter's sale were different, the net result was the same. One of the many offers from developers that had poured in since May's death drew acceptance from a majority of May's heirs.

In both examples, the proposed property transfers were met with vociferous objections from local community groups. Protesters were upset with the future plans of each developer. Edgewater's new owners envisioned a huge residential high-rise complex. At Tam, an industrial park was planned. In time, both developers settled for less.

Chicago politics contributed to the demise of the Rogers Park high-rise plan. One Chicago alderman was accused and later convicted of accepting unreported income after procuring favorable zoning law revisions for the developer. The front-page publicity that ensued, helped crystalize neighborhood opposition. The project was soon canceled.

In the end, the land went to the state and to the city of Chicago, though the $18 million cost was more than twice the amount originally paid to Edgewater's members. The Lawrence C. Warren community park now occupies the site. Included on grounds is an entirely new nine-hole course operated by the Chicago Park District and named after Robert A. Black. Opened in 1974, the facility represents the first new Park District course since Waveland's debut in the early '30s.

In Niles, the "Save Tam" committee wouldn't have quite the success as Edgewater's activists. In this case, Tam's new owner did give in somewhat by leasing a portion of the property to the Niles Park District. This 37-acre plot was eventually purchased by the village to create a community golf course. "Little" Tam incorporated a few of the old course's characteristics in its redesign and opened in the early '70s as a nine-hole course.

Clearly, the preservation mode of the times saved numerous golfing facilities. Clubs such as Chevy Chase had teetered on the brink of collapse for years. During the club's 50-year operation, several ownerships tried unsuccessfully to salvage the facility. Organized in the mid '20s by the Knights of Columbus, Columbian's early days suggested a promising future. By the early '40s, however, even the clubhouse sounds of cabaret acts and clanking slot machines couldn't keep the then-named "Bon Air" from closing—until 1949 when still another attempt to revive was made.

When the village of Wheeling purchased the rundown facility in 1977, it set out to resurrect the challenging layout. Fortunately for golfers, the village's efforts were successful.

Exhibiting a cooperative posture, two park districts joined forces in 1980 to solve their golf course objectives. When the original owners of Fox Bend expressed an interest to sell the facility for $1 million-plus, park districts in Oswegoland and Fox Valley raised enough capital for an initial down payment. The debt was eventually paid off completely. Today, the two local entities are again working together—this time in building a new course near Fox Valley.

Other towns during the '60s and '70s had no other alternative but to build from the ground up. Communities such as Villa Park, Elgin, Lake Bluff, Glen Ellyn, Palatine, Skokie, Dundee, Naperville, Arlington Heights and Waukegan searched for suitable sites. High land prices and limited open space necessitated some creative alternatives.

For Skokie, a landfill solved its search. Less than a quarter of a million dollars was required to turn the former site into a 22-acre park, 17 of them occupied by a par 3 nine-hole course. Although the Weber Park course measures less than 1,200 yards, its worth to Skokie residents is substantial. Few municipal golf course operations anywhere have been as aggressive in promoting the sport to residents.

Weber Park has become a golf classroom. Classes for all levels fill the Park District's calendar. While fun is an important requirement, competency is the goal. For youngsters, only those who successfully pass a proficiency test are allowed on the course.

It's hard to believe that back in 1972 some members of the community stated their disapproval to Weber Park. They argued that golf was too exclusive; others claimed there were better uses for the land. Nearly 20 years after Weber Park opened, it is unlikely any 22-acre plot could have been so singularly responsible for generating such massive community interest in golf. The small course also proved that beginners do not need a 150-acre layout to learn the game.

Elgin may have had more space than Skokie, but the far western suburb knew its task would be much more difficult than was true 70 years earlier. In 1907, the community took donated property from William Wing's estate and turned the land into a park and golf course. But establishing a site for Elgin's second layout required complex legal maneuvering. The desired parcel next to the Illinois State Hospital was mostly unused state-owned land. Community and city efforts, along with state support, helped reclassify the targeted property as surplus. After that important hurdle was cleared, it became relatively easy to acquire the site and build not only the Spartan Meadows 18-hole course, but also an adjoining junior college.

A different sort of bureaucracy confronted Arlington Heights. This time, it was the federal government that offered city officials both opportunity and repeated frustration. When Arlington Lakes Golf Club finally opened in 1979, the village had realized a goal it set exactly 15 years previously.

Land for the future course had been eyed by village officials in 1964. Believing a 100-acre parcel within a larger land mass used by the Army and Navy would be categorized as surplus, village expectations for a community course grew by 1966. That year, the federal government officially designated 100 acres of the Nike Missile Base as surplus. Almost immediately, however, the Navy declared an interest in 24 acres of the recategorized property. Hopes for an 18-hole layout fell, but then zoomed again when the Navy changed its plans three years later. With the village again in high gear to acquire the targeted site, the Navy flip-flopped again. This time though they sought not 24 but 51 acres of the so-called "surplus" property. By now, Senators Percy and Stevenson had entered the picture, and, in 1973, Arlington Heights took control of 13 acres.

In 1974, Representative Philip Crane became actively involved. As pressure mounted, the Navy acquiesced and offered to hand over their 51 acres to the village. Unbelievably, the base's other occupant—the Army—decided those 51 acres were needed for reserve training facilities. Soon afterwards, the president stepped into the fray and awarded the 51 acres to Arlington Heights.

At this point, the village controlled 64 total acres; however, the two 13 and 51 acre parcels weren't contiguous. Nevertheless, plans for a nine-hole course were established. The village also continued efforts to acquire at least 26 additional acres. A year later, the Army reluctantly accepted a city offer for the 26 acres in question. By 1976, village residents successfully passed a $1.5 million bond referendum to build the course, which was now to be 18 holes. In May 1979, the public facility opened for play.

One of the finest examples of a municipal golf facility was originally located on neither state nor federal property, but on a problem area known as a flood plain. Glen Ellyn officials knew that creating a housing subdivision would not be a good use for the low-lying land, yet as late as 1959, it appeared that new single-family homes would fill the troublesome site.

From the perspective of George Winchell, who was a village trustee, the planned construction seemed inappropriate. Instead, Winchell recommended an alternative.

This plan featured a recreational complex—anchored by a municipal golf course. He reasoned a properly built course would satisfy the growing call for a local layout. More importantly, it would serve as an effective control for flood waters. Winchell succeeded in convincing others to support the plan.

By 1967, an 18-hole course took root. Shortly thereafter, a nine-hole course was added. Both were designed by David Gill. Today, nearly 100,000 rounds are played annually on the $1.5 million facility.

Many who visit Village Links for the first time are frankly surprised at the difficulty of the 18-hole layout. Few municipally operated courses can claim, for example, that U.S. Open qualifying rounds have been held on their sites. What challenges all players here are the hazards. While there are at least 96 sand traps, it is the water hazards that stand out—21 lakes and ponds to be exact. To most visitors, this total does seem inordinately high. What's not recognized is how valuable the water hazards are in collecting and dispersing runoff. In this respect, the water hazards provide a far greater community benefit than just making the municipal course difficult.

While there are many who have contributed to this nationally acclaimed municipal facility, George Winchell's special leadership role has not been forgotten. Indeed, even the short road leading into Village Links pays homage. It is appropriately named "Winchell Way."

Taking their cue from community wishes, other Chicago-area villages established layouts in the '60s and '70s. Courses popped up in Des Plaines (Lake Park), Palatine (Palatine Hills), Deerfield (Deerfield Park District), Lake Bluff (Lake Bluff) and Villa Park (Sugar Creek). Although none of these, or others either newly constructed or acquired, provided as stern a challenge as Village Links, they did satisfy their community's golfing requirement. Today, each of the aforementioned municipal sites draws annually from 40,000 to 70,000 participants.

The various county forest preserve districts weren't ignoring golf's rapidly growing popularity, either. In 1965, the Cook County Forest Preserve District constructed the nine-hole Meadow Lark course in Hinsdale. As the first newly built forest preserve layout since the early '30s, Meadow Lark's success is easily illustrated by the 70,000 rounds played each year. Exactly 10 years later, in 1975, another forest preserve site was opened in Hoffman Estates. Highland Woods became the eighth forest preserve course within Cook County. To the north, Lake County's Forest Preserve District added the Countryside course in 1976. While formerly a privately owned daily-fee course, its acquisition reflected the expansionary mood of county forest preserve districts in general.

Another golfing option made its debut in this period. Combined hotel/resort courses were opening. Hardly mirror images of Florida or Arizona complexes, these new resorts were limited by winter weather. The local facilities did, however, offer summer weekend lodging packages, live stage shows and, most importantly, business meeting centers. In each case, golf worked as a primary marketing attraction.

First to appear here was the St. Charles-based Pheasant Run Resort, which opened in 1962. Several hotel/business meeting complexes followed, including Nordic Hills (Itasca), Indian Lakes (Bloomingdale), and Marriott's Lincolnshire Resort. North of the Illinois border saw the opening of the Americana Club. But while these sprawling outlets found a market, space constraints in other markets triggered particularly unique golf course design. Par 3 and executive-style, nine-hole layouts exploded in the early 1960s across the nation.

Two elements differentiated the par 3 and executive-style formats from conventional nine-hole layouts. These were indeed smaller facilities, making for shorter holes. Also, the courses weren't designed to be attacked with every club in a golfer's bag. Instead, iron play would be prioritized. For weekend enthusiasts, the iron practice would serve their overall game quite well.

But there was an overriding critical factor—namely, time. A round could be finished in 90 minutes or less; thus, the avid golfer could squeeze in a round before or after work. These mini-layouts were attractive to course owners in an area where land prices were sky high. Cheaper to build and requiring less land, they could be maintained for less dollars than traditional nine-hole courses. Finally, the mini-courses represent less intimidating learning sites for novices and beginners. No doubt many found their introduction to the sport on these user-friendly facilities.

During the six years from 1961 through 1966, an inordinate number of nine-hole layouts emerged locally. While a few were of the conventional nine-hole design, most took the form of these mini-courses. Today, the signs of change can be observed. Par 3 layouts have been converted to conventional nine-hole courses. Other courses that were originally nine holes have since expanded into regulation 18-hole layouts. While some are no longer around, here is a partial list of nine-hole courses constructed from 1961 through 1966:

Braidwood	Meadow Lark (Hinsdale)
Blackhorse (Westmont)	Park Forest
Calumet (Gary, Ind.)	Rolling Knolls (Elgin)
Concord Green	Shiloh (Zion)
(Libertyville)	Twin Ponds (Crystal Lake)
Greenshire (Waukegan)	Valley Green (North
Ken Loch (Lombard)	Aurora)
Marengo Ridge (Marengo)	Western Acres (Lombard)
	Willow Run (Mokena)

Other nines were added to existing facilities at Wilmette, Silver Lake (Orland Park) and Westgate Valley (Palos Heights).

Construction activities for all types of public-access courses remained brisk during the 1960s and 1970s. Indeed, 1962 was the first year in U.S. history when the total number of municipal and daily-fee courses had finally exceeded private layouts. The local area had benefited nicely. By 1980, no other region in the country could equal the quantity available to Chicago's public golfers.

But while some area enthusiasts were content with municipal and "pitch and putt" courses, others sought more upscale venues. Such challenging and high-profile facilities were defined as "championship" in makeup. Golfers gladly paid increased greens fees to compete on immaculately manicured grounds. Operated for the most part privately, these top-quality public courses provided a perfect medium between easier municipal layouts and inaccessible top-flight private facilities.

Among this new group were Plum Tree National (Harvard), Bon Vivant (Bourbonnais), Deer Creek (University Park) and Hilldale (Hoffman Estates). Midlane offered still another exceptional layout, having converted from a private facility in 1980. This collection of championship-styled layouts and others added at Country Lakes (Naperville), Pinecrest (Huntley), Urban Hills (Richton Park), Palmira (St. John, Ind.) and Scherwood (Schererville, Ind.) helped provide unprecedented quality-oriented options.

Rewarding as the 1961-1980 building period was, its importance would have been less had not two other public courses appeared. The introduction of Dubsdread and Kemper Lakes changed forever the perceptions of daily-fee layouts.

Before Dubsdread's debut in 1965, public courses had been considered as clearly inferior to their private course counterparts—and for good reason. Public sites weren't as well maintained. They offered few of the inherent challenges associated with championship-designed layouts. Furthermore, their aesthetic appeal was limited. They looked like public courses.

Wm. Daniels/The Photo Partners

Cog Hill's famous Dubsdread course and four of its many sand traps.

Dubsdread's founder, Joe Jemsek, had purchased in the early 1950s the 36-hole Cog Hill complex from its original owner—the Coghill family. The Nos. 1 and 2 courses traced their roots back to the late 1920s. In the early 1960s, Jemsek added Cog Hill's third layout and then, in 1965, built Cog Hill's No. 4—known as Dubsdread.

Jemsek ventured outside of the norm when he commissioned Joe Lee to design Cog Hill's No. 4 course. For years Jemsek had believed Chicago's golfing public would enthusiastically welcome and support an upscale championship-caliber daily-fee facility. His intuition proved correct.

While the course's $8 to $10 cost did represent the priciest public layout locally, its value was unquestioned. Finally, there existed a superb golfing challenge for the serious-minded public player. Featuring 123 sand traps, several water holes, tough greens and narrow fairways, the Dubsdread course was immediately recognized as the *creme de la creme* of local public sites. Naturally, it was also judged as one of the country's top 100 public *and* private 18-hole courses. While Chicago includes many outstanding public-fee courses today, Jemsek's pioneering efforts cannot be overstated. In fact, many in golfing's international fraternity refer to him as "the father of public golf."

By 1980, the designation of Chicago's premier daily-fee course switched from Dubsdread to Kemper Lakes. Ironically, Hawthorn Woods's championship-style venue was the farthest thing from anyone's mind when the property was purchased in 1966.

The Kemper Insurance Group's initial priority centered on relocating scattered Chicago-area offices into one headquarters. The acquired land featured one large parcel judged suitable for headquarters' buildings—the rest was filled with marshes and swamps. The low-lying areas were eventually excavated, then allowed to fill with rain and runoff. What resulted were more than 100 acres of lakes.

Additional buildings were considered, but prohibitive zoning laws stymied this option. Company chairman James Kemper Jr. later admitted that the golf course option was purely accidental. However, once Kemper made the decision, he spared no expense in building a public course worthy of PGA Tour play. Indeed, 10 years after Kemper Lakes opened its first nine holes, it hosted, in 1989, the first-ever PGA Championship played on a Chicago-area public course.

Representing the district's most expensive public course ($90 per round with cart), the Nugent-Killian-designed layout ranks as one of the premier sites anywhere. With multiple tees, immaculately groomed fairways, sand and oh so many water hazards, plus wonderfully "true" greens, Kemper's challenge is easily tempered by its natural beauty. While a high score is predictable here, most daily-fee golfers don't seem to mind. For many who play the site, Kemper Lakes is as close to "heaven on earth" as exists.

While new public course sites dominated the 1961-1980 period, private course construction did not fall somnambulant. Ironically, it was during this era that the "permanent" home of the Western Open championship took root.

Butler National

Just as had been true with Kemper Lakes and Dubsdread, Butler National came about through the inspirational efforts of one man—Paul Butler. Planned from its inception as a private club and one that would serve as the Western Open's home course, Butler National debuted officially in 1974. It coincided with the club's inaugural hosting of the Western. For 17 years, the Butler venue provided as stern a test for Tour professionals as any PGA Tournament site nationally. In Chicago, only Medinah's No. 3 course is arguably considered more challenging.

As part of an all-male private club, Butler National's members saw a trend beginning in 1990. Future PGA Tournaments were being scheduled at clubs with "less restrictive" membership policies. Consequently, it surprised no one when an amicable parting of the way occurred between Butler and the Western Golf Association. To speculate on whether Butler National will ever again host the Western Open or any other PGA event is, of course, just that—speculation. But don't be shocked to hear, in time, of a change in membership eligibility requirements. When this inevitable liberalization process transpires, a phone call from the USGA will be forthcoming. The local area's next

U.S. Open championship site could well be hosted in Oak Brook.

As noted, the 1961-1980 period wasn't a particularly prolific era for private courses. Some that were built—Butler National, Hillcrest (Long Grove), Ravinia Green (Deerfield), Stonehenge (Barrington) and Old Wayne (West Chicago)—were founded primarily to serve as golf clubs. This was a transitory period, though. Costs for land acquisition, course construction and maintenance, and clubhouse structures stretched beyond fiscal capabilities. From a practical standpoint, the stand-alone private golfing facility was becoming too expensive to build. Indeed, the concept of a stand-alone country club was also becoming outmoded.

Enter the economic alternative—the planned residential golf course community. Almost all private courses to be constructed from here on would be limited to those with an adjoining housing development.

There was at least one example of a residential golf course community prior to 1961. In 1938, the McIntosh family purchased land west of Palatine and developed custom homes on what is now considered Inverness. Included on the original property was an old golf course. It quickly was turned into the redesigned Inverness Golf Club. For more than a decade, homeowners within the affluent development were the exclusive members. Today, the private club's membership requirements are geographically less restrictive, although application to Inverness remains by invitation only.

In the '60s and '70s, golf-oriented residential communities grew in popularity. Membership opportunities varied. While some were restricted to property owners, others would include "out-of- development" applicants. A few even permitted public access. In some cases, property ownership provided no course privilege or invitation to become a club member.

Residential golf course communities were opening at Prestwick (Frankfort), Cress Creek (Naperville), Turnberry (Crystal Lake), Leisure Village (Fox Lake), Lake Barrington Shores (Barrington) and Indiana's Sand Creek (Chesterton). Mission Hills is a somewhat different example. The North-

Located in Northbrook, the Mission Hills Country Club was one of the first residential golf course communities to be built in the Chicago area.

brook course itself had existed since the '20s—operating for most of that time as a daily-fee facility. When the property's principal owner, Charles Nash, died in 1969, the course fell into liquidation proceedings.

In 1970, an attempt to acquire the site failed. Prospective purchasers failed to make an initial payment on the $2.4 million facility. Two years later, another group led by Eugene Corley bought the land with a plan to construct a 964-unit condominium/townhouse complex. The property's drawing card was a newly designed championship-style private golf course. Corley's success at Mission Hills surely prompted him to try in later years another local golfing community—Crystal Tree in Orland Park.

During this 20-year period of novel golf venues, the Chicago area continued to host major championships. In 1961, the PGA Championship was played at Olympia Fields. The Western Open returned in 1962 to Chicago-hosted sites after a 23-year absence. In 1974, the La Grange club hosted the U.S. Women's Open—marking the first time the event had picked a Chicago-area site. Actually, 1974 was a busy tournament year here. Besides Butler National's inaugural

Western Open, a Ladies Professional Golf Tour (LPGA) championship was played at Midlane (Wadsworth). Finally, in 1975, the U.S. Open revisited Medinah.

It is fitting that, as the game attracted more advocates during the 1960s and 1970s, the number and types of available public sites increased dramatically. For a sport that had once been primarily the exclusive domain of affluent men, golf had increased its appeal among the middle class. Furthermore, women began playing in greater numbers, as did retirees, children and teens. As the 1980s began, all vestiges of golf's regressive period had disappeared.

11

Residential Golf Course Construction: 1981-1990

There are some observers of the local golf scene who believe a golf course construction boom drove the 1980s. A few even suggest that this was the most prolific construction decade ever. Let's look at the real story.

Only 30 new sites were constructed from 1981 to 1990. Contrast that with the 1920s, which yielded more than 120 new layouts. The rate of course construction in golf's "Golden Era" has never been even remotely approached in ensuing decades. Not only were the 1980s far short of being the most productive era in terms of net golf course additions, there wasn't even a construction boom.

While the decade's 30 new golfing facilities represents a decent average of three openings per year, Chicago's historical annual average from 1893 to 1990 is, however, near four.

Why then is there this popular notion that the 1980s were unusually bountiful?

Two explanations come to mind. One involves time itself. Recent events are easily remembered and maybe even overstated. Since half the decade's course output occurred from 1988 to 1990, there may be a tendency to believe the entire decade was as active. It wasn't.

The second reason reflects worthiness. While the courses built during the 1980s may have been modest in quantity, they were exemplary in quality. In particular, the private clubs offered layouts designed in part by the sport's marquise names—among them PGA legends Jack Nicklaus, Arnold Palmer, Lee Trevino and Greg Norman. Area golfers lucky enough to visit these signature sites are often more interested in blessing the grounds than in playing them.

And who could blame them? Featuring grandiose clubhouses and bordered by million dollar homes, these golf course residential communities have evolved into the ultimate status symbols of our times.

Fortunately, public golfers found new upscale playgrounds, too. Four daily-fee sites built in the decade became recognized immediately as superb examples of quality-oriented championship-style design. In fact, Pine Meadow, Forest Preserve National, Golf Club of Illinois and Cantigny are ranked among this country's greatest public offerings.

Pine Meadow's debut in 1985 was applauded immediately. Less than a year later, *Golf Digest* voted the layout the best public course of 1986. With four tee box placements per hole, golfers can play a short 5,400-yard course to one measuring 7,100 yards. From its back tees, Pine Meadow is a severe test with a 74.3 course rating. Seventy sand traps, deviously placed, along with seven water hazards, add difficulty. The four par 5s average 549 yards. One par 3 requires a 245-yard poke to reach the pin.

Operated by the Jemsek organization, the land is leased from the Catholic Archdiocese of Chicago. Adjoining acreage, also under archdiocesan control, houses St. Mary of the Lake Seminary. Originally the inspiration of Cardinal Mundelein, the complex in the 1920s was envisioned to serve as the largest and most prominent Catholic university in the country. However, objections from other Catholic universities—Notre Dame and Fordham—dashed those early plans. Cardinal Mundelein settled on building the St. Mary of the Lake Seminary instead.

Totally self-reliant, the private facility satisfied the basic needs of a seminarian. The property even featured an 18-hole golf course. It was, however, limited to seminarians and other officials from the archdiocese. Over the years, participation waned, as did the funding for proper maintenance.

By the time Joe Jemsek won a 25-year lease in the early 1980s, fewer than 200 rounds were being played annually on the old course. Through the effort of architect Joe Lee, who had designed Cog Hill's Dubsdread layout 20 years earlier, the original St. Mary's course was completely transformed into Pine Meadow.

Greens fees today are $44, with an optional power cart for an additional $23. As a rare alternative, caddies are available for $12 per bag, although reservations for caddies must be made two days in advance. Pine Meadow is one of only a handful of public courses nationally that offer caddy service.

Forest Preserve National—also referred to as the "poor man's Kemper Lakes"—is another nationally acclaimed golf course built during the past decade. Designed by the architectural team of Dick Nugent and Ken Killian (which also crafted Kemper Lakes), Forest Preserve National is operated by the Cook County Forest Preserve. Dollar for dollar, the Oak Forest course represents one of the best golfing values in the Chicago area. Daily greens fees are $12; carts are only $16. While the weekend greens fees are four bucks higher, they along with a cart are still $58 less than a round at Kemper Lakes.

Wm. Daniels/The Photo Partners

One of the many water hazards at Forest Preserve National.

In playing Forest Preserve National, be prepared for a different sort of price to be paid. Considered by some experts to be the finest county operated course in the nation, the reservation policy—while fair—is extremely stringent. Unlike the vast majority of courses, Forest Preserve National accepts only daily reservations; furthermore, they must be made by at least one member of a playing foursome and in person. This rule represents a change from the facility's initial policy. Up until recently, enterprising youngsters were hired by eager golfers to wait in predawn lines for available tee times. Considering that lines form as early as 3:30 a.m., this circumventive maneuver was understandable. Today's policy acts to eliminate potential cheaters by hand stamping the player when reservations are finally secured. At the first tee, the ultraviolet identification must be on the hand of one member of the foursome.

This "first come, first served" policy wouldn't be necessary if tee times were abundantly available. They are not. Daily tee time allotments are filled quickly—often by 6:30 a.m. The mad rush to play the course isn't based on price alone; in fact, the county could charge three times as much and still draw to near capacity. Occupying nearly 300 acres, Forest Preserve National's layout is beautifully contoured. It is also extremely difficult. Though four tee placements exist on each hole, the county course provides a stern test from even its short tees. Sixty-three bunkers and eight lakes pose continual problems. For the back tees, the 7,170-yard course plays to a staggering 75.3 rating.

Because of its unique tee time policy, the course is probably ignored by many golfers in the district. While Forest Preserve National may represent a terrific dollar and cents bargain, many who have never played it must feel a 3 a.m. wakeup call is simply too high a price.

An entirely different experience awaits golfers at the Golf Club of Illinois. As the district's premier links-type course, Golf Club of Illinois replicates golf as it is found along the Scottish coast. Although the Algonquin site is landlocked, the other major components of a links design are found. For example, the course is treeless. Fairway perimeters are lined with tall grassy rough. Large double-holed greens are present. Typical of a links course, wind also plays a role here. As the course is located on one of the highest elevations within McHenry County, a stiff breeze is pretty much assured.

This is a strangely unique Midwestern course, requiring altered playing strategies. Golfers must adjust their game to avoid the 100-plus sand traps and especially the fescue-type "steel wool" rough. With no trees and only one pond, the course's hazards are sand and rough.

For golfers employing a conservative target-oriented style—one that prioritizes accuracy instead of distance—a round at Golf Club of Illinois will be enjoyable. Conversely, players taking an aggressive approach—those who never alter their game at any course—will assuredly be in trouble throughout the round. In all probability, they'll never return to the course, perhaps bemoaning its many "unfair advantages" to other golfers. While all courses require a proper mental strategy, a links layout absolutely mandates a well thought-out plan.

No doubt reacting to some believing Golf Club of Illinois is unfairly difficult, the club's new ownership—Dye Designs Inc.—is striving to provide a more user-friendly layout. One important modification will lessen the rough's severity. New management is also building shorter tee boxes, which will offer a 4,400-yard test. Fortunately, the long-tee box will remain in place, providing all the associated challenges of a 7,000-yard course—including the mammoth 678-yard par 5 No. 15 hole, the state's longest.

Originally designed by Dick Nugent, the course is different and difficult. But public golfers, especially, should play it, if for no other reason to have the opportunity to acquaint themselves with a links-type layout. With the natural beauty of its surroundings, unique course characteristics, relative ease of reservations and moderate cost—$28 to $33 plus $12 cart per person—Golf Club of Illinois is another example of a quality public course built locally during the '80s.

A recent and picturesque entry to Chicago-area golf is Cantigny. Open since 1989, the Roger Packard-designed course is already put in the same favorable light as Pine Meadow, Forest Preserve National, Kemper Lakes and Dubsdread. Any anonymity Cantigny may have had during its inaugural year quickly disappeared when *Golf Digest* named it Best New Course of the Year in 1989.

Surprisingly, Cantigny is not representative of the new breed of facilities that feature a maximum playing length of 7,000 yards or more. Instead, the layout's longest distance measures a "modest" 6,709 yards. This is no pushover course, however, as its 72.4 rating will attest.

Hazards include several lakes, one seemingly omnipresent stream and at least 75 bunkers. There are 10 traps on the 14th hole alone. But the site's most notable bunker is located on No. 18. There is to be found the carved likeness of Dick Tracy's face and hat. Packard added the signature trap at the request of Clayton Kirkpatrick, former publisher of the *Chicago Tribune,* which syndicates the Dick Tracy comic strip.

Cantigny's land had once been the summer estate of long-time *Chicago Tribune* publisher, Robert S. McCormick. The name he chose for the site, Cantigny (Can-TEE-nee), is taken from a victorious World War I site in France. It was on this Wheaton property that Colonel McCormick found time to create a fledgling tree farm that he hoped would lead to improved newsprint. To this day, the grounds are liberally anchored with thick clusters of mature trees. As such, Cantigny's "feel" is similar to a private country club. Limited to 200 rounds per day, the 18-hole course is not overrun by throngs of public golfers. Though there is an adjoining nine-hole course, the pace of Cantigny is clearly genteel. It has quickly become a first-class golfing environment. Upon entrance to the grounds, for example, players find that their bags are immediately transferred from car to cart by a well-trained staff. Other employees in the modern clubhouse, pro shop and grounds have clearly been schooled in customer care. Greens fees are $45 or $55 including cart. As the greens and fairways continue to mature, Cantigny will surely be considered on par with the great public courses found anywhere.

While Cantigny, Pine Meadow, Forest Preserve National and Golf Club of Illinois are the cream of the 1980s-type construction, there were other quality daily-fee courses built from 1981 to 1990. Owned by both private and municipal entities, these properties may not have established the fame of their more prominent counterparts but they have drawn loyal legions.

A listing of new public sites that opened in the last decade follows. Also noted are the number of course holes and inaugural year of operation. Municipal courses are designated with an asterisk.

*Arboretum (Buffalo Grove)	18	1990
*Boughton Ridge (Bolingbrook)	9	1981
Craig Woods (Woodstock)	9	1982
*Fox Run (Elk Grove)	18	1985
Glendale Lakes (Glendale Heights)	18	1988
Mid Iron (Lemont)	9	1985
*Naperbrook (Naperville)	18	1990
*Oak Brook	18	1981
Oak Brook Hills (Oak Brook)	18	1986
*Palos Hills	9	1990
*Settler's Hill (Batavia)	9	1990
*Streamwood Oaks (Streamwood)	9	1990
Tamarack (Naperville)	18	1989
*Walnut Greens (Schaumburg)	9	1989
Woodbine (Lockport)	18	1988

Among the new entries, Tamarack Golf Club merits further mention. Opening in 1989, the upscale daily-fee layout is certain to gain widespread fame. Featuring multiple tees, Tamarack's par 70 course plays to a 74.2 rating from its back tee yardage of 6,955. Even the more manageable 6,331 course length provides challenge—illustrated by its 70.9 rating. Built on a former cornfield, the David Gill-designed layout doesn't incorporate many trees; nevertheless, hazards abound. Water comes into play on virtually every hole. There's plenty of sand, too; in fact, 16 of the course's 75 traps are located on one hole alone.

Tamarack and its surrounding residential property evolved through the efforts of the Fry Development Company. Although the course represented its initial attempt in building a golfing facility, the company was quite successful developing real estate in the Naperville area. Familiarity with the community also proved to be an important asset—the Fry family can trace its Naperville roots back to 1854. But it wasn't until the early '50s that John Fry became active in local development. Among the company's earliest residential developments was Aero Estates—a housing subdivision featuring a private airstrip.

In 1978, Fry and his son Alan found a large parcel of Naperville real estate that, in their judgment, offered another housing/airstrip possibility. Although zoning changes were approved, the planned airstrip drew some local resistance. With interest rates at an all-time high, a decision was made to postpone all development of the property. During the early '80s, John Fry's insurance adviser expressed an opinion that the grounds would serve as a terrific golf course site. Intrigued by the thought, the elder Fry commissioned a feasibility study to investigate. Research confirmed the potential financial benefits of a combined residential/golf course community. By 1986, course architect David Gill already had submitted an initial design, but it had to be reconfigured when adjoining acreage was acquired. This additional property included a creek, which allowed Gill even greater creativity in course design. In Alan Fry's judgment, the original acreage would have yielded a good course setting. With the newly acquired parcel, however, the Tamarack site became an outstanding golfing site. Today, the 129-acre daily-fee course is bordered by 192 housing lots—a total of 325 acres.

As appealing as the newer upscale daily-fee sites are, many golfers remain loyal to less expensive municipal courses. Fortunately, for this cost-conscious constituency, the majority of the public courses built in the 1980s were developed by local municipalities. Furthermore, villages and counties continued to scrutinize existing courses for possible acquisition.

Particularly aggressive, the Du Page County Forest Preserve Commission purchased two former private clubs—Elmhurst and Brookwood, for reportedly $6.4 and $7.9 million, respectively. Earlier in the decade, the Cook County Forest Preserve acquired River Oaks, while Lake County assumed control of Brae Loch.

Local park districts were just as active. In 1981, Wheaton bought the 27-hole Arrowhead complex. Chicago reopened the historic South Shore club in 1985. Park Districts in Westmont (Twin Lakes) and River Trails (Rob Roy) became first-time golf course operators. Perhaps the most expensive property transaction in local golf history occurred in 1988. Schaumburg's Park District took control of the 27-hole Golden Acres facility—paying $15.5 million.

As for private clubs constructed from 1981 to 1990, only about a dozen new facilities were built. These few additions were, however, in marked contrast to conventional Chicago-based country clubs. The most obvious distinction was that nearly all 1980s-built country clubs were components of housing developments. Indeed, the recent decade represented the first in which planned golf course residential communities became the norm and not the exception. "Stand-alone" country clubs, those that had embodied Chicago's golfing scene throughout its history, simply had become too expensive.

What ultimately creates cost efficiencies for the developers in this era is the housing factor. Without this integral link, very few private clubs would emerge—and those would no doubt be modest on overall stature.

Typically, the formula characterizing the modern private development requires several prerequisites. As with any business venture, sufficient funding is critical. Equally important is a targeted market base. Other criteria are:

- Land availability—specifically between 300 and 750 acres. Centrally located near the population target, the land must also be conducive to providing an attractive playing site.
- Broad community acceptance and zoning approval for the eventual construction of 125-to-2,000 housing units.
- Well-organized marketing efforts to attract housing buyers willing to spend anywhere from $200,000 to $2 million per home.
- Championship-style design—preferably crafted by one of golf's recognizable names.
- Additional on-site recreational facilities plus a centerpiece clubhouse ranging in size from 20,000 to 50,000 square feet.

Planned residential golf course communities have long existed in more temperate climates hospitable to year-round golf. At these Southern locales, residential property owners include retirees, second-home owners and investors. This customer profile was quite different than the one evidenced locally. For Chicagoans, homes purchased at golf communities represented primary residences.

Early Pioneers

By most accounts, the area's first golf/residential development was Mission Hills. In 1972, a 144-acre site in

Northbrook was purchased by developer Eugene Corley and the Phoenix Mutual Life Insurance Company. The property included the busy daily-fee Mission Hills golf course—a layout built in the mid-20s. With a $50 million development fund, the developer constructed 820 condominiums and 144 townhouses around the old course, remodeled by noted architect Edward Lawrence Packard. The Mission Hills Country Club Village became the new name for the development.

Even before the Mission Hills Village debut, there were several examples of housing clusters directly associated with golf course properties. The Inverness Golf Club and its adjoining Inverness community is one example. Unlike Mission Hills, however, Inverness was not suddenly transformed into a golf course community; the process spanned several decades.

In 1938, the Arthur J. McIntosh Company purchased a sizable chunk of rural property, just west of Palatine. While most of the acreage was farmland, the site did include the nine-hole Meadow Grove course, built by the Cudahy Packing Company in the mid-1920s.

After McIntosh's acquisition, the layout became Inverness; during the following year it was lengthened to 18 holes. In the late '40s and '50s, upscale single family homes sprouted on the rest of the developer's land. Quite naturally, an important attraction for prospective home buyers was the private 18-hole course. Club members assumed full control of the Inverness golf course and clubhouse in 1955.

The McIntosh Company employed a similar formula when developing the Prestwick Country Club with its adjoining residential property in the early '60s. A decade later, the company tried again at Turnberry. In both cases, as with Inverness, the golf courses were the catalyst to the developmental success.

In a looser sense, residential golf course properties can trace their local existence back to 1900. Early in that year several members of the Glen View Club organized a syndicate with a stated objective to purchase 82 acres of property adjoining the course and also east of the "Golf" train depot. This newly acquired land was then subdivided into housing lots. Cottages were soon constructed, forming a mini-village, inhabited by club members.

While Olympia Fields Country Club featured "summer home" cottages on its property, in 1926 news regarding a planned community appeared in the club's monthly magazine. *The Olympian's* December issue reported, "Now there is to be the town Olympia. The desirability of the surrounding territory of the world's greatest golf club has attracted attention and the Illinois Central electrification brought the prospect to distinct reality." The community is there today—Olympia Fields.

Several years earlier the same railroad had created a subdivision just west of the Homewood club—its marketing appeal no doubt enhanced by the club's proximity. Not surprisingly, club members were aggressive purchasers of the new homes.

Interestingly, the local residential golf course communities of today are governed by a cornucopia of guidelines and policies. As will be noted, home ownership within the development does not always guarantee golf club eligibility.

At this juncture, a closer examination of the communities built since 1981 gives a peek into how different they really are.

Wynstone

Located in North Barrington, this opulent development is perhaps the most successful of all recent golf course communities—certainly it's the most publicized. Occupying nearly 750 acres, the site is synonymous with Jack Nicklaus. Not only did the Jack Nicklaus Development Corporation of Illinois build Wynstone, the famous golfer designed the course itself—choosing the final plan after rejecting the initial 43 designs.

The 7,003 yard, par 72 course opened in 1989—the same year Nicklaus established the course's current record of 66. Featuring a course rating of 74.2 and a slope rating of 139, Wynstone will soon be ranked as one of the region's most difficult sites.

Regarding membership, only property owners are eligible to join. The one exception is the allowance of a limited number of corporate memberships—one already taken by the Michael Jordan Company. Recent membership costs ranged from $40,000 for property owners to $44,000 for corporate members.

Wynstone's housing density is comparably light. Slightly more than 400 home sites have been or will be built; of this total, 320 are custom-designed properties. Prices will range from $500,000 to more than $2 million. Jack Nicklaus does in fact own a "modest" villa home. This 3,200 square foot retreat was reportedly purchased for $650,000. Included on its first level is a mini-garage for his golf cart.

The entire Wynstone property is replete with nature preserves, a bird sanctuary and marshlands. Including the course acreage, about one-third of the development is defined as open land. There's also a 37,000 square foot clubhouse (costing more than $8 million), plus swimming, tennis and community park facilities.

White Eagle

Part of another 750-acre development, this 18-hole course is associated with Arnold Palmer who helped in its links-type course design. Featuring rolling mounds, plenty of bunkers, several water hazards and penalizing rough, the course can play to a short 5,200 yards, or at its maximum—7,185. From the long tees, the par 72 plays to a 73.9 rating and 132 slope. While White Eagle is a different kind of layout than the Nicklaus creation, the major contrasts between the two are the size of the developments and their relative costs.

Geographic locations dictate specific marketing philosophies. High-end housing costs of $1 million to $2 million may be commonplace in North Barrington, but in Aurora and Naperville, where this residential/golf course community is located, housing costs are less. As such, prices at White Eagle's 1,100 single-home and multi-family unit complex range from $140,000 to $1 million. About 30 separate builders are involved. Approximately one-third of the development had been sold by mid-1991.

Farmland as recent as 1985, the site reportedly cost the primary developer—the Macom Corporation—about $11,000 an acre. Land for the golf course, construction costs, Palmer's fee and the 51,000 square foot Williamsburg-styled clubhouse were said to have totaled more than $13 million. White Eagle's development also includes other nongolf recreational facilities, including clay tennis courts, a regulation-sized pool and Illinois' first "zero-depth" pool. This pool's depth actually ranges from zero to 3-1/2 feet—perfect for the community's many children.

White Eagle's golf course members are comprised of residents and nonresidents alike. While rates are always subject to change, initiation fees are approximately $24,000.

Of peculiar note is that the White Eagle development lies in two counties—Du Page and Will—and is also considered part of Aurora and Naperville. Sometimes this duality presents confusion. For example, the Naperville Park District services the White Eagle complex and Naperville also represents the development's mailing address. On the other hand, police and fire services are provided by Aurora. Residents pay Aurora taxes and vote in local Aurora elections. For these reasons, White Eagle's location is referred to as "Aurora-Naperville."

Stonebridge

Still another 700-plus acre development, this Aurora-based residential golf course community will include upon its completion more than 1,700 housing units. Townhomes and condominiums will be available, but the vast majority of residential housing will be in the form of single-family homes—priced from $250,000 to $1 million. The entire complex is being developed by Aurora Venture.

The golf course doesn't appear to exhibit the characteristics of a layout only two years old. Instead, Stonebridge is mature—a virtue generally unknown at new sites. A priority from the onset, mature acreage was incorporated into architect Tom Fazio's design. Fazio's reputation as one who could craft a course among natural terrain was well known—his most notable local example is Butler National where he assisted his uncle George. Only about 20 percent of the development's housing lots border the course—

Wm. Daniels/The Photo Partners

Stonebridge played host to the 1991 Ameritech Senior Open.

an exceptionally low percentage. Tall oak and elm trees are abundant. Credit should also go to the developer, which prioritized course aesthetics when it would have been just as easy to sell additional wooded housing sites.

The course itself has the "feel" of a Butler National if not the extreme difficulty. Multiple tee boxes afford a course length anywhere from 5,300 to 6,900 yards. It's been said the golf course and the 30,000 square foot clubhouse cost $13 million. Adjacent to the clubhouse is a swim and tennis center.

Membership is limited to property owners, although some corporate memberships were available initially. Initiation fees were quoted in the range of $20,000 to $27,000.

The Stonebridge course does represent a "first" among recently built golf course/residential communities. It hosted in 1991 the Ameritech Senior Open. This PGA-sanctioned tournament represents the first major golf tournament contested at any of the local region's golf course residential sites.

Bull Valley

When Vignocchi and Associates acquired this 500-acre site southwest of McHenry, an important decision was made. Unlike other developments, all initial efforts would be directed to building the 18-hole course. Housing sites were to be allocated later.

With this creative flexibility at hand, course architect Dick Nugent designed a championship-style 7,228-yard layout. Built on unusually hilly terrain, the 172-acre course weaves through natural wetlands and balanced preserves of mature oak and hickory trees. Already established as one of the region's top challenges, the back-tee course rating is a sobering 75.9. Even the shorter tees of 6,228 yards play to a 72.3 rating.

The first phase of housing has begun. Plans include 177 single-family homes built on lots from 3/4-acre to a full acre. Prices per lot were quoted in the range of $60,000 to $155,000. Additional building phases will include townhouses.

Bull Valley club membership at one time included provisions for nonresident eligibility. Resident and corporate memberships are also available. Though the course is three years old, it was not until 1990 that the club's 37,000 square foot clubhouse opened.

Royal Fox

A 142-acre course is the centerpiece attraction of this $240 million development in St. Charles. Designed by Dick Nugent, the 6,816-yard championship-style layout plays to a 72.6 rating. With more than half of its par 4 holes exceeding 400 yards, and only one par 3 under 200 yards, Royal Fox is deceptively long. The four par 5s average 542 yards. The course's par 5 finishing hole is one of the most difficult in the Chicago region. Its 560-yard test ends on an island green. Nugent feels the Royal Fox site will be judged in time as one of his best. Construction costs for the course were said to be in the neighborhood of $6 million.

Vincent Solano Jr., a partner in the Robin Hill Development Company, is the man most responsible for Royal Fox's success. Experienced with other residential golf course communities and an exceptional player himself, Solano and his group purchased the 300-acre site in 1987.

Housing plans include the eventual construction of 291 single-family homes on lots of 1/2 acre to one acre. Lot prices were recently quoted in the $77,000 to $195,000 range. Custom-built homes of $400,000 to $1 million are being constructed.

The grounds include a 30,000 square foot Monticello-style clubhouse, which contains an indoor swimming pool, fitness center, formal and casual dining rooms and locker facilities. Next to the clubhouse is a larger outdoor swimming pool. Total cost for the clubhouse complex surpassed $7 million.

Members primarily own community property. Initiation fees are in the neighborhood of $30,000. Royal Fox is also at the forefront of courses pushing to permit women to join as full members and not just spousal or associate members.

Crystal Tree

In the early 1970s, Eugene Corley helped develop one of the area's first residential golf course communities—Mission Hills. Now almost 20 years later, Crystal Tree in Orland Park represents his second. The 282-acre site is smaller than most Chicago-area golfing communities, yet its 18-hole course takes up more than one half of the development's space.

Designed by internationally known Robert Trent Jones Jr., Crystal Tree represents his first Illinois project. Understanding that the playing proficiency of future club members could vary widely, Trent Jones crafted a layout to challenge all levels of play—enjoyably. The course can play to a long 6,706-yard length or one measuring 5,149 yards. Nowhere is the layout's flexibility more apparent than the par 3 No. 11 hole. Seven different tees exist. The upshot is that Crystal Tree is a championship-style design that's fun to play. Considering many of the current members are "empty-nester" types, the broad appeal of the $4 million course served as an important selling point.

About 400 housing units were initially present at Crystal Tree including 100 single-family homes, which were gobbled up quickly. Townhouse prices ran from $180,000 to almost $300,000. Single-family homes started at $400,000. About 85 percent of the units border the course.

Resident membership initiation fees were quoted in the $22,000 range. A few nonresident memberships were also available initially—for about $32,000.

Boulder Ridge

Encompassing 436 acres, this Lake in the Hills residential golf course community opened its 18-hole facility in 1990. Unusually spacious, the 200-acre layout is one of the Chicago region's largest.

The architectural team for this 7,130 yard, par 72 creation is Bob Lohmann and Fuzzy Zoeller. Lohmann's name is relatively unfamiliar to those outside his profession. Born in 1952 Lohmann learned his craft under the tutelage of Dick Nugent and Ken Killian and was instrumental in Forest Preserve National's design during the early 1980s. But because Lohmann's name was not widely known and hence, wasn't strong enough to attract potential buyers to Boulder Ridge, the effervescent and high-profile Fuzzy Zoeller was brought into the equation.

Though strictly a design consultant, Zoeller's name is the one that has been hyped. It's Fuzzy's photograph in the Boulder Ridge ads; it was Fuzzy who met the media in publicity sessions. If nothing else, linkage with a well-known PGA pro reflects the high-stakes atmosphere present at multimillion dollar golf course properties. The association of a popular PGA figure with contemporary golf course communities has become a common marketing strategy.

Par Development, a subsidiary of the Plote Company, is serving as the primary developer. Upon completion of its several planned building stages, the site will contain single-family homes, patio homes and townhouses. Initial single-family, one-half acre lots were priced in the $83,000 to $170,000 range. Custom-built homes of $400,000 and up will be commonplace throughout the community.

Boulder Ridge property owners will be the primary members of the golf club—with initiation fees in the $20,000 range. Some nonresident memberships at $25,000 were also available.

Carillon

Unlike Wynstone or White Eagle or for that matter the other area golf course residential communities, Carillon's appeal doesn't hinge exclusively on its golf course amenities. Instead, the development's 18-hole layout serves as just one more recreational activity available to the residents of one of the largest housing complexes ever planned in Illinois. Upon completion of its final phase, Carillon will represent a sizable community within Will County. About 7,500 housing units, comprised of single-family, townhouses and condominiums, are being built by Carillon's primary developer—Cenvill Illinois Corporation. Housing prices range from $78,000 to more than $150,000. Clearly, buyers of Carillon's property are not CEOs of major corporations or LaSalle Street bankers. Here, the targeted demography includes empty-nesters or retirees. Still, the Carillon golf course provides a good but fair test for all age levels.

Designed by Greg Martin, Carillon's two separate nine-hole courses play to lengths of 3,121 and 3,486 yards. A third nine may be added in the future. Ready for play in 1990, the course will eventually be limited to Carillon residents. In the interim, public players are invited to enjoy the layout. Reservations are required, however, a step necessary to gain entrance onto the private grounds.

The new course doesn't have many trees but other hazards—including water and bunkers—are evident. To those who have never played it, Carillon may conjure up images of a course befitting only seniors but in truth the layout offers challenge for all golfers.

While planned residential golf course communities multiplied during the late '80s especially, a local facility did take root early in the decade. Located in Schererville, Ind., Briar Ridge's 18-hole course is another private layout surrounded by a housing development. It represents still another example of a Dick Nugent/Ken Killian design.

Actually, the private Woodmar Country Club in Hammond, Ind., also debuted in the early '80s. This course and the Algonquin-based Terrace Hill Country Club were among the very few golfing facilities built during the last decade not associated with residential developments. As stand-alone entities, they were clearly the exceptions of private club growth from 1981 to 1990.

More to Come

Combined residential/golf course communities continue to be built. For example, four more private or semiprivate golfing communities are set to open this year. Three are in Lake County, the other near Lake Geneva.

Wisconsin's representative is the Geneva National Golf Club, a mammoth 1,600-acre site being developed by the Anvan Development Corporation. Upon completion, the development will have 1,900 homes. Homesites of one-half to 2 acres are currently being offered at prices from $53,000 to $250,000. Costs will no doubt increase as Chicagoans and other potential buyers learn about the diversity of Geneva National's appeal.

For starters, much of the site—about 95 percent—will be preserved as open space. Woodlands, streams, a lake, equestrian trails and three separate 18-hole courses will only partially comprise the open acreage. The golf courses will be opened to the public, officially on a semiprivate basis. Public fees in 1991 will range from $57 to $63 with cart.

Courses No. 1 and 2, designed in part by Arnold Palmer and Lee Trevino, opened in mid-1991. Palmer's layout features four tees per hole, the longest offering a 7,220-yard test. Trevino's course, from the back tees, runs 7,235 yards, with two other tee box alternatives. A third course designed by Gary Player will debut in 1992.

The club's golfing centerpiece, a 56,000 square-foot clubhouse, opened in 1991. On three levels, the clubhouse contains a litany of amenities geared to membership needs.

While fees are subject to change, property owners gain membership eligibility by paying $10,000. Nonresident initiation fees are $15,000.

At the three new Lake County golf/residential complexes, the public isn't invited. What's surprising, though, is that property ownership at The Merit Club, Conway Farms and the Ivanhoe facilities do not afford club membership. While some residents will eventually be allowed to join, their eligibility will be gained by invitation only.

Ivanhoe opened first. Comprised of members of the former Thorngate Country Club, Ivanhoe's 18-hole course was designed by Dick Nugent. Once the property of the Smith family (as in Smith Brothers cough drops), the Brook-Ridge Development Company has plans for 90 homes, costing from $500,000 to $1 million each.

Courtesy of Conway Farms/Sandy Stuart

Designed by Tom Fazio, Conway Farms' 18 hole private course debuted in 1991.

The Conway Farms Golf Club opened its Tom Fazio-designed 18-hole course in 1991. Located at Lake Forest's western border, the 500-acre development will eventually include 350 homes and a 100-acre office and research park. The project represents a joint partnership effort by the Stuart, Hart and Gordon Smith families.

Residential property in the new community will not be inexpensive—as much as $150,000 and up for lots alone. Still, this is a value in Lake Forest, one of Chicago's most affluent suburbs. There is, however, no linkage between property ownership and golf club membership. In fact, only about 250 members will comprise the club's exclusive roster. Though the course is very new, the early reviews are extremely complimentary.

The Merit Club is located north of Lake Forest in Gurnee. Here, 21 holes are expected to open in late 1992. Incidentally, the three "extra" holes will be used for instruction. Bob Lohmann and Ed Oldfield share design responsibilities for The Merit Club. The Globe Corporation is the project's primary developer. Single-family units are in the project's plan, although they will not border the course's holes. Membership will be limited and not necessarily offered to homeowners.

Aerial view of Seven Bridges Golf Club in Woodridge. Designed by Dick Nugent, the public course opened in July, 1991.

All players can, however, gain entrance to another golf course residential community, this one being the Seven Bridges development located in Woodridge. Debuting July 1991, Seven Bridges features a wonderfully designed 18-hole layout by Chicago's premier course craftsman—Dick Nugent. Four tee box placements per hole offer playing flexibility from 5,200 to more than 7,000 yards. Weaving through mature oaks and a meandering stream, the daily-fee course is contoured over rolling terrain. It's a challenging test but also one offering scenic vistas.

Although the development is new, a golfing legacy does exist. Indeed, a portion of the 395-acre site once housed the now defunct Woodridge Golf Club. Built in the '20s, the 36-hole public layout was among the earliest of Chicago's daily-fee facilities. Extremely active as a golfing venue, the Woodridge name was so well known that the newly incorporated village took the course name as its own in 1959.

Understandably, there was some resentment among village residents when the Forest City—Harris Group bought the old site for $14 million in 1986. When the group announced plans to develop a $400 million residential/retail/corporate park/golf course complex, it was clear the Woodridge course was headed to extinction. Sensing initial community resentment, the developers worked hard to alleviate concerns. Efforts were made to maintain the landscape's integrity by saving as many mature trees as possible. Land engineers and Nugent helped design a water-retention basin along with preserving the site's natural wetlands. This step helped to win over naysayers, since the old course and surrounding property frequently experienced flooding.

When its initial residential phase is completed, Seven Bridges will have more than 300 single-family homes, priced from $250,000 to $400,000. In keeping with the theme, all will have addresses on lanes and courts named after Bobby Jones, Patty Berg, Sam Snead, Walter Hagen, Chick Evans and other legendary golfers.

Several other currently active PGA greats are adding their names to soon-to-be-opened residential golf course communities. Two-time U.S. Open champion Curtis Strange is co-designing The Odyssey Golf Club in Tinley Park. Architect Harry Bowers and the Inter-Continental Development Company represent the major thrusts behind the long awaited 18-hole daily-fee facility—set to open in late '91.

Another two-time Open champion—Andy North—is providing his expertise at Geneva, Ill.-based Eagle Brook. The private community is being developed by Joe Keim Builders. Occupying a portion of the 563-acre site is a 187-acre 18-hole course, primarily designed by Roger Packard. Packard's recent local works have included Cantigny's 27-hole layout and redesign at Medinah's No. 3 course just prior to the 1990 U.S. Open.

A third development—Royal Melbourne—finds the popular Greg Norman and noted architect, Ted Robinson, sharing design responsibilities. Located in Long Grove, the upscale community will have only 125 homesites, each 3/4 acre to one acre. Recent prices for the lots alone were between $200,000 and $400,000. About half of the 315 total acreage will be covered by the 18-hole course. Resident initiation fees exceed $30,000.

From the Senior PGA Tour comes another recognizable name to jump into the local residential/golf course mix. As with Trevino and Player at Geneva National, Nicklaus at Wynstone and Palmer at White Eagle, the affable Chi Chi Rodriguez lends his design perspectives at Broken Arrow. Developed by Robin Hill (of Royal Fox fame), the 27-hole $250 million Lockport-based complex should be ready in a year or two. Almost 1,500 residential units are planned.

A further twist is construction of a 100-plus unit hotel/ business conference center.

Still more courses are in the early building or planning stages as the 1990s roll on. Pete Dye is designing Ruffled Feathers in Lemont. The seemingly omnipresent Dick Nugent is busy at work planning the Dunham Club in Wayne, Ill. New entries in South Barrington, Aurora, West Chicago and Lisle are also expected soon.

Golf course introductions in 1991, and those projected for '92 and '93 debuts, signal continued growth. While variables such as the economy, environmental concerns and golf's participatory levels will ultimately dictate the future, there is one certainty as the 21st century begins: The Chicago area will continue to have more golf courses than any other metro market, thus maintaining its long-held title as the country's golfing hub.

CHAPTER

12

Putting Down Roots— Early Tournaments

In the first six decades of American tournament golf, Chicago had become the favorite stop. From 1895 through 1950, 10 U.S. Opens, nine U.S. Amateurs and six U.S. Women's Amateurs took place here. No other market in the country came close. In fact, Chicago's closest challenger as a tournament center was the *state* of New York, which hosted 22.

In the early days, tournament organizers weren't eager to stage national tourneys out "West." To Easterners, Chicago was too far removed to attract the sport's best players. But after the success of the Chicago area's first (and second) tournaments, the three aforementioned national events stopped here regularly. Only throughout most of the '40s did tournament activity cease, due in large part to World War II. By 1949, the U.S. Open returned to Chicago, specifically to Medinah.

Other important championships also toured area courses. The Western Open played its first tournament in 1899. The same year, the Western Amateur started. When the PGA kicked off their inaugural championship in 1916, it didn't take long to schedule a Chicago stop. This tournament came to Flossmoor in 1920.

Understandably, it would be purely subjective to state Chicago-based major tournaments were the "best ever." Still, they were exciting. Many were historically important. Others were simply unusual. The following pages will highlight two of the earliest years in Chicago's tournament golf history, 1897 and 1928. These two years, however, do not take into account all the great moments and all the illustrious champions who had played in Chicago-hosted tournaments. There is no mention of Virginia Van Wie, Chicago's greatest female golfer, or amateurs Chandler Egan

and Robert Gardner. These three players are probably unfamiliar to most fans today, but in their day, their names
were nationally known. Chicago tournaments have been
important to golf's development. And, in 1897, it all began.

A September of Surprises

Fittingly, the Chicago area's first chartered golf club—
Chicago Golf Club—was also the first to host a major national championship. In fact, the Wheaton-based club
hosted not one but two championships during the same
week: the U.S. Open and the U.S. Amateur. Incidently, 1897
marked the last year that each tournament was held at the
same site, during the same week.

For the Chicago Golf Club to be awarded the host club
honors was, in itself, a coup. Most USGA members were
initially opposed to staging the contests west of the
Allegheny Mountains. Those who belonged to Eastern
clubs felt, "It is too early in the history of the game to go
so far away." Others stated, "The East is the place of greatest
convenience. . .golf sprang up in the East and obtained its
greatest impetus here." While the Chicago Golf Club was
one of the five original members of the USGA, the club's
eventual selection as the 1897 tournament site would not
have been without the efforts of one key individual.
Through his influence and reputation, Charles Blair Macdonald singlehandedly convinced fellow USGA members
to grant his Chicago Golf Club host site privileges.

Those who reluctantly went along with Macdonald still
believed both 1897 championship fields would be weak. To
their astonishment, the respective entry fields for the third
annual U.S. Amateur and third annual U.S. Open were the
best assembled in each event's three-year history.

Of the two contests, one clearly had top billing. The
Amateur event took four of the five days of the week's proceedings. Conversely, the 36-hole U.S. Open was a one-day
affair, played on the off-day of the U.S. Amateur. Tournament organizers knew the Open had less spectator appeal,
so they scheduled a long-drive exhibition on the day of the
U.S. Open. To keep the crowd interested, the exhibition
took place, by design, in the late afternoon as a sort of
"grand finale."

Why did the Open play second fiddle to the more prestigious U.S. Amateur? It came down to each tourney's participants. The Open's field included "professionals," which in those times often meant men of limited education and questionable pasts. Some were heavy gamblers or drinkers, often expressing themselves by using profanities on the field of honor.

Contrast that roster with the more genteel group who participated in the Amateur event. Well educated and successful, these men were sportsmen who simply enjoyed a good challenge. Unlike their professional counterparts, the amateur players sought the recognition and trophy, not any monetary reward. For those who followed golf in 1897 and for several years afterward, the Amateur contestants were the respective heroes of the game.

The U.S. Amateur's field included 58 qualified participants. One was C.B. Macdonald, himself, the pretournament favorite. He had won the 1895 U.S. Amateur, just missed reclaiming the title in 1896 and fully expected to prove his supremacy again. After all, he knew the Chicago Golf Club grounds well. Remember, he had designed the course. Furthermore, he held the course record.

Macdonald's major competition was thought to be, among others, Foxhall Keene. Keene was a good golfer but also the country's most famous polo player. Otto Hoehmeyer Jr. was another expected to challenge Macdonald. Hoehmeyer was the only one of the 58 entrants who had ever "holed out in one."

Still another threat was H.J. Whigham—the 1896 Amateur champion. Whigham played most of his golf at the Onwentsia Club but knew the Chicago Golf grounds well. He had, in fact, occasionally played with Macdonald at CGC. A few years later, Whigham would became even closer to Macdonald when he married his daughter. Whigham worked as a reporter for the *Chicago Tribune*. Not only did he seek to defend his Amateur title at the Chicago Golf Club in 1897, he also had the responsibility to report the week's events to *Tribune* readers. Interestingly, *Tribune* readers followed the stories but they never knew that Whigham wrote these accounts. There was no identifying byline.

Courtesy of Chicago District Golf Association

H.J. Whigham was the U.S. Amateur's first two-time winner—in 1896 and 1897.

During the days leading up to the two championships, the Chicago newspapers (all nine of them) increased their golf coverage. Interest ran high in Wheaton, in part because of the many social functions held in conjunction with the national tournaments. But for many Chicagoans, the media focus of the national event led to one commonly asked question: "What is golf?" No doubt the intense media coverage during the 1897 tournaments helped introduce the game to the masses.

On Sept. 14, 1897, the U.S. Amateur competition began. The first-day format was best score (medal play). By day's end, only the 16 lowest scores would advance to the next day's round. Macdonald posted the low score of Day One, an 86, although it was still nine strokes higher than his course record.

Day One produced two major surprises. The scores were higher than expected, primarily due to rock-hard fairway conditions. The club had an underground water system—but only for the greens. With no rain for seven weeks, the unyielding fairways had players' clubs bouncing off the hard ground, resulting in many balls being

topped. The second surprise of Day One saw the dismal
showing of the local amateurs. Unlike their Eastern com-
petitors, the locals had played the Chicago Golf Club
previously and were expected to hold an advantage. After
Day One, however, only four "Westerners" had qualified
for the second round. They were Macdonald, Whigham,
D.R. Forgan and G.S. Willis.

*Findley Douglas lost to Whigham in
the semi-finals in 1897; he also
finished second at the 1899 U.S.
Amateur at Onwentsia.*

On Day Two, the U.S. Amateur competition switched
to a match play format. In the morning round, the 16
qualifiers paired off. The eight winners then paired off
again in an afternoon round. By the end of Day Two, four
golfers remained. In one semifinal match to be played on
the following day, Macdonald would play against a Yale
University student, W.R. Betts. The other semifinal group
would have Whigham going against a strong Eastern player,
Findley Douglas.

On Sept. 16, the third day of the U.S. Amateur, the
summer drought ended. Though the rain stopped before

either semifinal match began, the sudden downpour had been quite unexpected. It wasn't the last surprise of the day.

Day Three attracted about 600 fans. Most waited for the Whigham-Douglas match. The other semifinal attracted less interest, since Macdonald was expected to win easily.

As it turned out, Whigham defeated Douglas quickly—so quickly that the day's first match was still in progress. In that match, Betts had a one hole advantage with only the 18th hole to go. With several hundred spectators now gathered, both Macdonald and Betts were on the green in two. Macdonald needed to win the hole just to tie Betts. When Macdonald failed to do so, the match ended. The young amateur had won his match against one of golf's earliest legends. But did he?

Macdonald hated to lose at anything, especially a U.S. Amateur competition. He immediately filed a protest, claiming Betts had broken a rule on the fifth hole. Indeed, Betts did commit an infraction, albeit a minor one. Betts' first shot on the fifth hole had sailed out-of-bounds. With golf's new out-of-bounds rule in effect, Betts took another drive. His error, according to Macdonald citing local club rules, was that Betts hit his second shot off a tee. Instead, Betts should have re-hit after dropping his ball on the ground.

After a short consultation, the tournament organizers ruled in favor of Macdonald's challenge. The match would proceed. Betts was furious, feeling that Macdonald should have made his official protest at the fifth hole. Tournament officials disagreed. Given a "second" chance, Macdonald wasted the opportunity. Betts won on the first hole. The hard-fought victory earned him a spot against Whigham in the Saturday finals.

Friday represented an off-day for the U.S. Amateur competition. Instead, the U.S. Open and long-drive contests were held.

The Open had a 35-man field, including a few amateur invitees. Among the professionals were 1895 and 1896 U.S. Open champions, Horace Rawlings and James Foulis, respectively, plus Joe Lloyd and 18-year-old "boy" professional, Willie Anderson. Local oddsmakers pegged Foulis the favorite. He was not only the defending champion but also the local club pro and greenskeeper at the host club.

At the Open's halfway point, Anderson's score of 79 led Foulis by a stroke. Both played poorly in the afternoon's 18-hole round. The upset winner turned out to be Joe Lloyd. Shooting a three (or one better than bogey) on the last hole, he beat Anderson by one shot. When pressed for a quote on his near miss, Anderson simply said, "Some other time." Prophetically, "some other time" turned out to be 1901, 1903, 1904 and 1905.

James Foulis, the club pro at the Chicago Golf Club during the late 1890s, won the U.S. Open in 1896.

Joe Lloyd, an English pro representing the Essex Country Club in Massachusetts, won the 1897 U.S. Open at the Chicago Golf Club and the first place prize of $125.

The long-drive contest winner was H.M. Harriman, with a drive of 244 yards, though the longest drive of the day took place in the Open itself. Joe Lloyd's tee shot on the 36th hole traveled 270 yards.

On Saturday, 900 people gathered to watch the Amateur final. Oddsmakers made Whigham a 3 to 1 favorite over Betts. Whigham proved them correct, in a match that was never close. With the win, Whigham—the

Chicago Tribune reporter—collected his second and last U.S. Amateur title.

The Chicago Golf Club had passed its test with flying colors, negating previous fears that sites outside the East could not run a big tournament. The club went on to host two other U.S. Opens and three U.S. Amateurs. To this day, no other Chicago-area club has hosted more.

An Olympian Effort

Chicago golf buffs had eagerly awaited the summer of 1928 since the U.S. Open and Western Open were in town. As a bonus, five prominent amateur events also were slated at Chicago-area clubs. Of the five, the Walker Cup competition in late August was the jewel. It marked the first (and only) time this international golf contest would choose the Midwest.

Though the plethora of tournaments drew the sport's best, one golfer's entry in the U.S. Open and Walker Cup matches captured the most attention. Bobby Jones would be coming to Chicago. Only 26 years old, he already was being compared to golf's immortals. His legion of local fans wouldn't be disappointed by his exploits in '28.

Olympia Fields, then the world's largest country club complex, hosted the U.S. Open. It had been six years since the Open had last visited—at the Skokie Country Club. There, Gene Sarazen won the title when he defeated Jones by one stroke. It also was the first time USGA organizers charged an admission fee.

Olympia Fields never had hosted an event of this magnitude. And few "experts" could predict how the game's best would perform on the club's 6,700-yard No. 4 course. The field included a U.S. Open record 1,064 entrants. Among the 144 qualifiers were Jones and Sarazen, plus others, such as Walter Hagen, Macdonald Smith, Al Espinosa and Johnny Farrell.

The 1928 Open's first-place prize of $500 wasn't a goal for the amateur Jones. By profession, Jones practiced law. He balanced his occupation with his golfing avocation and, by choice, entered few tournaments annually. In fact, Jones hadn't played in Chicago since the 1922 Open. Nevertheless, his limited schedule from 1923 to 1927 had netted the Georgian two first-place finishes in the U.S. Open, three in the U.S. Amateur and two in the British Open. On three other occasions he finished second in the majors.

He got off to a quick start at Olympia Fields. By the halfway point, his even par score of 144 led the field by two strokes. The tournament's third day saw all who survived the cut playing 36 holes. After posting a morning round of 73, Jones had maintained his two-shot margin, but in the afternoon he stumbled. It was the worst time to card a 77.

During the final 18 holes, Jones was paired with Walter Hagen. With a crowd of 5,000 watching these two golfing greats struggle through their round, the possibility loomed that someone else could win the U.S. Open. The crowd heard murmurs that Roland Hancock had posted a 60 through 16 of the final 18 holes. The 22-year-old North Carolinian had not only caught Jones but led by three strokes with only two holes to play. But the pressure finally caught up with Hancock on the 17th. He double-bogeyed the hole, then bogeyed the 18th.

Meanwhile, another player had toured the course in relative anonymity. Johnny Farrell's morning gallery was an even dozen. In the afternoon, three spectators had followed him in the final round. When the event's scores were tallied, however, he and Jones had ended in a 294 deadlock. Both would compete the following day in the first 36-hole playoff in U.S. Open history.

The Sunday playoff was one of the game's greatest head-to-head matches ever witnessed. Each player took turns leading. On six separate occasions, the contest was tied, the last time on the 33rd hole. On the next hole, Farrell's long par putt found the center of the cup. Jones meanwhile lipped his five footer and settled for a bogey five. Needing a birdie to catch Farrell, Jones calmly stroked a 25-foot shot into the 35th hole. After the crowd roar subsided, they then watched Farrell also birdie the hole. Johnny Farrell remained one up going into the 36th and final playoff hole.

USGA Museum & Library

Johnny Farrell upset Bobby
Jones in the 1928 U.S.
Open at Olympia Fields.

Both players executed superb approach shots to the green. Jones' ball rested only two feet from the hole; Farrell's, just seven. If Farrell missed and Jones sank his short putt, the match would be tied again. Another 36-hole playoff would be scheduled on Monday. But Farrell closed it out by making his seven-footer. His two-round playoff total of even par 144 bested Jones by a single stroke. It would be Johnny Farrell's only major golfing championship victory.

Bobby Jones, on the other hand, would go on to win the Open in 1929 and 1930. In 1930, he also captured the British Open, British Amateur and U.S. Amateur titles. At the conclusion of this four-event "Grand Slam" triumph, Jones retired from competitive golf at a youthful 28 years of age.

Western Open at North Shore

When the Western Open hosted its tournament at the relatively new North Shore Country Club in Glenview, most of the field from the recently held U.S. Open were on hand. There were two notable exceptions. Bobby Jones had left the Western off his abbreviated schedule; the other big name no-show was Walter Hagen. His omission was unusual, as he was the defending champion. Instead, Hagen chose to enter the Canadian Open—an event he had never won.

Courtesy of Chicago District Golf Association

Abe Espinosa won the 1928 Western Open at the North Shore Country Club.

The Western Open's 250 participants didn't seem to mind golf's two most formidable players weren't present. Johnny Farrell was on hand. So were the Espinosa brothers, Abe and Al. With the field being so large, one half of the group played the 6,772-yard layout on Day One. On Day Two, the other half completed their first round. After all players had finished the initial round, the best scorers moved on to the next day.

The leaders entering the final day's 36-hole double round were the Espinosas. Abe had earlier posted a course record 68, which helped give him a one-shot margin over his younger brother Al. By tourney's end, Abe Espinosa withstood not only his brother's challenge but also that of Farrell. Interestingly, Al Espinosa would tie Bobby Jones in the U.S. Open a year later. The two then competed in a 36-hole playoff, where Jones soundly defeated Espinosa by a 23-stroke margin (141-164). Ironically, the trouncing still netted Al the biggest U.S. Open paycheck up to then. The amateur, Jones, couldn't collect the cash award. The $1,000 prize was given to the next highest finisher. No wonder many of the era's professionals hoped Bobby Jones would forever stay an amateur.

Amateur Events

While the first half of the 1928 summer season would see professional golfing championships, the second would be limited to amateur events. The 1920s represented the last decade that amateur championships were considered equal in stature to the pro's game.

Chicago's tournament roots were firmly entrenched within amateur events. The Western Amateur, for example, debuted here in 1899. Its stature ranked only behind the prominent U.S. Amateur. The same was also true of the Women's Western Amateur, which began in 1901, or six years after the first U.S. Women's Amateur. The Western Junior tournaments for boys and girls were founded and first played locally in 1914 and 1920, respectively. Though each of these amateur events had been held from time to time at clubs outside of Illinois, all were scheduled on area courses in 1928. It was a banner year for Chicago golf and a busy summer for four host clubs—Glen View, South Shore, Indian Hill and Bob O'Link.

Bob O'Link had a peculiar challenge in staging the Western Amateur. The club was all male. Quite naturally though, women were expected to comprise part of the gallery. The club, therefore, amended its policy and permitted female spectators on the course. It was the one and only time women were allowed at Bob O'Link.

As to the Western Amateur itself, spectators viewed an entry field considered one of the best ever assembled. Several British amateurs competed as they tuned their games for the upcoming Walker Cup team competition. Among the other 200 entrants were eight-time winner Chick Evans and the defending champions from each of the prior two years—Ben Stein and Frank Dolp. Though many spectators were pulling for Evans, Dolp defeated Evans in the semifinal round, then beat another Chicagoan, Gus Novotny, in the finals.

Walker Cup

By late August, one event was left on Chicago's 1928 golfing calendar. The Walker Cup, a biannual team competition played between U.S. and British Isle amateur golfers, was hosted by the prestigious Chicago Golf Club.

On his way to Chicago, the U.S. team captain stopped first at Pinehurst in North Carolina to tune his game. Bobby Jones played five rounds. Judging by his scores, he didn't

Chicago Historical Society DN 67,763

Chicago Golf Club as it appeared in 1928.

need to make many adjustments, as his last four rounds were all below 70.

Once he arrived in Chicago, Jones set up a practice routine for the coming week. First, he visited the Old Elm Club. Though Jones never had played its course, he posted a 68—a new course record. The next day he shot another 68, this time at CGC. It too set a course record. On the following day, Jones played a morning and an afternoon round. First, he posted a course-record 67; then, presumably weakened, shot a 68.

The practice week concluded with a charity tournament at Flossmoor. Recording his ninth consecutive round under 70, Jones established yet another local course record with a 67. With his pre-tourney rounds liberally covered in the local press, Bobby Jones had simply amazed the general public. Even those not familiar with the game knew who Bobby Jones was.

On Aug. 30, Jones and seven teammates gathered at the Chicago Golf Club to prepare their Walker Cup defense. All prior competitions had resulted in American team victories—an increasing embarrassment to the British delegation. Certainly, the American supremacy hadn't been expected when competition began in 1922. After all, the original intent of staging the Walker Cup event had been to stimulate international golfing interest after World War I. Thus far, the respective outcomes were proving anything but stimulating to British egos.

USGA Museum & Library

Bobby Jones dominated the Chicago golf scene in 1928.

Nevertheless, hopes of the foreign team were high in 1928. Results from the 1926 matches were close, though the British team had lost 6 to 5. Furthermore, their confidence was buoyed by the 1928 golf site itself—a links-course, exactly the type of layout most suitable to their game. The one concern that couldn't be discounted, though, was the American superman—Bobby Jones.

The competition's two-day format was structured in such a manner that pairs would play against pairs in match play on Day One. Day Two included eight individual match play rounds.

By Day One's conclusion, the American team led 4 to 0. None of the matches was close. Jones and his playing partner, Chick Evans, were easy victors. All the American team needed on Day Two was two single's match victories and one tie. If accomplished, they would capture a fifth consecutive Walker Cup title.

Jones played his match first on Day Two. The outcome resulted in the most lopsided margin in Cup history. The scheduled 36-hole contest had been decided by the 24th hole, with Jones up 13 holes with 12 to play. Throughout his match with T. Philip Perkins, Jones had lost only two holes. Interestingly, on one of the two he lost, Jones picked up his ball and conceded the hole. If he would have sunk his short tap-in putt, his front side 18-hole score would have been 69. As it was, Jones recorded a 70. The "non-attempt" had prohibited him from shooting his 10th straight sub-70 round.

All but one of the other American amateurs followed with easy victories. The lone American loss occurred on the 36th and final hole, where T.A. Torrance executed a brilliant approach shot to defeat local hero Chick Evans. For Evans, it marked the only Walker Cup single's match he would ever lose. It was also to be his last time in the competition.

The American team's 11-1 triumph in 1928 represents the greatest Walker Cup rout in history. The Americans continued their dominance until 1938, when the British golfers finally won at St. Andrews in Scotland.

Recent Classics

While the organizers of the U.S. Open and U.S. Amateur didn't ignore Chicago club sites altogether from 1951 through 1991, they selected local venues far less. Golf's two oldest championships came to Chicago 19 times from 1897 through 1950 but only four times since. Knollwood and North Shore entertained the U.S. Amateur in 1956 and 1983, respectively. In 1975 and 1990, the U.S. Open revisited Medinah. But beyond these, Chicago clubs continued to host other major tournaments over the past four decades.

First, there were golf's richest tournaments—the famous World Championships at Tam O'Shanter. The '60s started with the PGA Championship at Olympia Fields. In 1962, the Western Open returned to area courses after a 23-year hiatus. Butler National became the Western's annual site in 1974. That year, for the first time, the USGA scheduled a Chicago club for their U.S. Women's Open.

The '80s saw other tournament firsts. The USGA Senior Open visited Medinah in 1988; the following year, the PGA Championship returned to Chicago—this time at a public course, Kemper Lakes. And in each year during the 1980s, Butler National hosted the Western Open.

The current decade is off to a great start. In 1991, fans have witnessed 1) the first Western Open at Cog Hill; 2) a Seniors event—the Ameritech Senior Open at Stonebridge; and 3) the first LPGA Shoot-Out at the Oak Brook Golf Club. In the four-year stretch between 1988 and 1991, there have already been 10 major championships held (this includes the 1989 U.S. Public Links). Tournament golf is, indeed, alive and well in the Chicago area.

This chapter will focus on just two of the past 41 years: 1974 and the 12-month period from June 19, 1989 to June 18, 1990.

Spotlight on Women

When the USGA selected the La Grange Country Club as the host site of the 1974 U.S. Women's Open, it marked the first time in the tournament's 28-year history that it came to Chicago. Amazingly, it was also the first time that this well-respected club—established in 1899—hosted a major championship.

Among the entrants were the game's stars as well as future luminaries. The new breed included 17-year-old amateur Nancy Lopez, tour rookie Pat Bradley and second-year player Jan Stephenson, then only a few years removed from her Hales Secretarial School background. All three went on to make the 36-hole cut but, in the end, this Open was fought for by the tour's veterans.

In their careers, Joanne Carner, Carol Mann, Sandra Haynie and Kathy Whitworth have combined for more than 200 Tour victories. In 1974, all had a legitimate chance to win the Open as they entered the fourth round. For three of the future Hall of Famers, the difference between winning and losing at La Grange came down to one hole—the 395-yard par 4 16th.

Kathy Whitworth won 88 championships in her golfing career. She would have possibly won her 89th and first U.S. Women's Open if she had not taken a double-bogey on 16. Whitworth finished two shots back as did Joanne Carner. Carner had also double-bogeyed 16. Carol Mann finished one shot behind the winner. Mann also double-bogeyed the tough 16th. Sandra Haynie took first-place honors, with the 16th hole proving decisive. Although she didn't birdie or par 16, her bogey was, still, one shot better on the hole than her three nearest challengers. With a four-round total of 295 or seven over par, Haynie took the tournament with one of the highest winning scores in U.S. Women's Open history.

The U.S. Women's Open returned to La Grange in 1981 with Pat Bradley the eventual champion. Her winning score of 279 curiously represented one of the lowest in U.S. Women's Open history.

Western Open Calls Butler Home

No tournament is more Chicago than the Western Open. Still, only 27 of the first 70 Westerns had been played here prior to 1974.

When the Western took to the road, it landed in all parts of the country, including California, Arizona, Utah, Texas, New York and Pennsylvania. This, of course, was by design. Clubs from nearly every state belonged to the Western Golf Association; consequently, many wanted to host its Open.

But Chicago is still the association's home. It was here the earliest Western Opens were played. By 1962, association directors felt the Open would benefit best by remaining within the Chicago area. From '62 through '73, Sunset Ridge, Tam O'Shanter, Midlothian and Medinah, among others, served as hosts.

In 1974, the Open's nomadic nature stopped. The plan was to roost at a single local venue. Directors chose Butler National. Though Butler National was private, the club from its inception was planned to serve as the Western Open's permanent home. Paul Butler, the multi-millionaire who developed much of Oak Brook, was the major force behind the creation of the Butler facility. Still active at age 82 in 1974, Paul Butler had many interests, including aviation, real estate and finance. He was also an avid sportsman.

During the 1930s, he founded the Butler Sports Core. Included among the many recreational options on the complex was the daily-fee York Golf Club—built in the '20s. In fact, Butler designed the public course himself. In the late '60s, Paul Butler incorporated the course acreage, along with additional portions of the Sports Core, to establish Butler National.

The new Butler facility was appealing to Western Golf Association directors for several reasons. They already had determined some years earlier the tournament's annual site changes were counter-productive. Logistically, the club rotation from 1962 to 1973 proved cumbersome, organizationally difficult and confusing to local fans.

Choosing a permanent Western site also was expected to help secure more advantageous PGA Tour dates. For several years, the tournament was contested prior to the British Open. As a result, many of the sport's big names skipped the Western—instead, using this time to practice overseas. With an absence of many stars, fan interest waned. The networks reduced broadcast coverage. This, in turn, forced the WGA to limit purses as well as cut back on charitable contributions.

Seeking to rekindle interest in American golf's second-oldest professional tournament, the WGA chose Butler National not only for the club's regional accessibility and crowd capacity but also because of the course's challenge. This was a beautifully crafted and tough layout. Course architect George Fazio later referred to Butler National as the most difficult playing course he had ever designed. Substantiating this claim, the course rating of 76.9 easily ranked Butler National among the toughest courses in the country.

Butler National Begins Tournament Play

When the entry field arrived at the first Butler-held Western Open in 1974, it marked the third consecutive week the PGA Tour had played a severely challenging layout. On the heels of the U.S. Open at Wingfoot, then the Firestone Championship in Akron, golfers were clearly in no mood to compete over another monstrous course. Most voiced concern over Butler's length. The majority preferred using the shorter tee lengths—but these were still 7,002 yards. Others, such as Palmer and Weiskopf, wanted tourney officials to select the longer tees—7,300 yards. To the relief of the majority, PGA officials chose the shorter tees. In retrospect, the final scores were so high, it really didn't matter what tees were used. Players were simply overmatched by the new layout.

In 1974, the PGA Tour was experiencing a changing of the guard. Prior to the Western Open, newcomers to the Tour were winning almost one of every two championships. Others like Ben Crenshaw, Larry Nelson, Tom Watson and Tom Kite were still seeking their first tournament wins. The four had qualified for the 1974 Western Open. The year's top three money winners—Johnny Miller, Hubert Green and Jack Nicklaus—had all decided to skip the event.

Of the 147 qualifiers who did participate, only three would better par of 71 on Day One. Bob Goalby, Frank Beard and Gary McCord posted 70s, a stroke better than the 71s registered by Tom Weiskopf, Hale Irwin and Gary Groh. The challenging Butler layout took its greatest toll on 32 others, who had shot 80 or worse. For example, Crenshaw scored an 81, then withdrew. He wasn't alone. Several other golfers failed to show up for their tee times on the following day.

On Day Two, 24,000 witnessed the tournament's best scores of the week. Five golfers broke par; three would actually score in the 60s. Little known Tom Evans had the day's best score, a course-record 67. Meanwhile, first-round leaders faltered. After two days, Tom Weiskopf led. Behind him were Al Geiberger, Watson, Palmer, Trevino, Irwin and Kite. Entering the final two rounds, 78 golfers survived the cut, although defending champion Billy Casper wasn't among them.

Butler National's early reputation as a difficult layout was most evident on Day Three. Not one player posted a sub-par round; only four golfers matched par. The par round by J.C. Snead helped him move to second place, a jump of 13 places from the day before. Snead still trailed Weiskopf by five shots. Watson and Beard were six behind Weiskopf entering the final round.

A record fourth-round Western tournament gallery of 32,000 watched as Tom Watson played brilliantly to score 69. It was the only sub-70 round of the day. It was enough to put him into the clubhouse as the early leader. Third-round leader Tom Weiskopf stumbled, but still had one last chance to tie Watson with a par on 18. Instead, Weiskopf took a double-bogey. Tom Watson had won the Western Open and his first professional event. Several of Butler's inaugural Western field would go on in later years to win at the Oak Brook site, including Weiskopf, Nelson, Irwin and Geiberger.

A Million, a Mellowing and Monday Overtime

For the first time, the Western Open had a purse exceeding one million dollars in 1989. It was five times the amount of the 1974 contest at Butler. But money alone was not the only reason the touring pros came calling.

Over the years, the once ferocious course had matured. In fact, the course had mellowed. Specifically, Butler National's greens were easier to read and easier to score on. Also, the course's length didn't pose the threat it once did in 1974. As a result, scores posted in the 1989 Western Open were much lower than in 1974.

Included in the 1989 field was every Western Open winner since 1974 except one (Geiberger had joined the Senior Tour). Defending champion Jim Benepe was present, though unlike the prior year, he wouldn't need a sponsor's exemption to gain entry. Another in the field was Lee Trevino. This would be his last Western before joining the senior circuit in 1990. The week's participants also included those playing in pre-Western pro-am events. Celebrity amateurs teamed with the pros. Celebrities included Chicago's most popular sports hero, Michael Jordan. The obviously talented Jordan went on to dazzle the huge gallery by shooting a respectable 79.

When the Western Open concluded Day One activities, 24 golfers scored under 70—compared with only four sub-70 rounds for the entire 1974 event. Day One's leader Chip Beck had a 65, one off the course record. Other big names shooting scores in the 60s were Payne Stewart, Hale Irwin, Mike Donald and Mark McCumber. However, defending champion Jim Benepe shot a 78.

Friday's second round included 21 more sub-70 rounds. Three-time Western champion Tom Watson was among them but still couldn't make the cut. Benepe's second-consecutive 78 placed his total far above the one-over-par-cut level. Trevino's two-round even par total left him in the field, though he trailed leaders Paul Azinger and Mark McCumber by nine strokes.

On Saturday, five golfers shot 67—the day's lowest score. Larry Mize's 67 earned him a tie with Mark McCumber as the co-leader.

Trevino, though six months short of his 50th birthday, also had a 67, placing him only five strokes back. This next-to-last round was particularly fulfilling in a tournament never kind to the gregarious veteran. For 29 years, Trevino was among the sport's best—winning more than $3.5

million along the way. In the Western events, however, he had collected a mere $12,000.

The previous year, Trevino was still trying, albeit unsuccessfully, to capture his first Western. In 1988, he could do no better than a tie for 41st place. Predictably, most fans associated Trevino with one infamous incident at Butler. During the 1975 tourney, lightning struck him and two other golfers. Those two—Jerry Heard and Bobby Nichols—never won another golfing championship after 1975. Trevino would remain successful, although, he too suffered some aftereffects from the accident. Certainly, no one would express surprise if he chose to avoid any more Westerns. But there he was in 1989, shooting a third-round 67 and barely off the lead.

On Sunday, Trevino posted a respectable 69. It was not enough to catch the leaders but this fourth-place tie and $38,000 check represented his career's best showing at Butler.

Through 72 holes, the event's co-leaders were McCumber and Peter Jacobsen. The tie necessitated a Monday sudden death playoff, which required all of 15 minutes. McCumber's second Western Open title in the decade was decided on the first hole. He shot par while Jacobsen's three-foot par attempt literally circled the hole but stayed out.

Wm. Daniels/The Photo Partners

Peter Jacobsen's putter helped him get to a playoff in the 1989 Western Open—he lost after one hole.

From Second Place to First in Fans' Hearts

Weeks after the Western, the season's second tournament was generating the most anticipation. Though the PGA Championship had not held its annual contest in Chicago since 1961, the main attraction of the 1989 PGA Championship was the host course itself. For the first time, a public layout was used. Bogey golfers, who had played on Chicago's priciest daily-fee course at Kemper Lakes, could now watch a major championship unfold on a course that they themselves had struggled over. Now, they waited for the pros to do the same.

Olympia Fields had been the last Chicago host of the PGA Championship. There, Jerry Barber, a diminutive 5 foot 5 inch, 135-pound veteran, captured the 1961 championship in the PGA's first-ever playoff.

In 1989, the likelihood of a small framed golfer successfully attacking Kemper's 7,197-yard layout seemed improbable. Only once before had the PGA Championship been contested on a longer layout. Furthermore, there were other obstacles present, including more than 125 acres of lakes and ponds. The most serious challenge facing the field, however, was also the least predictable. Wind would play a role in determining scores. The question, though, was how much?

Since Kemper Lakes had never hosted a PGA event, pretournament opinions varied as to what the eventual winning score would be. Most touring professionals simply weren't acquainted with the site; indeed, few had even played the 10-year-old facility. Against a backdrop of unfamiliarity and course unpredictability, the 1989 PGA Championship began.

Day One didn't disappoint. Sharing the lead was a golfer ranked 184th of 185 players measured in the driving-distance category. It didn't figure Mike Reid and his 150 pounds would score six strokes under par at Kemper. It didn't figure Reid's co-leader would be Leonard Thompson, either. All Thompson could show for his last 12 years on the Tour was one victory. It didn't figure Arnold Palmer, who was just short of his 60th birthday, would record a sparkling 68. It didn't figure for Greg Norman, too. Posting a first-round 74, he had perhaps the most experience of any touring professional at Kemper. In fact, Norman held the current course record of 67.

Mike Reid came ever so close to taking home the 1989 PGA Championship trophy.

With the air still, Kemper Lakes offered little challenge on Day Two. Reid took over sole possession of the lead, though Craig Stadler's new course record 64 highlighted the day's events. Through two days, the field averaged barely one over par. Surprisingly, the cut level was exactly one over par—the lowest in PGA Championship history. The giant, at least in public golfers' minds, had been tamed.

Rain and a violent electrical storm halted play on Day Three. Fewer than half the remaining field completed their third rounds.

It wasn't until Sunday, the tournament's fourth and final day, that Mike Reid finished round three. After 54 holes, he was still three strokes ahead. He maintained the three-shot advantage through 15 holes of the final round, but on 16, his first shot landed in the water. Still, Reid scrambled for a bogey. His lead was now down to two, with two holes to go.

On the par 3 17th hole, Reid's drive easily cleared the large water hazard, but landed in short rough some 35 feet from the hole. From there, Reid's dream of winning his first major turned into a nightmare as he required an unbelievable four shots to finish. The double-bogey was Reid's first during the event.

By the time Reid walked to the 18th tee, he was now in second place. Clubhouse leader Payne Stewart had fired a 67, taking just 31 strokes over the last nine holes. Needing a minor miracle to tie Stewart, Reid's attempt to sink a long birdie putt wasn't even close. Stewart had captured the PGA Championship. Reid's collapse, on the other hand, had won the heartfelt sympathy of all who watched.

Wearing the Chicago Bears colors, Payne Stewart captured the 1989 PGA Championship at Kemper Lakes.

While most local enthusiasts were genuinely disappointed for Mike Reid, all were totally shocked by Kemper's lackluster defense. During the tourney, 153 sub-par rounds were played—a PGA Championship record. For millions who watched the televised event, there may have been an impression formed that Kemper Lakes was too easy a course for a PGA Championship. This belief is mistaken, however. The absence of typically breezy August winds plus the rain-softened greens allowed the game's premier players to perform under optimum conditions. It's too bad that few out-of-town golfers will ever visit Kemper Lakes to find out first hand how challenging the course is.

Western Preps for U.S. Open

Less than nine months later, the 1990 Western Open was held. The Western's field was particularly strong, augmented by many big-name stars fine-tuning their games for the following week's Medinah-hosted U.S. Open. Indeed, many tour pros rented area homes for a month and it was not uncommon for golf-savvy suburbanites to bump into stars of the game at area stores. Several foreign-born contestants added to the glitter. Nick Faldo, Seve Ballesteros, Jose Marie Olazabal and Jumbo Ozaki were among the most recognized.

Also included in the 156-man field was little-known Wayne Westner. The South African professional had earned his way into the tournament as one of four qualifiers.

After Day One, the three other qualifiers were far down the leader board; however, Westner's play earned him a sixth-place tie. A day later, his two-under-par 70 round placed him five shots back behind leader Ray Stewart. At the halfway mark, Westner remained a legitimate contender. Few in the crowd followed him, choosing to chase Ballesteros, Faldo and Ozaki—in spite of the fact that Westner's two-round total placed him ahead of the famous trio.

But it was to be a different Wayne, in this case Wayne Levi, to go on to an easy Western Open victory. With this, his first Western title, Levi won $180,000 or about twice the amount Billy Casper had collected in nearly 20 Western Opens—and Casper had won four Western titles during his career.

As to Westner, his respectable showing clearly underscores one important fact of tournament golf. That is: there are proficient professionals who toil in the relative obscurity of qualifying events. During 1990, a bevy of qualifying tournaments was played locally. For those who enjoy watching the game's best golfers compete, these qualifying events are arguably the best venues to watch in comfort. Crowds are generally small, thereby making for intimate views of players and their skills. Furthermore, qualifying events are free. In fact, just two days after the Western's final day, qualifying rounds for the U.S. Open were held at the private Lake Shore and Skokie Country Clubs. Jim Benepe emerged from these trials as a qualifier for the U.S. Open, eventually finishing in a 14th place tie at Medinah.

Fitting Excitement for Final Chapter

The Open—the last of the four local 1989-1990 events—was the most memorable. Each year, the Open seems to provide a suspense far superior to other golf championships. This certainly was true at Medinah, as huge galleries saw several new U.S. Open records.

Curtis Strange and his quest for a third straight U.S. Open title was the main prologue to the 1990 Open. Only Willie Anderson had won the event three consecutive years—some 85 years previously. Admittedly, the odds for Strange to duplicate this feat were high but, at least, the possibility served as a magnet for media and fan attention.

Then, consider the incalculable improbability of 45-year-old Hale Irwin winning the 1990 U.S. Open. No 45-year-old had ever captured an Open before. Certainly, no one had ever won the Open via a sponsor's exemption for entry. Finally, no Open winner had done so in a sudden-death format.

A closer examination of the 91-hole, five-day tournament offers insight into Irwin's accomplishment. By the time the record entry field had been pared down to the final 156, Irwin still was considered a 75 to 1 longshot. He had been winless during the previous five years. In reality, the odds probably would have been higher had not his steady play on difficult courses been factored.

On Day One, Irwin recorded a respectable 69, but it was three shots behind the first-round leader. At Day Two's finish, Irwin trailed by four strokes. His 74 on Day Three kept him four back and mired in the pack tied for 20th. With one round to go, Irwin needed not only to charge but also hope no other challenger got hot.

On Day Four, a large gallery followed. At first, they hardly noticed Irwin, instead focusing on his playing companion—Greg Norman. Through nine holes, Irwin shot no better than even par. On the other hand, Norman had played the front side three under par.

On the back nine, Irwin's play became spectacular. He birdied four consecutive holes. Through the 17th hole, he had charged ahead of Norman and others. Still, he needed one last birdie to post a fourth-round total *capable* of winning the Open. Of the more than 8,000 shots taken in the U.S. Open championship, none was more important than Irwin's successful 45-foot birdie putt on 18. Can anyone there or watching on TV forget the emotion of the usually stoic Irwin as he high-fived several in the gallery in a lap around the green. His final day round of 67 was enough to tie third-round leader Mike Donald and force an 18-hole playoff on Monday.

Wm. Daniels/The Photo Partners

Making birdie on 18, Hale Irwin takes a jubilent gallop around the green.

Throughout the tournament, organizers drew high praise. A new U.S. Open attendance record was established, and crowd and player logistics were handled smoothly. If there was any lament, it directly related to the comparative ease of Medinah's course. Posted scores were low, too low for the internationally famous No. 3 layout.

With little wind, inch-shorter than usual deep rough and rain-softened greens, the Open saw scores in the red, well throughout the first four days. Area golfers were befuddled to see one of Chicago's most difficult courses brought to its knees. In fact, Medinah's layout allowed more sub-par rounds in U.S. Open history, a record members of the club found embarrassing.

Chances are that Medinah's members will instead remember the Monday playoff round. With conditions featuring faster greens and brisk wind, Irwin and Donald recorded 74s. For the first time in this Open, the course played up to its difficult reputation.

Wm. Daniels/The Photo Partners

Mike Donald can't hide his disappointment after losing the 1990 U.S. Open to Hale Irwin.

In tying Donald through 18, Irwin had to make up a two-stroke deficit with three holes to play. Once he had achieved this small miracle, his birdie on the first playoff hole in U.S. Open history beat Donald. For the third time, Hale Irwin had won the Open. Only Willie Anderson, Jack Nicklaus, Ben Hogan and Bobby Jones—each with four victories—had more.

What follows is a complete listing of major Chicago-area hosted tournaments, their winners, club sites and year-played. The championship listings are limited to the U.S. Open, U.S. Women's Open, U.S. Amateur, U.S. Women's Amateur, the PGA Championship, the Western Open, the World Championship of Golf and the Walker Cup.

U.S. Open

1897	Chicago Golf	Joe Lloyd
1900	Chicago Golf	Harry Vardon
1904	Glen View	Willie Anderson
1906	Onwentsia	Alex Smith
1911	Chicago Golf	John McDermott
1914	Midlothian	Walter Hagen
1922	Skokie	Gene Sarazen

1928	Olympia Fields	Johnny Farrell
1933	North Shore	Johnny Goodman
1949	Medinah	Cary Middlecoff
1975	Medinah	Lou Graham
1990	Medinah	Hale Irwin

U.S. Women's Open

| 1974 | La Grange | Sandra Haynie |
| 1981 | La Grange | Pat Bradley |

U.S. Amateur

1897	Chicago Golf	H.J. Whigham
1899	Onwentsia	H.M. Harriman
1902	Glen View	Louis James
1905	Chicago Golf	H. Chandler Egan
1909	Chicago Golf	Robert Gardner
1912	Chicago Golf	Jerry Travers
1923	Flossmoor	Max Marston
1931	Beverly	Francis Ouimet
1939	North Shore	Marvin Ward
1956	Knollwood	E. Harvie Ward
1983	North Shore	Jay Sigel

U.S. Women's Amateur

1903	Chicago Golf	Bessie Anthony
1907	Midlothian	Margaret Curtis
1910	Flossmoor	Dorothy Campbell
1915	Onwentsia	Florence Vanderbeck
1933	Exmoor	Virginia Van Wie
1938	Westmoreland	Patty Berg

PGA Championship

1920	Flossmoor	Jock Hutchison
1925	Olympia Fields	Walter Hagen
1961	Olympia Fields	Jerry Barber
1989	Kemper Lakes	Payne Stewart

Western Open

1899	Glen View	Willie Smith
1901	Midlothian	Laurie Auchterlonie
1906	Flossmoor	Alex Smith
1907	Hinsdale	Robert Simpson

1909	Skokie	Willie Anderson
1910	Beverly	Chick Evans
1912	Idlewild	Macdonald Smith
1915	Glen Oak	Tom McNamara
1917	Westmoreland	Jim Barnes
1920	Olympia Fields	Jock Hutchison
1924	Calumet	Bill Mehlhorn
1927	Olympia Fields	Walter Hagen
1928	North Shore	Abe Espinosa
1933	Olympia Fields	Macdonald Smith
1939	Medinah	Byron Nelson
1962	Medinah	Jacky Cupit
1963	Beverly	Arnold Palmer
1964	Tam O'Shanter	Chi Chi Rodriguez
1965	Tam O'Shanter	Billy Casper
1966	Medinah	Billy Casper
1967	Beverly	Jack Nicklaus
1968	Olympia Fields	Jack Nicklaus
1969	Midlothian	Billy Casper
1970	Beverly	Hugh Royer
1971	Olympia Fields	Bruce Crampton
1972	Sunset Ridge	Jim Jamieson
1973	Midlothian	Billy Casper
1974	Butler National	Tom Watson
1975	Butler National	Hale Irwin
1976	Butler National	Al Geiberger
1977	Butler National	Tom Watson
1978	Butler National	Andy Bean
1979	Butler National	Larry Nelson
1980	Butler National	Scott Simpson
1981	Butler National	Ed Fiori
1982	Butler National	Tom Weiskopf
1983	Butler National	Mark McCumber
1984	Butler National	Tom Watson
1985	Butler National	Scott Verplank
1986	Butler National	Tom Kite
1987	Butler National	D.A. Weibring
1988	Butler National	Jim Benepe
1989	Butler National	Mark McCumber
1990	Butler National	Wayne Levi
1991	Cog Hill	Russ Cochran

World Championship of Golf

1943	Tam O'Shanter	Harold McSpaden
1944	Tam O'Shanter	Byron Nelson
1946	Tam O'Shanter	Sam Snead
1947	Tam O'Shanter	Ben Hogan
1948	Tam O'Shanter	Lloyd Mangrum
1949	Tam O'Shanter	Johnny Palmer
1950	Tam O'Shanter	Henry Ransom
1951	Tam O'Shanter	Ben Hogan
1952	Tam O'Shanter	Julius Boros
1953	Tam O'Shanter	Lew Worsham
1954	Tam O'Shanter	Bob Toski
1955	Tam O'Shanter	Julius Boros
1956	Tam O'Shanter	Ted Kroll
1957	Tam O'Shanter	Dick Mayer

The Walker Cup

1928	Chicago Golf	United States

14

Heroes and Legends and Architects

When watching a current-day PGA Tour event on television, a few Chicago-area golfing faithfuls still look for Gary Hallberg's name. They have, since 1980, the year the Barrington native first joined the Tour.

Fresh from a four-year career at Wake Forest University, Hallberg's credentials were impressive. He was a four-time All-American and had won the individual championship in the NCAA Division I tournament. Three years after joining the Tour, Hallberg won his first PGA Event, the Andy Williams-San Diego Open. Not even 24 years old at the time, Hallberg appeared ready for golfing stardom. Chicago golf fans couldn't wait. After all, it had been more than three decades since they had witnessed a legitimate golfing hero, one who had come out of the Chicago ranks.

Unfortunately, the dream has yet to materialize. Hallberg has realized some success (he also won the 1987 Greater Milwaukee Open) but, in truth, is just another Tour journeyman. This is not meant to denigrate his skills—he is, indeed, one of the country's top 125 players. Still, Hallberg's name isn't one of the Tour's biggest. It is, however, more prominent than other Chicago-associated Tour hopefuls—Rick Dalpos, Gary Pinns and LPGA player, Deedee Lasker. Before this current crop, Chicago golf fans rooted in the '80s for David Ogrin, Roy Biancalana and Lance Ten Broeck and in the '70s for Bob Zender.

If Chicagoans feel the absolute urge to pull for famous golfers who have at least a quasi-Chicago link, they can focus attention on two native North Carolinians. One is Ray Floyd, the Tour's No. 1 Cub fan. The other is Chip Beck. Beck currently lives in the northern suburbs, having recently married a woman from the Chicago area.

Perhaps the golfer most associated with Chicago is Michael Jordan. Although Jordan's reputation is more court than course-oriented, his golfing prowess is known to millions nationally.

Today's dearth of big-name Chicago players is in stark contrast to the sport's first half century. In 1916, for example, Chick Evans guaranteed his place among golf's immortals by winning the U.S. Open and the U.S. Amateur. In doing so, he added his name to a surprisingly long list of former U.S. Open and U.S. Amateur champions, who, at one time or another, called Chicago home.

Before Evans' historic feat, seven of the first 21 U.S. Amateur competitions were won by Chicago-based players. The first three were captured by C.B. Macdonald and H.J. Whigham. In 1904 and 1905, H. Chandler Egan of Exmoor took home the first-place trophy. In 1909, Robert Gardner of Onwentsia defeated Egan in the finals at the Chicago Golf Club. Then just 19 years and five months old, Gardner remains the youngest U.S. Amateur champion ever. Six years later, Gardner won again. The following year, he lost to Evans in the 1916 U.S. Amateur finals.

Evans' U.S. Open win in 1916 represented the first for a Chicago native. Prior to 1916, foreign-born professionals dominated the event. Still, six early U.S. Open champions did have some local ties. All one-time professionals at area clubs, the list includes Jim Foulis, Fred Herd, Willie Smith, Willie Anderson, Laurie Auchterlonie and Fred McLeod.

In 1920, another foreign-born club pro, Jock Hutchison of the Glen View Club, won the 1920 PGA Championship at Flossmoor. A year later, Hutchison captured the British Open title.

From the '20s through the '40s, more than two dozen nationally known golfing legends worked in the Chicago area as club pros. Medinah employed two of the biggest names—Tommy Armour and Ralph Guldahl. Among their combined career totals were three U.S. Opens and one Masters, one British Open and one PGA Championship. The Chicago District had others of note. Horton Smith, host professional at the Oak Park Country Club, won the first Masters Tournament in 1934 and won again in 1936. Denny Shute of Westward Ho won the 1933 British Open. In 1936 and 1937, he took home back-to-back titles in the PGA Championship. Still others who kept Chicago in the national limelight during the '30s through '50s were Johnny Bulla, Harry Cooper, Abe and Al Espinosa, Jim Ferrier, Jim Foulis Jr., Dutch Harrison, Ky Laffoon, Lloyd Mangrum, Bill Mehlhorn, Dick Metz, Ed "Porky" Oliver and Frank Walsh.

Johnny Revolta may have been the one, however, who was most closely associated with Chicago golf. For almost all the last 50 years, Revolta was the host pro (later professional emeritus) at the Evanston Golf Club. Capturing 19 PGA-sanctioned tournaments in his Tour career, Revolta's best year came in 1935. He won the PGA Championship and ended the year as the Tour's leading money winner—exactly $9,543.

As Tour purses increased in the '40s and '50s, golfing professionals chose one of two paths. Those having the competitive skill, intestinal fortitude and financial backing concentrated on Tour competitions. The vast majority of professionals, however, stayed closer to home, becoming teaching pros at local clubs.

Some of Chicago's current-day club pros did give the Tour a try before settling in to their present positions. In fact, Dick Hart of the Hinsdale Golf Club and Gary Groh of Bob O'Link each won a Tour event (the 1965 Azalea Open and the 1975 Hawaiian Open, respectively). Others such as Bill Ogden (North Shore), Errie Ball (Butler National) and Hubby Habjan (Onwentsia) competed in numerous U.S. Opens, Western Opens, Masters, PGA Championships and World Championships. Indeed, a good number of Chicago's club pros have acquitted themselves well in selected Tour events.

Mostly though, the local club pros limit their competing to state events, which are sponsored by the Illinois Section of the PGA. These include the Illinois Open, PGA Medal Play, PGA Match Play and Assistants Championship. Ogden, in fact, won all four events in 1953/1954—the only player to hold all titles simultaneously. In addition to the "Grand Slam," Ogden has been awarded the Illinois PGA Player of the Year Award an unprecedented six times.

When the Illinois Section initiated its Illinois PGA Hall of Fame program in 1989, the year's list of inductees, along with others added in 1990, included 15 legends and luminaries. Among these are the recognizable names of Chick Evans, C.B. Macdonald, Johnny Revolta, Errie Ball, Hubby Habjan, Dick Hart and Bill Ogden. Seven of the remaining eight are:

- Charles Bartlett—award-winning former *Chicago Tribune* golf writer who helped found the Golf Writer's Association of America.

- Herb Graffis—publisher of *Golfdom* and later *Golfing,* Graffis and his brother, Joe, were the guiding lights behind the formation of the National Golf Foundation.

- Carol McCue—the "First Lady" of Chicago golf who served as the Executive Director of the Chicago District Golf Association during the '50s, '60s and '70s.

- David Ogilvie III—Flossmoor Country Club's head pro who was recognized in 1986 as the National PGA Professional of the Year.

- Mike Spinello—founder of the Illinois Junior Golf Association.

- Zigfield Troy—former Illinois Golf Professional of the Year, Illinois PGA President and Tour player in the '30s.

- Robert Williams—former President of the Midwest and the International Association of Golf Course Superintendents.

The Final Name

From the first class of Illinois PGA Hall of Fame inductees is Joe Jemsek. As Chicago's only honest-to-goodness living legend, Joe is recognized by the golf world as the pioneer of public championship-styled golf courses. His introduction of Dubsdread in 1964 unequivocally proved to a national golfing industry that the average golfer would gladly pay a premium to play on a superior layout. Today, more than 25 years after the "Dubs" debut, public operators around the world continue to flood local markets with "country club-like" public course facilities.

Michael Medland &
Chicago District Golfer

Chicago legend, Joe Jemsek (on the right) talks with 1990 U.S. Open tournament director John Lattin. Lattin is also the tournament director of the LPGA Chicago Shoot-Out.

Born in Chicago on December 24, 1913, Joe Jemsek might be thought of as the best Christmas gift local golfers have ever received. Every decade of his life has been spent, in one way or another, assisting and promoting the sport's development.

First a caddy, then a club parking lot attendant, Joe was only 19 when he became a club pro at Cog Hill. The year was 1933, the same year he served as one of the original instructors in the *Chicago Tribune*-sponsored golf school.

The following year, Jemsek won a long-drive contest at the 1934 Chicago World's Fair. Hitting off a 168 foot-high platform, Jemsek took advantage of a favorable wind and bested nearly 60 other contestants with a 501-yard drive. As Jemsek likes to tell the story, the following day he had a line of people seeking personal lessons "from here to your house."

Though he did play several Tour events in the '30s, his major goal was to own a golf course. The opportunity arose in 1939. Having left Cog Hill in 1937, Jemsek became the club professional in 1938 at the St. Andrews Country Club in West Chicago. When Frank Hough, the club's owner, died shortly thereafter, Jemsek purchased the 36-hole facility from Hough's heirs. Learning the management side of the business from the ground up, he worked in all aspects of the operation—pro, manager, greenskeeper, caddy master and, for a time, head chef.

It was during the '40s, however, that the Jemsek name began to gain prominence among the sport's insiders. After World War II, he was active in the formation of the Illinois Section of the PGA. And in 1949, Jemsek and Charlie Nash of Mission Hills helped create broadcast history. Together, the two pioneered the first nationally televised golf program called "Pars, Birdies and Eagles." The 30-minute syndicated program featured an entertaining mix of celebrity interviews, golfing tips, rules discussion and viewer mail. The show gave way to another one, the long-running "Shell All Stars of Golf."

During this time, Joe continued to look for more area clubs to run. And in the '50s he found two—Fairlawn (which he renamed Fresh Meadow) and Cog Hill. The Fresh Meadow venture was a leased operation, while Jemsek purchased Cog Hill outright from Marty Coghill. Although Joe doesn't operate Fresh Meadow today, his company does manage two other leased courses—Pine Meadow and Glenwoodie.

While Jemsek is closely associated with championship-style courses for the public, he is also known as a generous individual who rarely says no to charitable organizations, amateur golfing associations and high school golf teams. For the acclaim he has deservedly earned during his lifetime—with a little pleasure mixed in—Joe has clearly given more to the game than he has taken from it. His generosity has not gone unnoticed.

Throughout his many years, he has received countless awards and honors. In addition to being inducted into the Illinois PGA Hall of Fame, Joe Jemsek was:

- The recipient of the Herb Graffis Award from the National Golf Foundation.

- Given the Distinguished Service Award from the Chicago District Golf Association.

- Named the Illinois PGA Professional of the Year.

- Awarded the Gold Medal of Appreciation from the Western Golf Association.

- Recognized by *Golf Magazine* as one of golf's 100 heroes.

- Recognized in 1991 by *Golf Digest* as one of the game's 36 most powerful figures.

- The first from the public golfing sector to serve on the USGA's Executive Committee.

Not one to rest on his laurels, he remains active in all phases of his golfing empire. It isn't unusual to see him at all of his clubs on a daily basis during the summer months. While his son Frank is now the company's primary administrator, Joe has no plans to slow down. In fact, the elder Jemsek continues to blaze new trails.

In 1991, his Dubsdread course played host to the Western Open. It represented a dream come true for Jemsek—never before had one of his courses held a PGA event. And if Joe has his way, the Western Open will never leave.

Architects

Some residents may recall the days when the PGA and the National Golf Foundation had Chicago headquarters. Though both now operate out of Florida, Chicago is home to another service organization whose members are among golf's biggest names. The organization is the American Society of Golf Course Architects (ASGCA).

Even before the society's formation in 1947, Chicago had benefitted by the presence of celebrated architects. Though H.S. Colt, Alister Mackenzie and Donald Ross were only visitors, when they finished their project and departed, they would always leave another fine example of early golf course architecture.

Those Chicagoans who were part of the architectural trade made their impact, too. Clearly, C.B. Macdonald heads this list, although he left Chicago for good in 1900—but not before leaving his current legacy in Wheaton.

It fell upon the shoulders of H.J. Tweedie, James Foulis and, later, Tom Bendelow to carry Chicago's golf course architectural load from the 1890s to 1920. While these Chicago residents didn't achieve the critical acclaim of Macdonald or Ross, they were, at least, busy. Among the three, they laid out most of Chicago's earliest courses.

During the robust building years of the 1920s, the quality of new layouts improved dramatically. Bendelow, then in his architectural prime, laid out all three Medinah courses plus those at the Lincolnshire and Naperville Country Clubs. Other local architects such as Bill Langford (Bryn Mawr, Ridgemoor, Riverside and Ruth Lake), C.D. Wagstaff (Tam O'Shanter and the current-day Twin Orchard) and Joe Roseman (Barrington Hills and Crystal Lake) further enhanced the reputation of Chicago course architects. These men, along with Len Macomber, Charles Maddox, George O'Neil, Ed Dearie Jr. and Stan Pelchar were Chicago's architectural masters. For most, the 1920s represented their final decade of glory.

By the time the Depression and World War II had passed, the holdovers were few, only Langford, Pelchar and Maddox. There was one other local architect making his national mark—Robert Bruce Harris.

It was Harris who pushed the hardest to organize a national association of fellow architects. Mission accomplished in 1947, fellow members voted Harris ASGCA's first president. In addition to his leadership role, Harris led the way in designing courses that could be economically maintained. For example, a Harris course would often feature many oval-shaped bunkers. Aesthetics aside, they were designed primarily to allow cutting mowers an easy and quick one-time pass around their perimeters.

Perhaps his most important contribution was as a teacher. Harris trained many who would go out on their own as successful course architects. Those with a strong Chicago connection are Edward Lawrence Packard, David Gill, Ken Killian and Dick Nugent. These four have dominated the Chicago architectural scene ever since leaving the Harris wing. Packard was the first to design local golf course residential community courses. Gill's résumé includes Village Links of Glen Ellyn and Tamarack, among others. Killian and Nugent were Chicago's most successful designing team ever. Though they dissolved their partnership in the early '80s, each has remained active.

In particular, Dick Nugent Associates has zoomed into national and international prominence. Locally, Nugent's recent works include: Seven Bridges, Bull Valley, Ivanhoe,

Glendale Lakes, Arboretum, Oak Brook Hills and Royal Fox. Furthermore, this Highland Park native works with the Cook County Forest Preserve District in redesign projects on its courses. Add to this list his out-of-state projects and it's easy to understand why many consider Nugent the top Chicago-based architect today.

Two others making their presence felt are Roger Packard (Edward's son) and Bob Lohmann. Packard has a résumé that includes Cantigny, Eagle Brook, the redesign at Medinah No. 3 and projects in Texas, Indiana, Wisconsin and the Far East. Lohmann (who worked in the Nugent/Killian concern) was the primary architect at Boulder Ridge and is working with Ed Oldfield at The Merit Club. No doubt Packard and Lohmann are the heir apparents to the Nugents, Gills and Killians.

Rules and Rule Makers

When the Chicago District Golf Association (CDGA) held its 50th anniversary "Golden Tee" dinner in 1964, the evening's highlight was an awards ceremony in honor of three men. Filled with names representing Chicago Who's Who, the audience that night included Mayor Richard J. Daley, announcer Jack Brickhouse, columnist Irv Kupcinet and golfing legends Walter Hagen and Byron Nelson. On this occasion, though, the spotlight was on the three award recipients: Bob Hope, Bing Crosby and Tom McMahon.

As golf's unofficial goodwill ambassadors, Hope and Crosby had earned the CDGA's recognition because of their many appearances at local fund-raising events. The evening's other celebrant, Tom McMahon, wasn't as famous. In fact, few current-day golfers probably recognize McMahon's name. But the former president of the CDGA did leave an important legacy: he is credited with creating the modern golf handicap system.

His handicap formula is a good example of what Chicago-based golf associations have done, and continue to do, for area golfers. For the most part, Chicago's golfers just want to play golf. They don't pay much attention to the structure behind their sport. While most have heard of the CDGA, Western Golf Association, Illinois Junior and Women's Western Golf Association, among others, the typical player has little idea what these groups really do.

Associations "promote golf." They have, through the years, contributed greatly to the growth and vitality of the sport. It's important, then, to look at why associations formed, what services and programs they provide and how all local players are influenced by them.

But this chapter is not only about associations. In addition to analyzing the McMahon handicap system, the following pages look at the new slope system, why a golfer

Courtesy of Chicago District Golf Association

*A.W. Hale, Tom McMahon and Sam Byrd at the 1946
Chicago Victory Open. McMahon was the father of the
modern-day handicap formula.*

should establish a personal handicap, the rulebook—the
important tool most golfers lack, golfing etiquette and
Village Links' pioneering "Keep Pace Program."

McMahon's Handicap System Breakthrough

Handicaps are the "giving of strokes" that permit
players of unequal skills to compete against each other fairly. Although handicap systems have been a part of the sport
since the 18th century, it wasn't until 1912 that the United
States Golf Association adopted its own procedure for
determining a handicap.

In the 1930s, Tom McMahon introduced a new factor
to correct what he felt was a basic inequity. In the old
system, two golfers who shot identical scores were considered equal in ability. Since both golfers were "equally"
skilled, neither was allowed a handicap or extra strokes,
at least when playing against each other. McMahon saw
a problem with this logic. He reasoned that if Andy Ander-

son scored 72 on Chicago's toughest course and Bill Baker took his 72 on Chicago's easiest course, the scores may have been the same but the players' respective skill levels weren't. Andy was the better golfer. He should give some handicap to Bill. But what?

Enter McMahon's modification to the handicap system—the course rating formula. By taking into account respective scores and factoring in course difficulty, McMahon sought to establish a fairer handicap system.

McMahon established that there would be a standard or reference point—a course rating—that would be tied directly to how an excellent or scratch golfer would score. For example, a scratch player might shoot 76 on Chicago's most difficult course and a 66 at the easiest. If these were the respective course ratings, Andy Anderson would have to offer 10 strokes to Bill Baker. Thus, what was an apparent inequity had become quantifiable and correctable with the McMahon system.

Today, nearly every course has a course rating. Where there are multiple tee boxes per hole, offering different course lengths, there are multiple course ratings. Most courses also are rated for women golfers. Note the four course ratings and course lengths at Kemper Lakes:

Distance (yards)	Course Rating
7,217	75.7
6,680	73.1
6,265	71.1
5,638 (women's tees)	73.5 (women's course rating)

Assuming McMahon's excellent (male) golfer played to his normal ability, he would shoot almost five strokes higher on the 7,217-yard layout than the shorter 6,262-yard layout. Does this mean that longer courses are always tougher than shorter ones? Not necessarily. The following Chicago courses all have a 70.1 course rating for at least one of their playing lengths. But look at the yardage:

Site	Course Yardage
Carriage Greens	6,451
St. Andrews No. 2	6,425
Village Links	6,361
Ridge	6,224
Forest Preserve National	6,175

Forest Preserve National, 276 yards shorter than Carriage Greens, has the same rating of 70.1. Obviously, there must be other elements on its course that add difficulty.

McMahon tried to incorporate in his formula all the components of a course that add to its challenge. The length of a course is only one consideration. He added 10 more:

1) Topography—difficulty of stance in landing area and the vertical angle of shot from landing area into the green.

2) Fairway—effective width and depth of landing area, which can be reduced by a dogleg, trees or fairway slope.

3) Recoverability and rough—near the landing area and the green.

4) Out-of-bounds—near the landing area and around the green.

5) Water hazards—near the landing area and around green.

6) Trees—strategic location, size, height and number.

7) Bunkers—how many and how near the landing area and around green.

8) Green target—size, firmness, shape and slope of green in relation to the normal length of approach shot.

9) Green surfaces—contour and normal speed of putting surfaces.

10) Psychological—mental effect on play created by obstacles near the target area.

McMahon's formula first went into effect locally. Not long afterwards, the USGA incorporated his system, along with others who added their own twists, into the USGA's official handicap formula. The course rating factor went a long way to perfect the handicap system. But a further refinement came along, this one a little more complicated.

The Slope System

In 1982, the USGA introduced a major change in the handicap system. It took a few years to implement nationally, but as of March 1, 1991, the USGA's slope system became the law of the land.

Slope didn't replace course ratings; instead, it strengthened the basic handicap formula. "Slope," by the way, does not refer to a course's contour, but rather to a line on a graph that shows that, as the difficulty of the course increases, an average player's score increases at a higher rate than the scratch player's score. In other words, the more difficult the golf course is, it becomes increasingly more difficult for the less skilled player than it does for the player who normally scores well. Slope is a new word in golf today. Naturally, its meaning and application still create confusion.

First, let's eliminate one source of confusion. Slope is not a substitute for course ratings. Course ratings indicate the degree of difficulty between courses—specifically, how a scratch golfer would play each one. They can be thought of in terms of strokes. They continue to be used to determine handicap. Slope ratings, on the other hand, offer the average or bogey player an idea of a single course's difficulty in relation to the difficulty faced by a scratch golfer on the same course. Slope ratings are now also used to determine handicap.

There are courses in Chicago that have slope ratings below 100. The highest slope rating in Chicago is 147, at Medinah's No. 3 course—played from its championship tees. The USGA considers courses having a 113 slope rating as moderate; 125 and above, a high slope rating; and below 100, a low slope rating. What do these numbers really mean?

Consider a few examples. Imagine an 18-hole course with no traps, no thick rough and wide-open fairways. All the holes (except for the par 3s) measure 380 yards and have a small stream dissecting each fairway exactly 280 yards away. The scratch golfer is apt to average drives of 250 to 260 yards. The bogey golfer will hit his drive 180 to 190 yards. For each golfer's second shot to the green, the small stream has no effect. The hole, and others on this course, presents an obstacle that leads to the course having a moderate slope rating. In other words, the degree of obstacle difficulty for both golfers is the same.

In the second example, the stream is now located 190 yards from the tee, on every hole (an omnipresent stream). While it again has zero effect on the scratch golfer, the bogey golfer is affected. Since his drive will not clear the stream, he must "club-down," so his drive will roll short of the stream. In turn, this results in a long second shot, where his ball will probably not land on the green. A course exhibiting a disadvantage for the average player, in comparison to the scratch player's game, is defined as a high sloped course.

The final example finds the stream 250 yards out from every tee; it is exactly where the scratch golfer's drive would land. Now he must club-down. The average player is not threatened by the stream, either for his drive or second shot to the green. In this case, the course has a low slope rating.

It's important to avoid the common misconception that the term slope represents course difficulty. It doesn't. McMahon's course rating remains the exclusive definition of a course's respective difficulty. Slope is only a reference of difficulty faced by the average compared to the scratch player on a particular course.

In the Chicago area, measurements to determine a course's slope are taken by a CDGA rating team and then computed mathematically. The same obstacle factors that determine course ratings are evaluated at each hole. Point values of zero to 10 are assigned each factor, zero suggesting no obstacle and 10, the greatest obstacle possible. The points are totaled and then averaged for each hole. This is done first from the view of a scratch player and then, a bogey player. It is the difference in these averages totaled for all 18 holes that determine slope rating. The maximum slope any course could have is 180 (10 times 18 holes). The highest slope rating in the country is 150 at Pine Valley in New Jersey.

Let's review the slope ratings of the five courses used in the course rating example. Each had a 70.1 course rating.

Course	Distance	Slope
Carriage Greens	6,451	119
St. Andrews No. 2	6,425	112
Village Links	6,361	117
Ridge	6,224	127
Forest Preserve National	6,175	121

These slope numbers offer a hint of how each course's obstacles would affect an average and a scratch player's game. An average player would find that his score would be negatively influenced at Ridge. On the other hand, the average golfer is less affected by St. Andrews' various obstacles. There is, in fact, the likelihood the average player will post his normal score, while the scratch golfer's score might be a stroke or two higher than his norm.

The slope handicap system is employed to create fairness in the handicap system for average golfers. Take two golfers of different skill levels and direct them to a course exhibiting equal obstacle challenges. If they play their normal game, chances are their final scores will reflect their typical 18-hole margin. Now put the same two golfers on a course where the various hole obstacles affect the less-skilled player to a greater degree. The difference in their 18-hole margins will widen. Without the benefit of the slope factor in handicap computation, the less-skilled player always will be at a disadvantage. Since the handicap concept is to "equalize" players of different abilities, the slope handicap system does provide for additional stroke compensation.

To illustrate slope in practical terms, two friends venture from their normal neighborhood club and accept an invitation to play Medinah's No. 3 course. At his home club, Gil Goodplayer normally shoots 80, while Ned Notsogood shoots 100. The course there has a slope rating of 120. Gil gives his friend 20 strokes to make their Medinah match equal. Is this fair?

Based on the pre-slope system, 20 strokes would have been too many actually. With the new slope formula in effect, however, Ned needs a 25-stroke margin to equalize the match. Medinah's slope rating is a high 142; it is much tougher for a less-skilled player.

The following week, the two players visit Westgate Valley. Gil Goodplayer again gives 20 strokes to Ned. In this example, Gil has been too generous, since the course has a 113 slope rating. Instead, only 19 strokes are necessary to provide an equal match.

The pre-slope system and the current slope system for determining respective handicaps follow:

Pre-Slope

Handicap differential =
Adjusted score – USGA Course Rating

1) Average 10 lowest handicap differentials of last 20 scores

2) Multiply by 0.96

3) Round off to the nearest whole number

4) Identify as USGA Handicap Number

With Slope

Handicap differential

$$= \frac{(\text{Adjusted score} - \text{USGA Course Rating}) \times 113}{\text{Course Slope Rating}}$$

1) Total lowest 10 handicap differentials of last 20 scores

2) Multiply total by 0.096

3) Delete all numbers after tenths digit

4) Identify as USGA Handicap Index

Once a golfer receives an official handicap index, he consults the "Course Handicap Table" at the course to be played to get his handicap. Located in the locker room or pro shop, the chart contains conversion tables. The player's handicap index is converted to a new number, which indicates the number of handicap strokes the golfer is allowed on that particular layout.

Just as McMahon's course rating improvement achieved nearly 50 years ago, slope rating will further strengthen the handicap system. These two modifications provide, in combination, an accurate judgment of a golfer's handicap allowance. As such, they minimize pre-play debate on the game's age-old dilemma; namely, how many strokes should one player offer another. Considering friendly competition is ingrained in most golfers' characters and that a typical golfing foursome brings together players of different skill levels, the new slope system does provide a formula in which all players can compete fairly. The match's ultimate winner will be that golfer who performs the best within his normal standard—and isn't that the way it should be?

A handicap index—is it worth the effort?

Of the nearly one million golfers in the Chicago region, perhaps as many as 800,000 don't have an official handicap index. Many feel it's not a prerequisite to teeing off and they're right. But, it's also true the more seriously you take your golf game, the greater the need for a handicap index.

Chicago's private club members are more apt to carry an official handicap card than the public golfer. In fact, the majority of country club members use an official handicap. It's easy to see why. When a club member finishes his game, he gives his scorecard to the club pro, assistant pro or someone else who will then record his score. Whether a club employee or the Chicago District Golf Association calculates the handicap index and thus the member's official handicap is, in this case, irrelevant. What is important is that the member has this service provided to him.

The public golfer doesn't have it as easy. Some who play a home course regularly will also have the handicap service provided to them by the public-course operator. This is especially true at major public daily-fee and municipal courses such as Village Links, Pine Meadow, Cog Hill and others. If, however, a public golfer visits many different courses, without a "home site," the player must record his score, the course's slope rating and course rating. At this point, he mails the information to an independent handicap rating service that performs the various calculations. For most public players, the bother is just too great. While many public players would like to have an official handicap, they never follow through. Inertia soon sets in and the need for a handicap is rationalized away.

For informal matches among friends, a handicap isn't crucial, but it would probably settle a few pre-first-tee discussions. As illustrated earlier, two players normally separated by 10 strokes won't have a problem determining a stroke differential if they often play at the same course. When they visit a far tougher or easier layout, the stroke differential changes. This is where the discussion becomes sometimes heated as to what is "fair."

Sanctioned amateur events do require official handicaps. How else could there exist a fair system for evaluating the playing proficiency of a crowd of golfing strangers?

For those who will never compete in amateur tournaments or for others who don't play golf but once or twice a season, there is still an important reason to have a correctly calculated handicap.

This involves the instinctive desire to show skill improvement. Since handicaps reflect basic proficiencies, personal pride is enhanced by lowering a handicap over time—in other words, becoming better at the sport. Obviously, handicaps can also increase. While it is no fun to admit proficiency has slipped, a handicap in itself shouldn't be blamed for highlighting the bad news—remember it's just the messenger. Besides, the good news coming out of the bad is the benefit of receiving additional strokes.

Rules to golf by

Golf is one of those rare sports where the player keeps track of his own score. With the current 128-page USGA Rulebook containing 34 specific rules and 123 differentiations, it's highly unlikely few players, if any, know all of them.

When golf was far simpler, C.B. Macdonald and his friends played the game under golf's original 13 rules. No doubt, many who play today would welcome a return to the following:

The Original 13 Rules of Golf

1) You must tee your ball within a club length of the (prior) hole.

2) Your tee must be upon the ground.

3) You are not to change the ball which you strike off the tee.

4) You are not to remove stones, bones, or any broken club for the sake of playing your ball, except upon the fair green, and that only within a club length of your ball.

5) If your ball comes among water or any watery filth, you are at liberty to take out your ball and throw it behind the hazard six yards at least; you may play it with any club, and allow your adversary a stroke so getting out your ball.

6) If your balls be found anywhere touching one another, you are to lift the first ball until you play the last.

7) At holing you are to play your ball honestly for the hole and not to play upon your adversary's ball, not lying in your way.

8) If you should lose your ball by its being taken up or any other way you are to go back to the spot where you struck last and drop another ball and allow your adversary a stroke for the misfortune.

9) No man at holing his ball is to be allowed to mark his way to the hole with his club or anything else.

10) If a ball is stopped by any person, horse, dog or anything else, the ball so stopped must be played where it lies.

11) If you draw your club in order to strike and proceed so far with your stroke as to be bringing down your club, if then your club should break in any way, it is to be accounted a stroke.

12) He whose ball lies furthest from the hole is obliged to play first.

13) Neither trench, ditch, or dike made for the preservation of the links, nor the Scholars' Holes, nor the Soldiers' Lines shall be accounted a hazard, but the ball is to be taken out, teed, and played with any iron club.

These 13 rules with their succinct definitions were easy to understand. For example, the "lost ball" rule was basic, taking only 40 words to explain.

In today's game, this same "misfortune" encompasses several pages in golf's rulebook. Rule 25-1, for example, specifically relates to lost balls in casual water; Rule 26-1 explains proper procedures if balls are lost in water hazards; Rule 26-2b addresses lost balls in unplayable hazards and out-of-bounds areas. The definition of a "lost" ball is further studied in Rule 27. Though these lost ball rulings can be understood eventually, they probably aren't always followed. Considering the number of rules and their complexity, is there any doubt as to why so many are unaware of all the game's correct procedures?

Downers Grove Golf Course posts some of its course rules.

Scorecards at several area courses prominently display the phrase: "When the rules are broken, the game ceases to be golf." In the strictest sense, this is true. But the typical player adheres to the sport's laws about as often as the average cab driver follows the rules of the road.

Paradoxically, players adhere to "local club rules" more closely. In large part, the compliance is due simply to the course's scorecard where the local rules are outlined. Generally, the card's format will dictate that all USGA's rules apply, and then define any specific exceptions. Furthermore, local rules often provide options. At the Thunderbird Country Club, for example, club rules indicate "private property as out-of-bounds." For some players, this statement is apparently not emphatic enough, so Thunderbird adds: "Balls must not be played from private property." Even the most uninformed golfer gets the message.

Specific applications of USGA rules on local courses do solve dilemmas. Those who have watched the Palmers and Normans perform may encounter a situation never seen on televised events. At Foss Park and Deer Creek, local rules advise "Ball striking power lines must be replayed." Happily, no penalty stroke is subtracted.

Often, club rules save strokes. This explains why golfers read the fine print, predictably, at times when they've erred the most.

There always will be occasions to assess one-stroke penalties. But even then, the local club rules can be more advantageous than the standard USGA ruling. Perhaps the most common example is the out-of-bounds shot. At many local public courses, the penalty rendered is a stroke, whereas the national ruling is stroke and distance. It's an important benefit—one which is only noted by knowing local rules.

Local rules define broader topics such as general policy and expected course demeanor. Considering the sport's increasing appeal, many find the printed information to be a quick reference on the "dos and don'ts" in effect. Sometimes the printed rules are straightforward and fundamental. Other times they address potential infractions of a most peculiar nature. Following is a potpourri of local course rules ranging from the logical to the unusual. In truth, may clubs may have similar policies, but at the following courses the rules are specifically printed on their scorecards.

- No pets on course (Valley Green)
- No mulligans allowed (Brae Loch)
- Buying or selling balls on course is strictly prohibited (Evergreen)
- Climbing fences and wading in lakes is prohibited (Walnut Greens)
- No coolers on course (many)
- Excessive drinking will not be tolerated (Old Orchard)
- No profanity (Deer Creek)
- Bathing attire is not condoned (Renwood)
- No woods to be used on course (Lake Park)
- In case of lightning all golfers must evacuate golf course (Riverside Park)
- Ladies not allowed on course or green with high heeled shoes (Par Three)
- Don't wear shoes with heels less than two inches wide (Pistakee)
- No boots allowed (Boughton Ridge)
- All players must wear shirts and shoes (many)

- Ranger will enforce 7-stroke rule when necessary (Randall Oaks)
- Ranger will enforce 8-stroke rule from the tee to holing out (Villa Olivia)
- Each player must have his own set of clubs (many)
- All players must have at least five clubs (Deerfield)
- Each player must have a bag and at least 3 clubs plus putter (Urban Hills)
- All players must have at least 3 clubs (Boughton Ridge)
- Children under 14 not permitted unless approved (Urban Hills)
- No player under 12 without club pro permission (Lake Park)
- No players under 10 years of age (Walnut Greens)
- Golfers under 9 must be accompanied by a parent (Apple Orchard)
- No children under 8 (Park Forest)
- Children under 6 not allowed on course (Apple Orchard)
- All golfers must play with one ball (many)
- Playing with range balls prohibited (Park Forest)

As much as they might wish, course operators could never have the necessary scorecard space to educate golfers on etiquette. Printing the simple statement of "observe proper course etiquette" is about as close as most come. Other facilities may provide a few additional hints such as raking sand traps, repairing ball marks, replacing divots and avoiding tees and greens while driving or pulling carts.

Poor etiquette isn't exhibited by all golfers, but all golfers are affected by the few who either ignore the niceties of the sport or who have never learned them. Even the poorest player who recognizes accepted course behavior is a far more enjoyable companion than one oblivious to golf's code of conduct—regardless of his playing proficiency.

While an unraked bunker or an unrepaired divot on the green diminishes the game for fellow golfers, nothing so aggravates avid golfers as that primarily etiquette-related nemesis—slow play.

Playing behind the sport's most feared players, *the dalliers*, is the most dreaded fate of enthusiasts. Unfortunately, most golfers have suffered this painful experience.

Speed of play is a major problem facing golfers and course operators today.

"The Keep Pace Program"

Considered the brainchild of Matt Pekarek at Glen Ellyn's Village Links, the program's objective is to shorten the time for a round of golf. To achieve this, Pekarek devised a system defining a foursome's speed of play. Foursomes playing "slow" can be identified when the time intervals between groups increase from hole to hole. For example, the normal interval between two foursomes on the first hole may be seven or eight minutes. By the last hole, the gap may be 10 or 12 minutes. Though the difference is only a few minutes, all the following foursomes are similarly slowed. With *each* hole taking three to four minutes more to play, a typical four-hour morning round by late afternoon becomes a 5-to-5½-hour round.

Pekarek had observed this slowdown at Village Links in 1978 and wondered why all foursomes couldn't somehow maintain a regular interval. The Keep Pace Program accomplished this goal—amazingly, by changing the behavior of the golfing public.

The program's success was tied to communicating the benefits of a speedier round through a marketing effort highlighting the Keep Pace logo. Keep Pace timers delivered the message. The program was deemed an immediate success after its 1979 debut. Rounds of five hours turned into 4½-hour rounds from dawn to dusk. A post-season survey of Village Links' players indicated 88% endorsed the Keep Pace Program and requested its continuation. Respondents also suggested tougher penalties for slow players; therefore, the following year, foursomes were required to maintain regular intervals for at least two-thirds of their rounds. Consistently failing to keep pace resulted in the loss of regular tee times. By the end of the second year, rounds quickened to a four-hour pace—about the same as the 1991 pace. Today, the Keep Pace Program is successfully used nationwide.

Western Golf Association

Golf was in its infancy when the Western Golf Association formed in 1899. At the time, only a few clubs existed, all private, with the oldest not even six years old. In the broadest sense, the primary objective of the WGA was to further the sport's development in the "West." This geographical consideration led to the rejection of the initially proposed name, Associated Golf Clubs of Chicago. Indeed, the group's founders were cognizant of golf's unlimited potential and geographical expansion.

There were two additional factors behind WGA's formation. The first involved the United States Golf Association, which began in 1894. While the USGA was the sport's official national governing body, its headquarters were out East as were the vast majority of USGA's 139 golf club members. Concerned that "an autocratic body run by the East" would pay short shrift to clubs located elsewhere, the WGA began as a kind of intermediary between the national association and "western" clubs. The WGA's other priority was starting its own national Amateur and Open championship events. Before the year had passed, the inaugural Western Open and Western Amateur tournaments were in the books.

Somewhat surprisingly, the individual recognized as the "father of the Western Golf Association" served as the No. 2 man on the founding board. Arthur Bowen of the Riverside Golf Club spearheaded WGA's creation, but at its start was the association's vice president. Perhaps because of a feeling the WGA needed a nationally recognized name for its first president, Hobart C. Chatfield-Taylor from the prestigious Onwentsia Club gladly accepted. George R. Thorne (Midlothian Country Club) and Phelps B. Hoyt (Glen View Golf and Polo Club) filled the remaining two positions on the executive committee. Besides these four clubs, six others helped form the WGA: Evanston Golf Club, Skokie Country Club, and Chicago Golf Club, along with the now extinct Belmont Golf Club, Edgewater Golf Club and Westward Ho Golf Club.

By 1904, the WGA had extended its eligibility area to a 500-mile radius; consequently, the association's membership roster soared to 57 clubs. Growth continued briskly throughout the next three decades, enough so that the Western Golf Association was regional in name alone. By the 1930s, a total of 525 clubs were members, from Buffalo to the West Coast and beyond. Even the Oahu Country Club in Honolulu was a WGA member.

Entrance to the Western Golf Association in Golf, Illinois.

During its long history, the WGA has endured, despite several crises and a number of thorny disputes. Perhaps predictably, one of WGA's major adversaries early in the century was the USGA. On a number of occasions, the USGA sought to consolidate all sectional and regional golfing associations under its rule. This never proved successful despite putting the WGA and other groups in a decidedly defensive posture.

The WGA did, however, fight back. For example, in 1921, the WGA initiated new rules for unplayable lies, lost balls and out-of-bounds rulings. It also approved steel shafts in its tournaments.

Proprietary pride aside, the WGA is most known for its annual championships and the Chick Evans Scholars Foundation. In truth, both are synonymous with the "Western" name.

The Western's first two tournaments took place in September 1899 at the Glen View Club. The amateur event drew the most attention. From an almost entirely local field, David Forgan defeated another Onwentsia Club entrant to win the first Western Amateur championship. The one-day 36-hole Western Open was held during the same week. A total of 18 participated—two amateurs and 16 local professionals. Willie Smith, the club professional at Midlothian, defeated another Scottish pro—Laurie Auchterlonie of the Glen View Club—to capture his trophy and $125 of the total $300 purse. While the Western Amateur was played the following year, the Open wasn't. Organizers were disappointed with the small entry field of the 1899 event.

Since then, however, the Western Open has grown beyond what its founders imagined. The country's second oldest major tournament and oldest PGA Tour event, its winners have included golf's biggest names—Hagen, Palmer, Nicklaus, Watson and Anderson—and along the way, the WGA awarded more then $10 million in prize money. Held locally through out its early years, the Western Open moved around outside the area—once never visiting a Chicago site for two decades. In the '60s, the tournament returned to Chicago and rotated its sites annually until finally settling in at Butler National from 1974 to 1990. The WGA added another chapter in the tourney's history in 1991, when Cog Hill's public Dubsdread layout hosted its first Western Open.

The Western Amateur, like the Open, also has visited different clubs in and out of the area. The Western Amateur's permanent site is Point O'Woods in Benton Harbor, Mich. Included among the Amateur event's champions are familiar names like Crenshaw, Nicklaus, Strange, Weiskopf and Evans. In Evans' case, Chicago's greatest golfer won the Western Amateur an unprecedented eight times. He also won the 1910 Western Open, but, as an amateur, was ineligible to collect the $200 first prize.

In fact, the issue of money took on a greater importance in 1916—the year Evans became the first golfer to register wins in the U.S. Amateur and U.S. Open during the same year. After consulting with his mother, Evans decided to remain an amateur forever. From that point on, the hardest decision was what to do with the income he received from instruction, phonograph record royalties and the escalating endorsement fees he earned. Evans later

Courtesy of Chicago District Golf Association

Chicago's most famous golfer ever—Chick Evans.

reflected that it was his mother's idea that the supplementary income should be directed to scholarships for former caddies.

In 1928, the WGA agreed to administer the Evans trust—two years later, the first two recipients entered Northwestern University. By 1935, the program turned into the Evans Scholars Foundation.

To date, the WGA and other golfing associations have raised enough money to provide more than 6,000 scholarships. There are, in fact, more than 5,000 college graduates of the program. The Evans Scholars Foundation is the largest individually supported scholarship program in the world. Funding is provided by several sources, including the Evans Scholars Alumni, the Western Open tournament and contributions of $10 to $100 from nearly 200,000 worldwide golfers of the "Bag-Tag" and the "Par Club" programs.

Evans, of course, learned the game as a caddy and was proficient enough to win a total of 54 championships in his six-decade career. But, as he said in 1977, the biggest thrill in his lifetime was the success of the Evans Scholars Foundation. Fortunately, through the efforts of the WGA, the legacy continues.

Women's Western Golf Association

The "other" Western golfing association also has played a prominent role for its member clubs. Organized in 1901, the Women's Western Golf Association spun off from the WGA and chartered its own organization in 1903. Although originally comprised of member clubs within a 500-mile radius of Chicago, WWGA now covers the entire country. More than 500 clubs are current members, representing 42 states. The Illinois contingent is the largest, however, accounting for more than 90 clubs alone.

During WWGA's 90-year history, the group has sponsored a bevy of prestigious tournaments, such as the Western Women's Amateur—the country's oldest uninterrupted championship event—the Junior championship and the Senior championship. The group also paved the way for the LPGA Open championship. This was discontinued in 1968, its membership instead opting to concentrate exclusively on amateur competitions.

Like its corresponding male association, the WWGA is active in charitable causes. In 1971, the group established an auxiliary organization—the Women's Western Golf Foundation, designed to advance women in scholastic and golfing endeavors.

While the WWGA, along with its foundation, is national in scope, it maintains a strong local bent. Nearly one-third of its 75-person volunteer board live in the Chicago area, and 39 of the group's 43 former presidents have been from the area.

The Chicago District Golf Association

With the WGA and the WWGA becoming broader in geographical makeup, it isn't surprising that another association would organize, its mission to concentrate on more local matters. The Chicago District Golf Association formed in 1914. Francis S. Peabody of the Hinsdale Golf Club, later the CDGA's first president, spearheaded the effort. There were 25 original member clubs:

Beverly	Midlothian
Calumet	Old Elm
Chicago	Onwentsia
Edgewater*	Park Ridge
Evanston	Ravisloe
Exmoor	Skokie
Glen Oak	South Shore (no longer
Glen View	private)
Hinsdale	Westmoreland
Homewood (Flossmoor)	Westward Ho*
Idlewild	Wheaton*
La Grange	Windsor*
Lake Shore	Winnetka (Indian Hill)

*No longer in existence

Today, the CDGA includes more than 200 member clubs, private and public, in four states. The majority are private and within the Chicago district.

Throughout its history, the CDGA has provided services for the local golfer, including legal advice, a base for golfing employment and caddy service standardization. Currently, the CDGA assists its 80,000 members representing more than 200 golfing organizations by:

- organizing tournaments
- processing handicap computations
- interpreting rules of the game
- measuring courses and determining course and slope ratings
- conducting seminars for member clubs
- providing general information for visiting and resident golfing enthusiasts

In 1944, the CDGA formed an auxiliary organization— the Chicago District Golf Foundation, which was responsible for the organization of the Chicago Victory National golf championships during World War II. Money collected from these events helped fund the construction of nine-hole courses at local VA hospitals. Other revenue received was given to organizations such as the Shriners Hospital for Crippled Children, Salvation Army and the USO. To date, more than $2 million has been raised and distributed to charitable groups within the Chicago area.

There is now another major thrust of the CDGF, this one intra-sport related. Involving turfgrass research, it assists member clubs in finding effective ways to combat one of the sport's greatest concerns, namely turfgrass disease.

If there's a common misconception about the duties of the CDGA, it is the belief the organization spends most of its time processing handicaps. While this is an important responsibility, it is not the most time consuming. Organizing tournaments is. In all, about 30 events are staged annually, highlighted by the Amateur and Illinois State championships. Other tournaments are also organized for a variety of men's and women's championships— for all age groups. The CDGA also conducts qualifying rounds of USGA events, including the U.S. Open, U.S. Amateur, U.S. Women's Amateur, and U.S. Junior and Senior Amateurs. The tournament program is funded entirely from entry fees paid by individuals.

Illinois Junior Golf Association

One of the region's newest associations, the Illinois Junior Golf Association, formed in 1967. Mike Spinello is its founder. During its first year, it held three Junior Open tournaments, capped off with a season-ending championship event. Reflecting the interest of golf by teenage boys and girls, the 1991 schedule features 19 tournaments— played in the following seven categories:

- Junior Open
- Illinois Junior
- "B" Division Clinic
- Father Son/Daughter Team
- Chick Evans Junior Open
- Junior Team
- Tournament of Champions

Golf's junior citizens need not belong to an organized club to enter events sponsored by the IJGA; they simply pay a nominal entry fee.

In 1991, the IJGA merged with the CDGA and the Illinois PGA organizations—a move that should strengthen its role in bringing tourney competition to interested youngsters.

As do other local associations, the IJGA aids junior golfers with scholarships. Currently, the IJGA awards three grants annually. A 30-person volunteer board governs the IJGA.

To Sum It Up

Golf, the social game it is, lends itself to being a sport influenced by golfing associations. It's also true that most area golfers don't belong to one. Whether these players ever seek the benefits of local golf associations is not the issue. What's important is that local golfers, regardless of any club or organization affiliations, are the beneficiaries of a very healthy golfing market and the structure that supports it.

16

The Long and the Short of It

Representing a Chicago milestone of sorts, 1991 marks the first year more than 5,000 different golf holes are available to play. That's a lot of flagsticks to shoot at! With at least 316 local courses, a golfing zealot could visit a new site every day of the year and take Sundays off. Before mapping a personal itinerary, though, consider four obstacles—time, money, private-club access and—probably the most troublesome—spouse approval.

Understandably, few residents will ever have an opportunity to sample such an expansive local golfing menu. But fortunately, there is an appetizing alternative. It is a meaty proposition, though, one that will test the stomach muscles of any challenger. The task at hand is to play Chicago's 18 longest holes—a par 72 behemoth measuring 8,342 yards.

Actually, this 18-hole "course" isn't conveniently located at one location but rather at 18 sites throughout the region. If a scorecard for the "Gargantuan Golf Course" were printed, it would read as follows:

Gargantuan Golf Course

Hole No.	Par	Distance yards	Site of Hole (and No.)
1	4	484	Fox Lake (No. 17)
2	4	479	Bon Vivant (No. 6)
3	3	250	Ken Loch (No. 3)
4	5	678	Golf Club of Illinois (No. 15)
5	4	477	St. Charles (No. 8)
6	4	472	Pine Meadow (No. 3)
7	4	472	Deerfield (No. 3)
8	3	250	Addison (No. 4)
9	5	626	Urban Hills (No. 16)
Out	36	4,188	

10	4	471	Medinah No. 3 (No. 12)
11	4	470	Village Links (No. 4)
12	3	250	Par Three (No. 9)
13	5	623	Butler National (No. 7)
14	4	471	Tamarack (No. 2)
15	4	471	Green Garden (No. 5)
16	3	250	Broadmoor (No. 18)
17	5	678	Palmira (No. 17)
18	4	470	Stonebridge (No. 4)
In	36	4,154	
Total	72	8,342	

The Gargantuan course features the only four 250-yard par 3s in Chicago. The 10 par 4s average 473 yards, while the par 5s average 651 yards. Playing the course with pin-point accuracy would require a four-and-one-half mile walk (or ride), and players spraying their shots might end up trekking twice as much. The golf club might even mandate a policy that all gas and electric carts be charged or fueled at the nine-hole turn.

While the attraction at Gargantuan is length, the layout isn't short of other hazards. Consider the par 5s, for example. The two 678-yard holes, Palmira and Golf Club of Illinois, each toss in trouble to go along with their mammoth length. Two streams dissect the Indiana monster, while the Illinois hole is bordered by steel-wool-like rough. Called fescue, its unique properties make a golf ball hard to find and even harder to slap out. Butler National's par 5 is the shortest of the quartet though its length is complicated by a dogleg right. There's also a winding creek traversing the Oak Brook hole's right side from the tee to the back of the green. Urban Hills is the "easiest" of the bunch. With two fairway sand traps and a pond near the green, scoring par here shouldn't be too difficult. All that's needed are three well-placed 209-yard shots and two putts. Who said golf was a tough game anyway?

On second thought, maybe three consecutive quality distance shots are pressing the odds—but then again only two are required on each of Gargantuan's 10 par 4s. For the 484-yard Fox Lake representative, two 240-yard pokes are needed to land greenside on the region's longest par 4. At Village Links' 470-yard hole, abundant hazards discourage par hopes. One pond and 10 bunkers—seven around the green—convince even the best players to forget about par and play instead for bogey.

Then there's the "natural" hole at Medinah, a 471-yard par 4, with no water hazards to speak of and nary a sand trap. When the world's best pro golfers played it at the 1990 U.S. Open, the hole computed as the second hardest on the Medinah site—4.31 strokes on the average. They even had the advantage of playing the hole from its shorter length of 462 yards.

In truth, the entire U.S. Open field would find all 4s on Gargantuan's course difficult to par. For Chicago's amateur enthusiasts, the only realistic strategy for scoring par would be to get to the long 4s *eventually* and use a single putt. Saving par with lucky one putts is simply the game's greatest reward.

Good golfing fortune—never in generous supply—might best be saved for the 250-yard par 3s. While some players are blessed with unusual strength, their successful drives to these long par 3s provide an example of golf's cruelest fate. Consider these occurrences as an illustration of the Darwinian principle in reverse. Off the tee, the big hitters are replicates of the perfect physical specimen—well postured, immaculately chiseled, having terrific golfing form and, in general, representing the most advanced species of golf's order.

Once reaching the green, however, the big hitter transforms into a gangling mass of shaky and confused protoplasm—all because of three frustrating putts from 25 feet for a bogey. This is very sad to see.

While the thought of playing such a humbling and potentially embarrassing 8,342-yard layout stirs the imagination, logistical complexities are obvious. With Chicago's longest 18 holes located everywhere from Fox Lake to Frankfort; from St. John, Ind., to Naperville, the "round" might best be arranged by a travel agent specializing in whimsical tours.

There's another, more practical alternative: in this example, a long-distance layout is readily available at Bon Vivant. If the 10-year-old course had been in existence during Horace Greeley's time, he might have uttered: "Go southwest (of Chicago), young man" to Bourbonnais where this staggering 7,498-yard course exists. From the back tees, Bon Vivant is the longest playing course in the Chicago area.

Yielding average 5, 4 and 3 par lengths of 588, 427 and 217 yards respectively, the par 72 course plays to a 76.2 rating. While it's an open layout, nine water hazards come into play—as do 46 well-placed sand traps. Consistent with Bon Vivant's overall theme, the 18 greens are also very large and definite 3-putt possibilities. The Championship course's hole by hole breakdown is shown:

Bon Vivant Scorecard

Hole	Distance, yards	Par
1	360	4
2	570	5
3	446	4
4	241	3
5	595	5
6	479	4
7	200	3
8	445	4
9	462	4
Out	3,798	36
10	598	5
11	419	4
12	403	4
13	200	3
14	348	4
15	442	4
16	233	3
17	469	4
18	588	5
In	3,700	36
Total	7,498	72

If ever there was a course demanding long drives, this is one. In fact, about 20 are needed—including the two for travel to and from the Bourbonnais site. Gasoline costs aside, Bon Vivant is not only a very, very long course, but also one of the best golfing values in the area. The weekday rate is a $12 bargain, although carts are additional.

Bon Vivant and the other 17 Gargantuan courses aren't the only sites to feature lengthy holes. Although some Chicago-area golfers may believe their favorite courses feature endlessly long holes, the majority of holes fall within acceptable distances. Nevertheless, it's interesting to look at a list of the longest holes in the Chicago region from their back tee yardage lengths. Two separate categories are provided—total hole length and total length by individual course hole number. While the following breakout is hopefully without error, it's important to remember clubs often rearrange course distances through remodeling. Golf course holes change. Furthermore, the author—while seeking total accuracy—may have overlooked a deserving entrant. Perhaps the list of Chicago's longest holes may resolve a few friendly arguments and provide a topic for 19th hole conversation.

Longest 3s By Distance

Rank	Distance, yards	Hole No.	Site of Hole
1*	250	3	Ken Loch
1*	250	4	Addison
1*	250	9	Par Three
1*	250	18	Broadmoor
5	248	7	Skokie
6*	245	7	Par Three
6*	245	3	Stonebridge
6*	245	5	Pine Meadow
9	243	15	Nordic Hills
10	242	3	Addison
11*	241	4	Ivanhoe
11*	241	4	Bon Vivant
13*	240	13	Palatine Hills
13*	240	5	Old Wayne
15	239	6	Tamarack
16*	236	9	Four Winds
16*	236	18	Antioch
18*	235	11	Ravisloe
18*	235	17	Fox Bend

*Tie

Longest 3s By Specific Course Hole

Hole No.	Distance, yards	Site of Hole
1	230	Addison
2	234	Edgebrook
3	250	Ken Loch
4	250	Addison
5	245	Pine Meadow
6	239	Tamarack
7	248	Skokie
8	233	Gleason Park & La Grange
9	250	Par Three
10	230	Antioch
11	235	Ravisloe
12	220	Brookwood & Briar Leaf

13	240	Palatine Hills
14	224	Boulder Ridge
15	243	Nordic Hills
16	233	Bon Vivant
17	235	Fox Bend
18	250	Broadmoor

Longest 4s By Distance

Rank	Distance, yards	Hole No.	Site of Hole
1	484	17	Fox Lake
2	479	6	Bon Vivant
3	477	8	St. Charles
4*	472	3	Deerfield
4*	472	3	Pine Meadow
6*	471	12	Medinah No. 3
6*	471	2	Tamarack
6*	471	5	Green Garden
9*	470	4	Village Links
9*	470	13	Village Links
9*	470	9	Silver Lake (North)
9*	470	16	Scherwood
9*	470	18	Hillcrest
9*	470	4	Stonebridge
15*	469	7	Seven Bridges
15*	469	13	White Eagle
15*	469	16	Kemper Lakes
15*	469	7	Ravinia Green
15*	469	15	Balmoral Woods
15*	469	17	Bon Vivant
15*	469	7	Pheasant Valley

*Tie

Longest 4s by Specific Course Hole

Hole No.	Distance, yards	Site of Hole
1	456	Americana (Brute)
2	471	Tamarack
3	472	Deerfield & Pine Meadow
4	470	Stonebridge & Village Links
5	471	Green Garden
6	479	Bon Vivant
7	469	Seven Bridges
8	477	St. Charles
9	470	Silver Lake (North)
10	468	Old Oak
11	455	Stonebridge
12	471	Medinah No. 3
13	470	Village Links
14	465	Highland Woods & Longwood
15	469	Balmoral Woods

16	470	Scherwood
17	484	Fox Lake
18	470	Hillcrest

Longest 5s By Distance

Rank	Distance, yards	Hole No.	Site of Hole
1*	678	15	Golf Club of Illinois
1*	678	17	Palmira
3	626	16	Urban Hills
4	623	7	Butler National
5	614	7	Joe Louis the Champ
6*	613	12	Tamarack
6*	613	11	White Pines (West)
8*	610	9	Big Run
8*	610	9	Shady Lawn (South)
10*	607	11	Americana (Briar Patch)
10*	607	18	Cedar Lake
12	605	17	Chapel Hill
13	602	17	Broadmoor
14*	598	10	Bon Vivant
14*	598	7	Hinsdale
16	595	5	Bon Vivant
17	594	8	Four Winds
18*	593	2	Pinecrest
18*	593	1	Barrington Hills

*Tie

Longest 5s By Specific Course Hole

Hole No.	Distance, yards	Site of Hole
1	593	Barrington Hills
2	593	Pinecrest
3	580	Old Wayne
4	564	River Forest
5	595	Bon Vivant
6	591	White Eagle
7	623	Butler National
8	594	Four Winds
9	610	Shady Lawn (South) & Big Run
10	598	Bon Vivant
11	613	White Pines (West)
12	613	Tamarack
13	567	Oak Brook
14	583	Medinah No. 3
15	678	Golf Club of Illinois
16	626	Urban Hills
17	678	Palmira
18	607	Cedar Lake

Unusually long golf holes have traditionally attracted the average player's interest. Consider the initial exclamations of a first-time visitor at a site exhibiting such a mammoth hole. Inevitably, verbal disbelief turns into an expletive or two. Amusingly, players express these reactions well short of the anticipated challenge, often while scanning the scorecard in the clubhouse—before the round begins.

There exists in golf a certain macabre willingness to suffer. While the sport has been played for centuries, the exact reasons for a golfer's eager acceptance of self-inflicted flagellation remain unanswered—and should be left to the philosophers. Perhaps Aristotle said it best. Though his inherent wisdom preceded the times of the "cleek" or "brassie" or "Ping putter," the great Greek's utterance that "punishment is a sort of medicine" must apply to golfers. But then again Aristotle never once teed it up on a 678-yard par 5.

If a golfer's medicinal relief is only realized through anguish, logic would dictate short holes would provide an ideal elixir. This is not the case, however. Short holes—especially those of par 4 and par 5 variety—are perceived differently. Considered by golfers as almost indefensible, these little softies are approached with no hint of trepidation. Success is the expectation. Just as Sir Edmund Hillary wouldn't climb a foothill, or an accomplished marathon runner wouldn't enter a 5K race, a golfer shrugs off the challenge of a short hole with one of the game's well-worn cliche—"This one is a scoring opportunity."

The reality is these holes are easy only once par or better is attained. For the less successful golfer, playing the "shorties" can be bitterly disappointing. A poor score on such holes cannot be summarily rationalized by such common face-saving excuses as length and difficulty.

For its part, the short hole is honest and unpretentious. Its role on a golf course is sacrificial. In exchange for this assignment, the short hole enters in a kind of "bad joke" mentality with an approaching foursome. While the hole expects to be beaten and *should* be beaten, it should be allowed the privilege of laughing silently at those opponents who fail to register par or better.

As with Gargantuan, there is another Chicago course that is extreme. Referred to as the "Low Yardage Links," the 3,932-yard par 72 is a compilation of various area sites. A golfer must still put the ball in the cup to score but for those players who have never broken par, "Low Yardage Links" is the ultimate opportunity to shoot par.

Low Yardage Links

Hole	Par	Distance, yards	Site of Hole and No.
1	4	100	Barrington Park (No.1)
2	4	192	McArthur (No. 6)
3	3	54	Lake Park (No. 12)
4	5	433	Bonnie Dundee (No. 1)
5	4	227	Lansing (No. 4)
6	4	175	Barrington Park (No. 4)
3	3	55	Lake Park (No. 3)
8	5	432	Foss Park (No. 1)
9	4	228	Lansing (No. 5)
Out	36	1,896	
1	4	209	Chalet (No. 13)
11	3	49	Ramada O'Hare (No. 6)
12	5	425	Prestbury (No. 9)
13	4	215	McArthur (No. 2)
14	4	228	Twin Lakes (No. 1)
15	4	218	Rolling Knolls (No. 8)
16	3	61	Lake Park (No. 6)
17	5	436	Chalet (No. 7)
18	4	195	Barrington Park (No. 3)
In	36	2,036	
Total	72	3,932	

Chicago's single shortest 18-hole facility is the 1,515-yard par 54 Lake Park municipal course in Des Plaines. Featuring 18 wonderful little holes—the longest 115 yards—Lake Park is a fun place to play. While it's extremely busy and popular with all age groups, the course is very well maintained. This is evident especially with the putting greens. Furthermore, the sand traps (there are 24) are filled with legitimate golf course sand. Understandably, woods are not allowed. Actually, the only clubs players need here are a putter, sand and pitching wedge and maybe a 9-iron.

Lake Opeka, a man-made recreational pond borders four holes, though its presence is primarily diversionary— unless a golfer's 60-80 yard wedge shots slice right. By design, Lake Park isn't meant to be intimidating but its diminutive stature shouldn't be confused with ease. Playing this par 3 course in 54 and par would be a real accomplishment. Don't be surprised if a round in the 60s is taken here. The Lake Park scorecard is:

Lake Park Scorecard

Hole	Distance, yards
1	110
2	77
3	55
4	106
5	80
6	61
7	84
8	92
9	95
Out	760
10	115
11	64
12	54
13	100
14	111
15	76
16	85
17	79
18	71
In	755
Total	1,515

A list of Chicago's shortest par 3,4 and 5 holes by length and course hole number follows:

Shortest 3s By Distance

Rank	Distance, yards	Hole No.	Site of Hole
1	49	6	Ramada O'Hare
2	54	12	Lake Park
3	55	3	Lake Park
4	61	6	Lake Park
5	62	1	Ramada O'Hare
6	64	11	Lake Park
7*	65	2	Craig Woods
7*	65	2	Ramada O'Hare
9	68	2	Anets
10	70	7	Valley Lo
11*	71	18	Lake Park

11*	71	9	Ramada O'Hare
13	75	8	Winnetka (Par 3)
14	76	15	Lake Park
15	77	2	Lake Park
16	78	4	Ramada O'Hare
17	79	17	Lake Park
18*	80	12	Valley Lo
18*	80	5	Lake Park
*Tie			

Shortest 3s By Specific Course Hole

Hole No.	Distance, yards	Site of Hole
1	62	Ramada O'Hare
2	65	Ramada O'Hare & Craig Woods
3	55	Lake Park
4	78	Ramada O'Hare
5	80	Lake Park
6	49	Ramada O'Hare
7	70	Valley Lo
8	75	Winnetka (Par 3)
9	71	Ramada O'Hare
10	115	Lake Park
11	64	Lake Park
12	54	Lake Park
13	94	Nordic Hills
14	111	Lake Park
15	76	Lake Park
16	85	Lake Park
17	79	Lake Park
18	71	Lake Park

Shortest 4s By Distance

Rank	Distance, yards	Hole No.	Site of Hole
1	100	1	Barrington Park
2	175	4	Barrington Park
3	192	6	McArthur
4	195	3	Barrington Park
5	209	13	Chalet
6	215	2	McArthur
7	218	8	Rolling Knolls
8	227	4	Lansing
9*	228	1	Twin Lakes
9*	228	5	Lansing
11	232	13	Rolling Knolls
12	233	10	Rolling Knolls
13*	234	11	Villa Olivia
13*	234	8	White Pines (East)
15	235	13	Chapel Hill

16	236	13	Peter N. Jans
17	237	3	Silver Lake (Executive 3)
18	240	1	Hickory Knoll

*Tie

Shortest 4s By Specific Course Hole

Hole No.	Distance, yards	Site of Hole
1	100	Barrington Park
2	215	McArthur
3	195	Barrington Park
4	175	Barrington Park
5	228	Lansing
6	192	McArthur
7	255	Calumet (Gary, Ind.) & Pistakee
8	218	Rolling Knolls
9	251	Western Acres
10	233	Rolling Knolls
11	234	Villa Olivia
12	269	Edgebrook
13	209	Chalet
14	275	Rolling Knolls
15	249	Rolling Knolls
16	272	Phillips Park
17	276	Edgebrook
18	251	Rolling Knolls & Brae Loch

Shortest 5s By Distance

Rank	Distance, yards	Hole No.	Site of Hole
1	425	9	Prestbury
2	432	1	Foss Park
3	433	1	Bonnie Dundee
4	436	7	Chalet
5	440	10	Willow Glen
6	441	4	Oak Hills
7*	444	17	Glendale
7*	444	5	Foss Park
7*	444	13	Old Orchard
10	447	1	Cherry Hills
11	448	12	Prestbury
12*	451	7	Lake Hills
12*	451	9	Arlington Lakes
12*	451	6	Randall Oaks
12*	451	4	Gleason Park
12*	451	6	Hickory Hills
17	452	9	Pistakee
18*	454	7	Fresh Meadow
18*	454	9	Cherry Hills

*Tie

Shortest 5s By Specific Course Hole

Hole No.	Distance, yards	Site of Hole
1	432	Foss Park
2	469	Randall Oaks
3	462	Indian Boundary
4	441	Oak Hills
5	444	Foss Park
6	451	Randall Oaks
7	436	Chalet
8	460	Briar Leaf
9	425	Prestbury
10	440	Willow Glen
11	459	Indian Valley
12	448	Prestbury
13	444	Old Orchard
14	456	Tuckaway
15	459	Fresh Meadow
16	466	Joliet
17	444	Glendale
18	468	Orchard Hills

17

Oddities, Anecdotes and More

Chicago is a serious golf town. In spite of this, or perhaps because of it, unusual and sometimes comical events have taken place here over the past 100 years. This chapter examines some of these. The following tidbits provide a sample:

- Twenty years after the phone company set up phone lines in Park Ridge: the police station had a three-digit number; the local bank, a two-digit number; and the Park Ridge Country Club had a one-digit number—1.

- During the Depression, clubs experimented with ways to attract customers. The public Woodridge Golf Club chose to give away each week $25 in gold.

- Today's clubhouses lack at least one fixture commonly found on club grounds in the '30s to '50s: a slot machine.

- When J.M. McEvoy drove from the third tee at the Midlothian course in 1924, his ball ended up in a donkey's ear. McEvoy took a one-shot penalty. The animal had already taken his.

Caddies

Automation has pushed golf's caddy onto the endangered list. While it's true many private clubs still provide caddy services, their numbers are declining every year. At daily-fee courses, the caddy is virtually extinct. What was once as common on a golf course as wood-shafted clubs or rubber-cored balls, the caddy is being replaced with the golf cart. Since their introduction in the '40s, carts have won over course operators and players alike—each for different reasons. Club operators derive additional profit.

Players benefit by motoring through a three-to-four mile course in comfort. Still, many golfers do lament the caddy's declining role in golf today. No doubt these traditionalists would agree with the pro-caddy position of Dick Haskell, executive director of the Massachusetts Golf Association.

Caddy	Cart
Has name, will respond	Just sits there
Will signal and wave	Doesn't understand
Moves out ahead	Always with you
Holds flagstick	Cannot go on greens
Hands you a club	You get it yourself
Weighs 140, no track	Weighs 750, makes ruts
Will caddy rain or shine	Course closed to carts
Finds your ball	Never even looks
Wipes your club	Bangs up your clubs
Tires but never stops	Runs out of juice and quits
Picks up clubs	Runs over them
Can judge distance	Blind as a bat
Says nice shot	Has no interest
Cleans your ball	Could care less
Can walk anywhere	Has restricted areas
Rakes bunkers	Watches you do it

Regardless of which side you take in the debate, it's clear that caddies have been an integral part of the golf scene. For example:

- Turn-of-the-century caddy rates were 10 cents to 15 cents per hour. At the end of a nine-hole round, a young caddy received between 20 to 30 cents. Today, the costs are 100 times higher. Depending on whether one or two bags are carried and the gratuity offered, an average round nets a caddy about $20 to $40.

- When the Lake Forest health department issued a quarantine against Onwentsia's caddies in 1903, the club members had only one option if they wanted to play golf: they carried their own bags.

- In 1919, Amos Alonzo Stagg, president of Olympia Fields, suggested a "First Caddy Field Day" for local caddies. A survey indicated local clubs employed over 12,000 registered caddies in 1919. Just a few years later, Olympia Fields employed 2,000 caddies by itself.

Chicago caddies circa 1902.

- During the mid-1920s, Keith LeKander earned 35 cents per hour, caddying at the Chicago Golf Club. In 1928, the club hosted the Walker Cup competition, with LeKander assuming caddying responsibility for Bobby Jones. Upon the event's conclusion, Jones gave the young man a $25 tip.

- At the height of the Depression, adults flocked to Chicago-area courses—not to play but to work as caddies. This was especially common at south side courses near manufacturing plants that had been forced to cut back their operations. At most courses, however, caddies were predominately young boys— often representing their household's only wage earner.

- Scorecards often had a printed statement that reminded members to "treat your caddy as you would your own son."

- While caddy strikes were common during golf's early years, with better pay and more considerate treatment, they became less frequent. However, one strike did take place at the Northmoor Country Club as late as 1942. Caddies wanted a 60-cent increase over the club's $1.25 per hour offer.

- In the spring of 1945, Vic Soitz needed caddies for Edgewood Valley's upcoming season. Speaking to boys at the Justice Elementary School in Chicago, Soitz delivered his pitch, only to find no takers. On his way out, 12 young girls volunteered their services, making Edgewood Valley the local pioneer in caddy equality. In a few weeks, the number of girl caddies increased to 150. Soitz later commented the girls caught on fast. They learned their new trade by looking for lost balls, which were hit by Soitz into the rough and trees.

- Issued for protection, baseball helmets were worn by caddies at the 1970 Western Open hosted by the Beverly Country Club.

- Hollywood's blockbuster movie, Caddyshack, featured Chicago comedian Bill Murray—a former caddy at Indian Hill. Eddie Murray, one of Bill's four brothers also working on the 1980 hit, had a few years earlier earned a scholarship from the Evans Scholars Foundation.

- There are many other former caddies who have gone on to lead successful business careers. To note just four: Joe Jemsek; Dick Nugent; Don Barr, former publisher of *Sports Illustrated*; and Robert Ranquist, currently developing Ruffled Feathers in Lemont.

- Bucking an industry trend, Pine Meadow became in 1986 the first new daily-fee facility in several years to offer caddy service. Through advance reservations, caddies are available to patrons for $12 per bag plus any gratuity given.

- Robert Todd Lincoln, the son of the former president, was a successful lawyer around the turn of the century and an enthusiast of the game. He also developed a reputation for being frugal. Lincoln belonged to several local clubs including Chicago Golf but in the winter would travel south to enjoy golf in more moderate climes. Herb Graffis cites one such round Lincoln played in his book, *The PGA*. Graffis points out the story may or may not be folklore. The narrative begins as Lincoln completes the round and offers his black caddy a 10-cent tip. "Excuse me sir, but northern gentlemen usually give me a quarter." Taken aback,

Lincoln is said to have responded, "Didn't my father do enough for you people?" Without hesitation, the caddy retorted, "I don't know. I never caddied for your father."

Hey Ray! What Was My Score When We Played Together On June 23, 1958?

In 1976, Raymond S. Blunt Jr. reminisced on his 55 years of playing golf. The 78-year-old veteran had more than his memory, though, to assist him. At arm's length were THE records: volumes of meticulously entered and precisely arranged statistical notations. Ray could tell anyone when he played, where he played, what it cost, what he shot and even supply the names and scores of his playing companions.

His initial entry showed a 137 on his very first round of golf—at Marquette Park in 1922. Later, he joined the Ridge Country Club—serving as president in the late '40s. In all, Blunt recorded 1,189 rounds at Ridge from a high of 120 in 1925 to a low of 75 in 1945.

Ray loved golf, but he also adored numbers. He had calculations for his lifetime stroke average, cost per stroke and total strokes taken—172,049 in all. Of course, Blunt didn't devote all his adult years to playing and reporting scores—his full-time job wouldn't allow it. Ray Blunt was by profession a CPA.

What...No Zoo Committee?

Country clubs require committees to serve their members—the bigger the club, the more committees it has. No club, however, featured as many as South Shore. With over 2,200 members at its peak and only a nine-hole golf course to play, committees promulgated during the club's 69 years. Ranging in titles from A to Y, here is a partial list of the club's various committees:

Admission	Billiards
Art	Boating
Automobile	Bowling
Aviation	Building
Baseball	By-Laws
Bath & Rowhouse	Entertainment
Beach	Equestrian

Chicago Historical Society ICHi-00409 Kaufmann-Fabry Photo

Social functions were always a part of South Shore's calendar; this one in 1917 raised money for the war effort.

Chicago's Most Amazing Round...or Was It?

Tom Doty was just another assistant pro toiling in relative obscurity in 1971. Few people outside the Brookwood Country Club had reason to note the 23-year-old's name. By 1973, however, that all changed. Tom Doty became a celebrity. From local newspapers to national magazines such as *Sports Illustrated,* his new fame spread. Fittingly, the magazine's two-page account of Doty's eye-popping golfing achievement ran in its annual swimsuit issue.

His notoriety came from as near perfect a round as any mortal could possibly play. It included two holes-in-one, two double eagles, three eagles and four birdies. Through a four-hole span, Doty carded scores of 2-1-1-2—or 10 under par; this four-hole total remains a national golfing record.

The round also included a scant 15 putts—one the result of a missed 18-incher. By day's end, Doty's score was an unbelievable 59.

His work day at Brookwood started routinely enough on the warm and windy November day. Tending to his pro-shop duties, Doty was invited by four club members to join their group. He quickly accepted the offer, but advised the four he would join them on the course as soon as he completed some pro-shop tasks. At the third hole, he caught the foursome and began his round—bogeying the par 3 hole.

It would be on the next few holes Doty's introduction to immortality would begin. He recorded first a double eagle—the result of a holed second shot on a par 5. He then aced a 360-yard dogleg left par 4. Another ace on the ensuing par 3 followed. On the next hole, he holed out in two on the par 4. Through these four holes he had scored 10 under par—never pulling his putter out of the bag. Doty went on to complete the round—joined by the four club members on Brookwood's first and second holes. The foursome wanted to witness Doty's two remaining holes to calculate for themselves the assistant pro's final score. Doty, of course, broke 60—even with a last hole bogey.

A chronological hole-by-hole recap of Doty's score over the 6,435-yard par 72 layout follows:

Hole Number	Par	Score	Result
3	3	4	Bogey
4	5	2	Double Eagle
5	4	1	Double Eagle
6	3	1	Eagle
7	4	2	Eagle
8	4	4	Par
9	4	4	Par
10	5	5	Par
11	4	3	Birdie
12	3	3	Par
13	4	4	Par
14	3	3	Par
15	5	4	Birdie
16	4	3	Birdie
17	4	3	Birdie
18	4	5	Bogey
1	5	3	Eagle
2	4	5	Bogey

It was an unbelievable golfing achievement. So astounding, in fact, its authenticity has been questioned. Controversy exists. Was it a hoax? as some have suggested. Indeed, several peculiarities do exist. One is that Doty posted the 59 on Nov. 10, 1971, yet nearly two months expired before the news reached the region's golfing community.

A second unusual aspect is that Doty joined the foursome on the third hole. Could he have possibly planted balls in holes No. 4 and 5, while he was "working" in the club's pro shop? Thirdly, there is the improbability of registering consecutive aces—especially one on a 360-yard dogleg. Today, 20 years later, old-timers at Brookwood (the club is now operated by the Du Page Forest Preserve District) are convinced the score was bogus.

There were Doty supporters—including the four witnesses—each vehemently attesting to Doty's round. Carol McCue, the former executive director of the Chicago District Golf Association, investigated the matter and concluded the score, though unbelievable, was factual. "I looked into Doty's eyes and saw the truth," she later noted. The CDGA later officially recognized the 13-under-par round.

Was it the greatest round recorded locally or was it an elaborate ruse? Regardless of its fact or fiction status, few Chicago rounds have ever been as widely noted and fiercely debated as Tom Doty's amazing 59.

Catching More Than the Golfing Bug

When the prominent retailer Marshall Field died in 1906, official cause of death was listed as pneumonia. A case can be made that his zest for playing golf led to his sudden passing. Only an average player, Field thrived on the competitiveness and camaraderie. Introduced to golf late in life, he played on average three times weekly—mostly at Midlothian or the Chicago Golf Club.

As testament to his fondness for golf, Field joined three companions for a friendly game at CGC in 1906. The date was Jan. 1. With temperatures near freezing and patches of snow covering the layout, conditions were anything but pleasant. But play began with each enthusiast using a red-colored ball. On the train ride back to Chicago, Field felt a cold coming on; nevertheless, he confirmed his desire to play another round on Jan. 3, which he did honor.

By week's end, his condition became worse. Boarding a train for New York, Field tired during the trip. His energy all but gone, he had barely enough strength to enter a New York hospital. The doctors regrettably announced that pneumonia had advanced beyond their medical capabilities. On Jan. 17th, Field died. It was two weeks after he enjoyed his final round of golf.

Holes-In-One

Through its Hole-In-One Clearing House, *Golf Digest* has been recording aces since 1952. In the 1980s, more than 350,000 "1's" were registered, at least 10,000 in Illinois alone. As to the number given up by Chicago courses since 1892—it would be anyone's guess—but assuredly the total is in excess of 15,000. Six of those Chicago-area "1's" are particularly noteworthy.

- Bob Hope's golfing career includes five aces, two in the Chicago area: at Bob O'Link and Butler National.

- During the 1950s, Michael Conley's round at the Winnetka Golf Club included two holes-in-one. He was immediately offered a guest appearance on CBS's popular Garry Moore television show.

- The first 15 holes of Sheldon Berman's round at Green Acres that day were relatively uneventful. Then, at the 16th, playing companion Larry Guilford aced the 130-yard hole. Berman literally jumped up and down in congratulatory delight. As the foursome quieted down, Berman walked to the tee box, teed up and swung. "I was just stunned," he later said. He too had just scored his first ace ever. Many golfers would also be impressed with Berman's par 4 at the next hole. (How many players lucky enough to score "1" remain focused? Guilford, in fact, took a 6.) Reality did finally set in for Berman on the day's final hole; he ended his round with a double-bogey 7.

Street Names

Every day local golfers and nongolfers alike navigate their way to work, school or the shopping mall over roads named for distinguished characters in history, regional destinations and yes even famous golf courses. In Coun-

Bunker Lane and Fairway Drive are two of the more common golf-related street names.

try Club Hills, for example, you can take a spin down streets named Idlewild, Ravisloe, Butterfield and Glen Oaks.

Orland Park has been the biggest proponent in using golf-related designations for its Avenues, Courts, Drives, Lanes, Places, Roads, Circles and Trails. More than 40 include golfing references. One of its streets is even called Chipshot Lane. Other examples include:

Baltusrol Drive	Merion Drive
Butler Court	Pebble Beach Street
Carnoustie Drive	Sawgrass Court
Coghill Lane	Spyglass Circle
Fairway Drive	Torrey Pines Drive

Following is a partial list of the more than 200 other golf-related street names that dot the greater Chicago area:

Armour Court (Woodridge)	Middlecoff Court (Woodridge)
Ball Avenue (East Dundee)	Oakmont Drive (Naperville)
Bobby Jones Lane (Woodridge)	Palmer Circle (Naperville)
Brassie Drive (Glenview)	Par Lane (Itasca)
Bunker Avenue (Flossmoor)	Patty Berg Court (Woodridge)
Caddy Lane (Joliet)	Pinehurst Drive (Naperville)
Casper Court (Elgin)	Putter Court (Joliet)
Chick Evans Lane (Woodridge)	Snead Court (Woodridge)
Evans Road (Flossmoor)	Swing Court (Joliet)
Hagen Lane (Flossmoor)	Tee Lane (Itasca)
Hazard Road (East Dundee)	Travers Avenue (Chicago Hts)
Hook Road (East Dundee)	Vardon Place (Flossmoor)
Knollwood Drive (Flossmoor)	Westward Ho Drive (Northlake)

The Fastest Local Golf Round Ever

Four-to-five-hour excursions didn't always represent a typical game's duration. In fact, 60 years ago player's sped through a round of 18 holes in two hours or less. Granted the courses were sometimes shorter or sometimes easier. Imagine, however, a single round's total duration being completed in 17 minutes and 20 seconds. In 1939, one such episode occurred and in the process established a record for the quickest 18-hole round in the United States.

The 6,400-yard layout at Tam O'Shanter provided the setting for this most unusual affair. An army of players gathered—their objective: to determine how quickly one single ball could be propelled around a standard-sized golf course. The participants stood on every hole at spots considered the most plausible landing areas. Others placed themselves in less likely resting areas just in case the prior stroke went awry. It must have been an amusing scene—club-carrying players scattered behind trees, in bunkers and near any other spot a ball might come to rest.

After each holed hit, a volunteer quickly recovered the ball from the cup and tossed it to the next teeing area—where another person immediately struck the ball again. With an elapsed time averaging less than 60 seconds per hole, a national record was set. It does fall short of the world record—9 minutes and 51 seconds—which 48 players helped set in 1988 on a 7,108-yard South African course.

A Hole By Any Other Name

In addition to being referred to by number, holes used to have names—often hinting of the challenges lying ahead. This practice has all but ceased today as scorecard maps and yardage booklets detail an individual hole's character. Gone are the days when early Chicago clubs tapped local newspapers or foreign countries for colorful monikers. Other clubs simply used less exotic names—sometimes employing a foreboding message such as: Dismal Swamp, The Growler, Isle of Woe, Trouble, The Fool, Devil's Ditch, Spookey, Trepidation, Hell and Bath Tub.

At least four area clubs maintain this age-old custom. One is the Golf Club of Illinois, which blends descriptive and state historical references for hole names. Adlai's Draw,

Daley Dilemma, Lincoln Trail, Sandburg Dunes and Abe's Elbow are a sampling. There's also an aptly named moniker for the longest hole in Illinois—the 678-yard par 5 is named Grant's March.

People's names are borrowed to designate holes at the Joe Louis the Champ Golf Course in Riverdale. These include: Lee Elder, Calvin Peete, Jackie Robinson and Cecil Partee.

Olympia Fields North and Americana's Briar Patch courses also feature names. The complete 18-hole list for each follows:

	Olympia Fields North Course	Americana's Briar Patch
1	Railroad	Away
2	Crook	Meadow
3	Ararat	Woods
4	Dardenelles	River
5	Narrows	Airport
6	Oasis	Dogleg
7	The Brook	Short
8	Sunset	Hidden
9	Halfway	Long
10	The Carry	Turn
11	Woodland	Bunker
12	Channel	Valley
13	Baby	Bogie
14	Caution	Ridge
15	Wilderness	Lake
16	The Pool	Road
17	Two Rivers	Willow
18	Home	Home

Do You Smell Something Burning?

One of Chicago Golf Club's house rules warned members, "Smoking or lighting matches in the locker room is absolutely prohibited. A fine of $10 will be imposed for violation." Considering many members commonly referred to the locker room as "cigarette alley," the no-smoking rule wasn't totally obeyed. The inevitable took place Aug. 22, 1912, when the locker room and clubhouse went up in flames. Exactly 11 days later—and on schedule—the club hosted the 1912 U.S. Amateur. Many referred to the competition as simply "the blazing championship of 1912."

Unfortunately, clubhouse fires are an infamous part of golf's local history as illuminated by the following examples:

Barrington Hills	1930
Beverly	1917
Bryn Mawr	1954, 1986
Flossmoor	1904, 1914
Gleneagles	1955
Glen Oak	1929
Hinsdale	1920, 1921
Inverness	1959
Itasca	1935, 1963
Old Orchard	1953
Riverside	1899, 1918, 1984
Silver Lake	1958
Skokie	1911
St. Charles	1943
Tam O'Shanter	1946
Wilmette	1952

All Aboard

With 33 different railroads using Chicago as a hub around the turn of the century, it's not surprising that their presence helped shape outlying community growth. As rural areas became more easily accessible, an ancillary benefit, in the form of a golf course, often took root. Sometimes, though, hamlets fought the railroads' approach; in effect, they also closed the door on golf club development. An example illustrates the point.

The residents in two Kankakee county villages—Bourbonnais and Kankakee—had diametrically opposed attitudes toward railway expansion. The Illinois Central Railroad wanted to extend tracks into Bourbonnais, but community objections forced the railway to change its plans. Eventually, the southern tracks passed through Kankakee instead. Just a few years later in 1916, Kankakee's first golf club opened. The isolated Bourbonnais hamlet didn't form its first club until 1980.

Throughout 100 years of Chicago golf, the railroad industry has dramatically affected the sport. Here are specific details of note:

- In lobbying USGA members to select the Chicago Golf Club as the first non-Eastern U.S. Open and Amateur venue, C.B. Macdonald made reference to Wheaton's rail access in 1897. "There are over 40 trains a day between (Wheaton and Chicago) and as the running time is between 40 and 50 minutes, there can surely be no just complaint on the subject of inconvenience." Macdonald had done his homework—there were exactly 41 available runs, to and from Wheaton, on the Chicago & North Western Railroad.

- Three decades later, the Chicago Golf Club hosted the 1928 Walker Cup. Access to the tourney site was even more convenient as the electrified Chicago, Aurora & Elgin Railroad built its Wheaton depot across the street from the club's entrance.

- Country club rosters have commonly included railroad employees, but few clubs topped the total at Olympia Fields. Railway executives of at least 13 lines played regularly during the 1920s at the south suburban club:

> Atchison, Topeka & Santa Fe
> Baltimore & Ohio
> Chesapeake & Ohio
> Chicago & Western Indiana
> Chicago & North Western
> Chicago, Milwaukee & St. Paul
> Chicago, Rock Island & Pacific
> Chicago, Indianapolis &
> Louisville
> Delaware, Lackawanna &
> Western
> Illinois Central
> Missouri Pacific
> Northern Pacific
> Pennsylvania

- The Glen View Club's founders lived in Evanston. A one-car trolley line operated between the club and Evanston from 1907 to 1935. Another area club—Westmoreland—added a stop on this line in 1913. Also tied to the rails, the Midlothian Country Club owned its railroad. Incorporated in 1901 for $25,000, the Midlothian & Blue Island Railroad operated on a three-mile-long track. A locomotive (referred to as "the mule") pulled two passenger coaches along 147th Street. While the railway was phased out in 1928, one of the early victims of automobile use, the golf club is believed to be the only one in the world to have run its own private railroad.

• In 1913, the Illinois Central operated 253 weekday trains on its south suburban lines. The railroad also featured "Golf Specials" to service members at six south side clubs. Departing downtown Chicago at 12:23, 1:25 and 1:40, the afternoon runs insured arrival in time to tee off at Homewood, Ravisloe, Idlewild, Calumet, Windsor or South Shore. Another run—the Country Club Special—left Chicago at 5:10 p.m., thus providing time for a late round or dinner. "Club Specials" are still a contemporary part of the railroad vernacular.

• Railroad companies have not always been the best ally of a golf club. In 1959, the Chicago, Milwaukee & St. Paul and Pennsylvania Railroads advised Bensenville's village board of their intent to purchase the Mohawk Country Club—to develop the site into an industrial property. Though residents of the adjoining Mohawk subdivision objected to the railway's plans, Bensenville took the first step by annexing the golf club in 1960. Within a decade, the village sold the property. The land is today an industrial site.

Railway access, though no longer crucial, continues to be important today. For example, some residential golf course communities are promising prospective buyers the construction of new train depots near planned clubs.

Put Your Seatback and Tray Table in their Original Upright Position

Of course, the aviation industry, soaring in the last half of Chicago's 100 golfing years, has also influenced the progress of golf locally.

• In 1911, only eight years after the Wright brothers escaped the sand trap near Kitty Hawk, North Carolina, the aviation committee of the South Shore

Country Club was awhirl supporting and promoting Chicago's great airplane race of the same year.

- For the most part, however, the relationship between golf and the airplane involves landing sites. In 1928, for example, Samuel Insull—a wealthy Chicago financier—formed a 26-man syndicate to purchase the former Mellody Farm estate for $2.5 million. Plans included construction of a golf club with an adjoining single airplane runway. Christened the Aviation Golf Club, the project collapsed in 1929—the result of the millions of dollars lost by the investment group in Wall Street's crash.

- Initially, Olympia Fields planned construction of a private airstrip, but this idea never took off.

- In 1937, the U.S. Navy purchased the Curtis Wright Airport in Glenview. By 1942, the Navy had taken control of adjoining property, including land housing the 36-hole Pickwick daily-fee club. Billed as the "north side's most beautiful playground," the 6,710 and 6,545-yard courses featured creeping bent grass greens and tees. Today, the base serves as headquarters for the Naval and Marine Air Reserve Training Commands and still has a golf course—the Naval Air Station Golf Club.

- Local courses have always stood in the direct flight path of aviation's development. Chicago's Municipal Airport had bordered Laramie Country Club—an early private golf club. By the '20s, the club converted to Chicago Meadows—a public-fee facility. In the '30s, the airport gobbled up this 18-hole course for expansion.

- The current "world's busiest" airport also found a nearby golf course site appetizing. Orchard Field (ever wonder why O'Hare's three-character designation is ORD?) was a tiny airstrip before the War Department purchased the land and leased it to the Douglas Aircraft Company for cargo plane production. In 1947, federal agencies awarded the city of Chicago 1,080 acres (the military retained 420 acres). By 1949, the city embarked on an aggressive campaign to acquire additional land and, within 11 years, the property totaled

7,000 acres. The tiny O'Hare Field Golf Club represented but a minuscule percentage of the newly acquired property.

- In Chicago, at least at this time, the third airport of note is Merrill C. Meigs Field. While the lake landfill site had no prior history of being a golf course—there is, in fact, a golf tie-in. Meigs Field is named after Merrill Chuck Meigs—the 1920 president of the Western Advertising Golfing Association. While the former Hearst newspaper publisher was an All-American under coach Amos Alonzo Stagg, Meigs was even more renown as one of this country's aviation pioneers.

- While golf courses have usually given way in the turbulence of the aviation storm, occasionally they do prevail. McHenry County's Skycrest Country Club Airport was named after its neighbor—the Skycrest Golf Club. Today, the airport is no longer around, but the golf course is, though remodeled, reorganized and renamed Twin Orchard. The same cannot be said of the Lansing Airport Golf Club—it's a county forest preserve today.

- While Bon Vivant includes a private airstrip, as does the Americana Club in Lake Geneva, Village Links does not. That still didn't stop Phil Capone from landing on the Glen Ellyn course early in 1990. Suddenly powerless in his 1962 Piper Cub, Capone had one chance to put the plane down safely, which he did on the facility's 470-yard par 4 hole. No one will ever convince the fortunate aviator that the course's No. 13 hole is anything but his luckiest at Village Links.

The golf/aviation connection gets another more down-to-earth venue as part of the Du Page Airport's $100 million expansion program. Expected to open in early 1993, the Robert Trent Jones Jr.-designed course just south of the airport will get many of its contours from dirt excavated for the airport's new runways. Architects have worked with the Federal Aviation Administration to keep errant golf balls on the course and driving range from interfering with airplane flight paths, so there'll be no need to yell, "Fore," to incoming pilots.

18

100 Years and Going Strong

Golf isn't all that different today than it was in the 1890s when Chicagoans were first introduced to the game. Foreign-born professionals were capturing golf's major championships. Other well-known players were actively laying out new courses. The average weekend golfer played for bogey. And while the courses today are slightly longer, the 18 cups still measure 4¼ inches in diameter, just as they did a century ago.

Though the game itself hasn't changed, the trappings have. Embellishments have been added—in such forms as technological advances in equipment, ten-million-dollar clubhouses, electric carts, improved turfgrass and bio-degradable tees.

Above all, though, the most important change is that golf has become an accepted part of Americana. No longer are questions asked about its survival. No one views the game as a passing fad. Clearly, the sport is here to stay and will probably continue to be one of the most popular recreational activities for another 100 years—but in what form?

For example, in the year 2092, will Chicago golfers play under glass-enclosed domes? Will there be illuminated 18-hole venues? Will there be more six-hole courses than nines or 18s? Will a golfer step forward from Chicago ranks and be judged the greatest local product ever? Will computer technology and an in-home driving net allow golfers to "play" the world's greatest courses in their basements? Will private country clubs charge one-million-dollar initiation fees? Will there even be private clubs then? Of course, at this time, we all can offer only guesses. And here are mine: No. Yes. Probably. Yes (and it's about time). Yes (the prototypes are out there now). Maybe two million. Of course.

About all that is safe to assume is that golf's second 100 years in Chicago will start with a bang! In 1992, five national tournaments will take place. The Western Open returns to Cog Hill while the Ameritech Senior Open and LPGA Shoot-Out are again scheduling Chicago venues. In August, Kemper Lakes will host the first U.S. Women's Amateur contested here since Patty Berg won at Westmoreland in 1938. And finally, the Legends of Golf—a new tournament for PGA pros 60 and older—makes its national debut at Bull Valley in August.

Meanwhile, the Chicago area continues adding to its already long list of golf course properties. Slated for 1992 openings are the Dunham Club (Wayne), Eagle Brook (Geneva), The Merit Club (Gurnee), Lisle Park (Lisle), Orchard Valley (Aurora), a second 18 at Countryside (Mundelein) and a third 18 at Geneva National (Lake Geneva, Wis.). Furthermore, 1992 will represent the first full season for Conway Farms (Lake Forest), Seven Bridges (Woodridge) and Odyssey (Tinley Park). Never before have so many fine courses existed in the Chicago area. Then again, never have so many golfers been as eager to play the game.

As golf enters its fourth consecutive decade of expansion locally, interest in the game has reached an all-time high. Still, there are those who simply wonder how long this unprecedented escalation can continue. Has the "red zone" been reached? Is the game, its participants and club operators due for some kind of temporary derailment? As we have seen, it has happened before. Indeed, the Depression of the '30s and the war years of the '40s proved that the sport is vulnerable.

Fortunately, the future offers no hint such despair, but the economic conditions of today do suggest that a shakeout, in some form or another, is imminent. The truth is that not all Chicago-area public and private clubs are financially secure.

Nevertheless, the 1990s will be marked with a celebratory air. Centennials are planned for several established clubs, while in 1999, the WGA reaches its 100-year milestone.

Chicago golf and its 100-year history may seem unimportant to resident nongolfers. It may even seem insignificant to golfers in Scotland, where the game has been played since 1457. But, as has been illustrated many times in this book, today's Chicago-area golfers are the beneficiaries of, as well as participants in, a great and continuing tradition. It is appropriate, then, to end with a chronology showing 100 years filled with historic and memorable milestones.

Milestones in 100 Years of Chicago Golf

1892   First area course laid out—seven holes in Lake Forest.

1893   Chicago Golf Club incorporates, in Downers Grove. Builds the area's first nine-hole course.

1894   Chicago Golf Club joins four Eastern clubs in formation of USGA.

1895   Chicago Golf Club moves to Wheaton. Builds first 18-hole course in the United States.

    First out-of-bounds rule in world is formulated at CGC.

    Onwentsia becomes first north suburban golf club to incorporate.

,96   Jim Foulis from CGC becomes first Chicago-based professional to win U.S. Open.

1897   Chicago Golf Club becomes first area club to host U.S. Open and U.S. Amateur.

    First use in country of creeping bent grass greens, at CGC.

1898   First south suburban club formed—Midlothian Country Club.

1899   Western Golf Association organizes. Stages first Western Open and Western Amateur at Glen View Club.

    Jackson Park Golf Course debuts—first public golf course in Midwest.

    Herbert Harriman becomes first native-born American to win U.S. Amateur, at Onwentsia Club.

1900   First foreign entrant wins U.S. Open—Harry Vardon at Chicago Golf Club.

1901   First Western Women's Amateur, at Onwentsia Club.

1902   *Golfer's Magazine* introduced—first Chicago-based golfing publication.

1903   Women's Western Golf Association spins off from WGA.

        First U.S. Women's Amateur played locally, at CGC.

1904   Pater-Filius starts at Midlothian Country Club— oldest father-son tournament in the U.S.

1905   Jim and Dave Foulis acquire patent for mashie-niblick. It's the forerunner of modern-day 7-iron.

1906   South Shore Country Club forms. It will eventually be the largest membership club in the area.

1907   First area public course outside of Chicago opens— Wing Park Golf Course in Elgin.

1908   Garfield Park Golf Course opens on Aug. 17 with little advance publicity, city officials not wanting to detract from the Cubs-Giants baseball game. The Cubs went on to win the World Series that year.

1909   Chicago-native Robert Gardner—19 years, five months old—becomes youngest ever to win U.S. Amateur, at Chicago Golf Club.

1910   First Chicago-area daily-fee course opens—Harlem Golf Club.

1911   First native-born American to win U.S. Open—John McDermott at Chicago Golf Club.

1912   Chick Evans reaches finals bracket in U.S. Amateur at Chicago Golf Club. Loses to three-time U.S. Amateur winner Jerry Travers.

1913   Joe Jemsek was born on Christmas Eve.

1914   Chicago District Golf Association forms. Holds first Amateur Championship, won by Chick Evans at Ravisloe Country Club.

1915   Cook County Forest Preserve District formally organizes.

1916   Amateur Chick Evans scores a first—wins U.S. Open and U.S. Amateur in the same year.

1917   To aid the war effort, the Red Cross and Western Golf Association schedule exhibition matches at golf clubs across the country, including several locally. Of the more than $300,000 raised, the Lake Shore Country Club donates the most—$35,000.

1918   Exmoor Country Club's clubhouse serves as temporary hospital as influenza epidemic hits North Shore.

1919   First Caddy Field Day for all 12,000 registered caddies in Chicago area.

1920   First PGA Championship held locally, at Flossmoor Country Club. Glen View Club pro Jock Hutchison wins event after gaining entry as alternate.

1921   Chicago's most prolific course construction decade begins.

1922   First U.S. Open to charge spectator fees, at Skokie Country Club.

1923   First issue of *Chicago Golfer* appears.

1924   Olympia Fields Country Club breaks ground for world's largest clubhouse.

1925   The 27-hole Jackson Park Golf Course drew 259,843 rounds. It was the busiest course in the world.

1926   Chicago's first International Golf Show held.

1927   Albert Lasker establishes Mill Road Farm. The 18-hole course on his private estate is arguably the toughest golf course built in Chicago's history.

1928   The Walker Cup competition comes to the Chicago area, at Chicago Golf Club.

1929   The stock market crashes in October. Golf is just one of the victims.

1930   First two Chick Evans caddy scholarship recipients enroll at Northwestern University—James McGinnis of the Indian Hill Club and Harold Fink of the Glen View Club.

1931   First Illinois Open held, won by Abe Espinosa.

1932   The long-anticipated opening of the Waveland Golf Course takes place on land reclaimed from Lake Michigan.

First pro shop in country to sell golfing apparel, at Medinah Country Club.

1933   Chicago's largest golf "classroom"—sponsored by the *Chicago Tribune.*

An amateur wins the U.S. Open—Johnny Goodman, at North Shore Country Club.

1934   Horton Smith, club professional at the Oak Park Country Club, wins inaugural Masters Tournament.

1935   Evanston Golf Club professional John Revolta finishes the year as the PGA Tour's top money winner—his total, $9,543.

1936   Chicagoans Herb and Joe Graffis form National Golf Foundation.

1937   First Chicago Open, at Medinah Country Club.

First visit to area of Annual Lefthanders Golfers Championship, at Olympia Fields.

1938   Sam Snead wins his first Chicago tournament—the Chicago Open.

1939   Fastest 18-hole round in U.S. is played, at Tam O'Shanter Country Club.

1940   Tam O'Shanter hosts its first important championship—Dick Metz wins the Chicago Open.

1941   First year of George S. May tournaments—at Tam O'Shanter.

1942   War halts all major tourneys except one—the Hale America Open at Ridgemoor Country Club. Won by Ben Hogan.

1943   Beverly Country Club hosts first Chicago Victory tournament. Won by former New York Yankee baseball player, Sam Byrd.

1944   The Aurora Country Club becomes first in area to feature motorized golf cart.

1945   Chick Evans, at 55, successfully defends his Chicago Amateur Championship title.

1946   Hansberger Tool and Die Company forms in Chicago, renamed Ram Golf Company in 1967.

1947   Ben Hogan wins the last Chicago Victory tournament—at Westward Ho Golf Club.

American Society of Golf Course Architects establishes headquarters in Chicago.

1948   PGA Tour's biggest first-place prize announced—
       $10,000 World Championship of Golf at Tam
       O'Shanter.

1949   Joe Jemsek and Charlie Nash launch first television
       golf show in country—"Pars, Birdies and Eagles."

1950   After a 10-year hiatus, the Illinois Open resumes
       play. Felice Torza gains the victory.

1951   Babe Zaharias wins the Women's World Champion-
       ship of Golf for the fourth consecutive year.
       Finishing second is Patty Berg, also for the fourth
       consecutive year.

1952   George May increases first prize of World Cham-
       pionship to unprecedented $25,000.

1953   First national television audience of major golf event
       sees Lew Worsham sink 103-yard wedge shot on
       final hole to win World Championship by a single
       stroke.

1954   First prize now $50,000 at World Championship plus
       additional $50,000 awarded to tourney champion for
       series of exhibition matches.

1955   Sunset Ridge Country Club pro Bob Harris shoots
       59 or 11 under par at Edgewater Golf Club.

1956   South Shore Country Club celebrates its 50th an-
       niversary. The club's membership at the time is more
       than 2,100.

1957   Dick Mayer wins the last World Championship of
       Golf at Tam O'Shanter.

1958   U.S. Public Links Championship visits Chicago for
       first time, played at Silver Lake Country Club.

1959   A new village incorporates in the western suburbs,
       taking its name from the Woodridge Golf Club.

1960   Future LPGA Hall of Famer Carol Mann wins
       Chicago Women's District Golf Association
       championship.

1961   Jerry Barber wins PGA Championship at Olympia
       Fields.

1962   Pheasant Run opens; it's the first hotel/golf resort
       in region.

1963   Arnold Palmer wins his first local championship—
        the Western Open at Beverly Country Club.

1964   Cog Hill opens its fourth 18, the only 72-hole facili-
        ty in region.

1965   Meadow Lark in Hinsdale opens—first new Cook
        County Forest Preserve course built since the 1930s.

1966   Sherman Finger wins NCAA All-American golfing
        honors for the third consecutive year. Finger cur-
        rently serves as the club pro at Knollwood Club.

1967   Illinois Junior Golf Association formed, by Mike
        Spinello.

        Jack Nicklaus wins his first Chicago PGA event, the
        Western Open at Beverly Country Club.

1968   Downers Grove Park District purchases course—
        now named Downers Grove Golf Club—that was
        the original site of Chicago Golf Club.

1969   The Branigar organization owns and operates five
        daily-fee sites—Mohawk Country Club, White Pines
        Golf Club, Indian Lakes Resort, Tally Ho Golf Club
        and Buffalo Grove Golf Club.

1970   First national tourney to issue baseball helmets to
        caddies for protection—the Western Open at Beverly
        Country Club.

1971   Brookwood Country Club is the site of Tom Doty's
        controversial 59 or 13 under par.

1972   Mission Hills property sold to new owners who an-
        nounce plans to develop a residential golf course
        community. It's the first in the Chicago area.

1973   Billy Casper wins Western Open for fourth time—
        at Midlothian.

1974   Butler National hosts its first Western Open. Tom
        Watson wins. It's his first Tour victory.

1975   Lightning strikes Lee Trevino and two other pro
        golfers at Western Open—at Butler National.

1976   First Cook County Forest Preserve-operated
        championship-styled course opens—at Highland
        Woods.

1977   Chick Evans birdies No. 18 at Glen View Club. It's
        the last round the 87-year-old Chicago legend will

ever play.

1978   Slow play at Village Links of Glen Ellyn prompts Matt Pekarek to conceptualize the Keep Pace Program.

1979   Kemper Lakes opens.

1980   Barrington's Gary Hallberg is the Rolex Rookie of the Year on the PGA Tour.

1981   Pat Bradley wins the U.S. Women's Open at La Grange Country Club.

1982   Forest Preserve National opens. Considered today the finest county-operated course in the country.

1983   Chicago native and former Medinah member Deedee Lasker joins the LPGA Tour.

1984   Chicago native Lance Ten Broeck wins the Magnolia Classic.

1985   Joe Louis the Champ Golf Course is country's first course to be named after a black sports hero.

Scott Verplank wins the Western Open at Butler National. He is the first amateur to win a PGA Tour event in 31 years.

1986   *Golf Digest* selects Pine Meadow as the country's best new public course.

1987   Floods wash out half of Butler National's course for Western Open. The tournament is played on the nine dry holes at Butler and the neighboring Oak Brook Golf Club.

1988   First USGA Senior Open played locally, at Medinah Country Club.

1989   Kemper Lakes hosts PGA Championship.

Golf Digest names Cantigny best new public course of the year.

1990   Hale Irwin is the first player to receive a special USGA exemption *and* win a U.S. Open—at Medinah. Irwin becomes the oldest U.S. Open winner ever.

1991   Three local clubs host tournaments for the first time: Cog Hill Golf Club—Western Open; Oak Brook Golf Club—LPGA Shoot-Out; and Stonebridge—Ameritech Senior Open.

SELECTED BIBLIOGRAPHY

Alft, E.C. *Elgin: An American History.* Elgin, IL: Crossroads Communications, 1984.

Arpee, Edward. *Lake Forest, Illinois: History & Reminiscenses 1861-1969.* Lake Forest, IL: Rotary Club, 1969.

Bakken, Timothy H. *Hinsdale.* Hinsdale, IL: Hinsdale Doings, 1976.

Barkow, Al. *The History of the PGA Tour.* New York: Doubleday—Div. of Bantam Doubleday Dell Publishing Group, Inc., 1989.

Bartlett, Charlie. *The New 1969 Golfer's Almanac.* New York: Bantam Books, 1969.

Blatt, Miriam Green. *The History of Itasca.* Itasca, IL: Itasca State Bank, 1976.

Bushnell, George D. *Wilmette: A History.* Wilmette, IL: Wilmette Bicentennial Commission, Village of Wilmette, 1976.

Chieger, Bob and Pat Sullivan. *Inside Golf: Quotations On The Royal And Ancient Game.* New York: Atheneum, 1985.

Cornish, Geoffrey S. and Ronald E. Whitten. *The Golf Course.* New York: The Rutledge Press, 1981.

Davis, Joe, ed. *Blue Book of Chicago Golfers.* Chicago: W.S. Chambers, 1925.

Dedmon, Emmett. *Fabulous Chicago.* New York: Random House, 1953.

Evans, Charles, Jr. *Chick Evans' Golf Book.* New York: Thos. E. Wilson & Co., 1921.

Fyfe, Gordon. *A Short History of the Village of Golf.* Golf, IL: Village of Golf, N.D.

Gibson, Nevin H. *The Encyclopedia of Golf,* Revised Edition. New York: A.S. Barnes and Company, 1958, 1964.

—— *The Golf Course Directory of Chicagoland.* Elgin, IL: Wing Publishing, 1990.

Graffis, Herb. *The PGA.* New York: Thomas Y. Crowell, 1975.

Harnsberber, Caroline Thomas. *Winnetka—The Biography of a Village.* Evanston: Schore Press, 1977.

Head, Alice G. Glenview at 75, 1899-1974. Glenview, IL: Glenview Area Historical Society, 1974.

Hope, Bob with Dwayne Netland. *Confessions of a Hooker.* Garden City, N.Y.: Doubleday & Company, 1985.

Houghton, George. *Believe It or Not—That's Golf.* London: William Luscome Publisher Limited, 1974.

Huggins, Percy, ed. *The Golfer's Miscellany.* New York: Harper & Row, 1971.

Jensen, George Peter. *Historic Chicago Sites.* Chicago: Creative Enterprises, 1953.

Kaiser, Blythe and Dorothy Vandercook. *Glen Ellyn's Story.* Glen Ellyn: 1976.

—— *La Grange Centennial History.* La Grange, IL: La Grange Area Historical Society, 1979.

LeKander, Keith. *Reminiscences of a Caddy.* Presented to DuPage County Historical Society, 1985.

Macdonald, C.B. *Scotland's Gift: Golf.* New York: Charles Scribner and Sons, 1928.

Martin, H.B. *Fifty Years of American Golf.* New York: Dodd, Mead and Company, 1936.

Pacyga, Dominic A. and Ellen Skerrett. *Chicago: City of Neighborhoods.* Chicago: Loyola University Press, 1986.

Parsons, Iain, ed. *World Atlas of Golf.* London: Mitchell Beazley Publishers Limited, 1976.

Pearson, Ruth Seen. *Reflections of St. Charles—A History of St. Charles, Illinois 1833-1976.* Elgin: Brethren Press, 1976.

Peper, George. *Golf In America: The First One Hundred Years.* New York: Harry N. Abrams, Inc., 1988.

Price, Charles. *The World of Golf.* New York: Random House, 1962.

Reichelt, Marie Ward. *History of Deerfield, Illinois.* Glenview Press, 1928.

Richardson, William D., ed. *The Golfer's Year Book.* New York: Lincoln A. Werden Publisher by The Golfer's Year Book Co. Inc., 1930.

Ringdahl, Anna and Lillian Tucker. *Highland Park: The First Hundred Years.* Highland Park Society Centennial Committee, 1969.

Ryan, Joseph Edmund G. *Golfers' Green Book.* Chicago: 1902.

Shapiro, Mel and Warren Dohn and Leonard Berger. *Golf A Turn-of-the-Century Treasury.* Secaucus, NJ: Castle, 1986.

Stoddard, William Leavitt. *New Golfers Almanac for 1909.* Boston: Houghton/Mifflin Publishing, 1909.

Tebbel, John. *The Marshall Fields: A Study in Wealth.* New York: E.P. Dutton & Co. Inc., 1947.

Thompson, Richard A. *DuPage Roots.* Wheaton, IL: DuPage County Historical Society, 1985.

Welch, Jane Faxon and Wade M. Welch. *The Golfer's Book of Trivia.* Boston: Quinlan Press, 1985.

Wind, Herbert Warren. *The Story of American Golf.* New York: Alfred A. Knopf, Inc., 1948, 1956, 1975.

INDEX